# Michigan

Dixie Franklin
with Bill Semion and Dan Stivers

Photography by Dennis Cox

COMPASS AMERICAN GUIDES
An Imprint of Fodor's Travel Publications

# Michigan
## First Edition

Copyright © 2001 Fodor's Travel Publications
Maps Copyright © 2001 Fodor's Travel Publications
ISBN 0-679-00534-X

**Compass American Guides, Inc., 5332 College Ave., Suite 201, Oakland, CA 94618, USA**

| | |
|---|---|
| Editors: Pennfield Jensen, Kit Duane | Designers: Christopher Burt, Julia Dillon |
| Managing Editor/Galley Layout: Kit Duane | Map Design and Production: Mark Stroud of Moon |
| Creative Director/Photo Editor: Christopher Burt | Street Cartography |
| | Production Editor: Julia Dillon |
| Production House: Twin Age, Ltd. | Manufactured in China |

10 9 8 7 6 5 4 3 2 1

COMPASS AMERICAN GUIDES ACKNOWLEDGES the following institutions and individuals for the use of their photographs and illustrations: **Ann Arbor Public Library** p.108; **Army Corps of Engineers** p. 250; **Art Gallery of Ontario** p. 21; **Bentley Historical Library, University of Michigan** pp. 13, 49, 51, 76, 106, 203; **Detroit Institute of Arts** p. 48; **Grand Rapids Public Library** p. 184; **Library of Congress** pp. 20, 33, 51, 291; **Mariners Museum of Virginia** p. 47; **University Archives, Milwaukee** p. 27; **Marshall M. Fredericks Gallery** p. 147; **Michigan State Archives** pp. 37, 39, 78, 85, 127, 176, 182, 236, 257, 260; **Motown Record Corporation** p. 81; **Museum of Art and History, Port Huron** p. 40; **National Archives of Canada** p. 28 (top); **National Gallery of Art** pp. 152-153; **Royal Ontario Museum** pp. 28 (bottom), 244, 248; **Smithsonian Institute, National Museum of American History, Peters Collection** p. 146; **Stroh Company Archives** p. 50; **Underwood Photo Archives, San Francisco** pp. 42, 66, 261; **William M. Clements Library** p. 83; **Wisconsin State Historical Society, Madison** p. 24.

   WE THANK **Rolf Peterson** for his piece on the wolves of Isle Royale, pp. 266-267. We also thank the following for use of their published works: Excerpts on pp. 26, 43, and 121 from *Michigan, A History,* by **Bruce Catton.** Copyright © 1984, 1975, by Bruce Catton. Used by permission of W. W. Norton & Company, Inc. Excerpt on p. 157 reprinted by permission of the publisher from *Blood Stoppers and Bear Walkers: Folk Tales of Immigrants, Lumberjacks, and Indians,* by **Richard M. Dorson,** 186-187, Cambridge, MA: Harvard University Press, Copyright © 1952 by the President and Fellows of Harvard College, Copyright © by Richard M. Dorson. Excerpt on p. 246 from *Iron Brew,* by **Stewart H. Holbrook;** MacMillan Co., 1939. Excerpts on pp. 72 and 236 are from *The Lost Continent: Travels in Small-Town America,* by **William Bryson.** HarperCollins, 1989.

   COMPASS AMERICAN GUIDES THANKS assistant editor **Beth Burleson,** copy editor **Pamela Evans,** proofreader **Ellen Klages,** and expert reader **Jay Platt** of West Side Books.

*Dedicated to my family and others whom I love, in memory of the good times.*

## AUTHOR'S ACKNOWLEDGMENTS

I owe deep gratitude to so many fine folks of Michigan who so generously shared information when I called time and time again with the opening phrase of, "One more question on the book." A heart-felt thanks to all the historians who worked at keeping me posted on the facts of the past, tourism agencies, Convention & Visitors Bureaus who helped define their main attractions, and so many more. So many friends and associates gave freely of their time and knowledge: Al Sandner, Bill Semion, Tom Nemacheck, Peter Fitzsimons, Renee Monforton and her able assistant Amber Kendall, Chris Dancisak, Carolyn Artman, Deb Pardyke. The list could stretch on and on. My thanks go to Leonard A. DeFrain whom I have never met and others like him who responded to my request for information by taking time to research almost forgotten ghost towns and other remnants of the past. Kay Boughner and other librarians at the small library in the village of Norway kept a constant flow of Michigan history books coming through interlibrary loans from Michigan to California. This book would not have been possible without the assistance of the fine editorial staff, especially Kit Duane, Pennfield Jensen, and Chris Burt. Thank you.

# C O N T E N T S

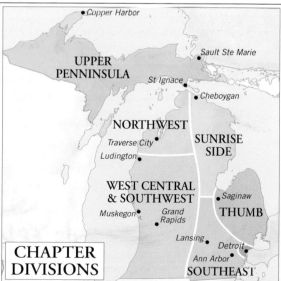

CHAPTER
DIVISIONS

## Topical Essays

## Literary Excerpts

# Maps

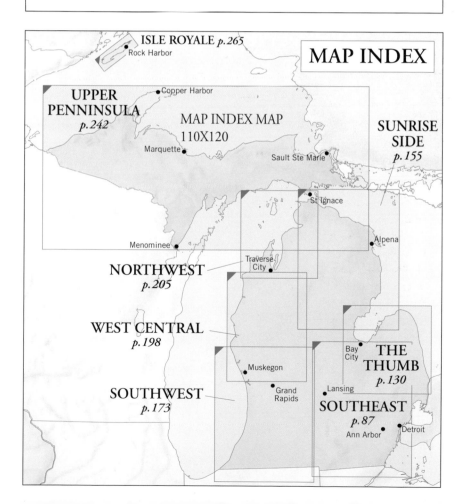

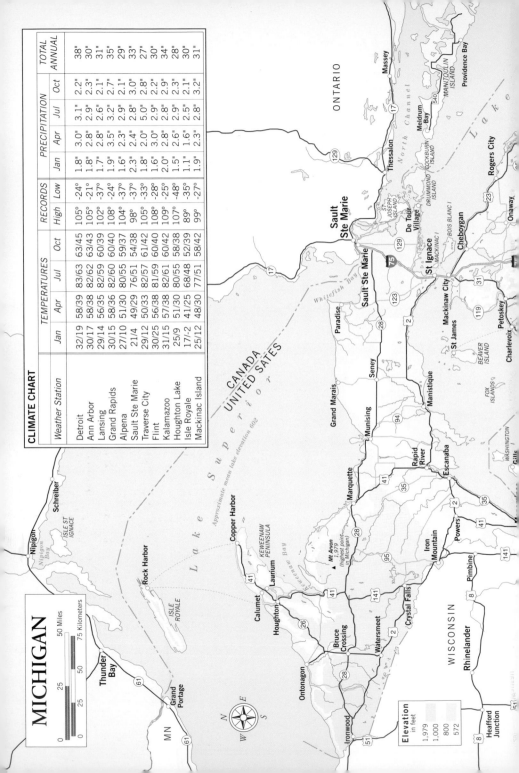

# MICHIGAN

## CLIMATE CHART

| Weather Station | TEMPERATURES | | | | RECORDS | | PRECIPITATION | | | | TOTAL ANNUAL |
|---|---|---|---|---|---|---|---|---|---|---|---|
| | Jan | Apr | Jul | Oct | High | Low | Jan | Apr | Jul | Oct | |
| Detroit | 32/19 | 58/39 | 83/63 | 63/45 | 105° | -24° | 1.8" | 3.0" | 3.1" | 2.2" | 38" |
| Ann Arbor | 30/17 | 58/38 | 82/62 | 63/43 | 105° | -21° | 1.8" | 2.8" | 2.9" | 2.3" | 30" |
| Lansing | 29/14 | 56/35 | 82/59 | 60/39 | 102° | -37° | 1.7" | 2.8" | 2.6" | 2.1" | 31" |
| Grand Rapids | 30/15 | 58/36 | 82/60 | 60/40 | 104° | -24° | 1.9" | 3.5" | 3.2" | 2.7" | 35" |
| Alpena | 27/10 | 51/30 | 80/55 | 59/37 | 104° | -37° | 1.9" | 2.3" | 2.9" | 2.1" | 29" |
| Sault Ste Marie | 21/4 | 49/29 | 76/51 | 54/38 | 98° | -37° | 1.6" | 2.4" | 2.8" | 3.0" | 33" |
| Traverse City | 29/12 | 50/33 | 82/57 | 61/42 | 105° | -33° | 1.8" | 2.0" | 3.0" | 2.8" | 27" |
| Flint | 30/25 | 56/38 | 81/59 | 60/40 | 108° | -28° | 1.6" | 3.0" | 2.9" | 2.2" | 30" |
| Kalamazoo | 31/15 | 57/38 | 82/61 | 60/42 | 109° | -25° | 2.0" | 2.8" | 2.8" | 2.9" | 34" |
| Houghton Lake | 25/9 | 51/30 | 80/55 | 58/38 | 107° | -48° | 1.5" | 2.6" | 2.9" | 2.3" | 28" |
| Isle Royale | 17/-2 | 41/25 | 68/48 | 52/39 | 89° | -35° | 1.1" | 1.6" | 2.5" | 2.1" | 30" |
| Mackinac Island | 25/12 | 48/30 | 77/51 | 58/42 | 99° | -27° | 1.9" | 2.3" | 2.8" | 3.2" | 31" |

Elevation in feet
1,979
1,000
800
572

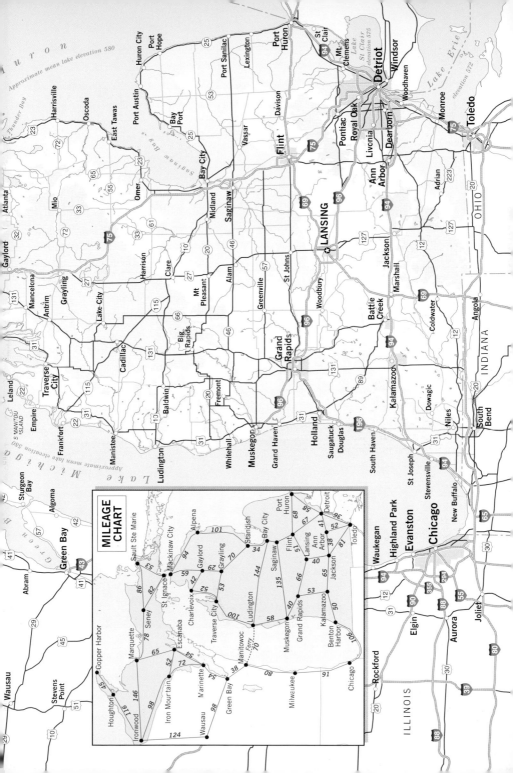

# O V E R V I E W

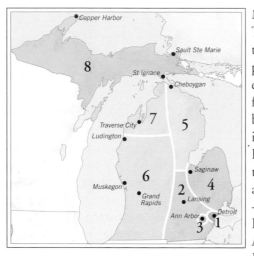

MICHIGAN IS MORE THAN CARS... The north is a landscape of lakes too wide to see across, mossy paths winding through deep forest, gurgling streams rippling fresh and clean over their pebbled beds, and waterfalls plunging headlong down rocky cliffs. Flat, fertile farmland rolls through the southeast, broken by the steel and concrete of industrial centers —especially Flint, Battle Creek, Lansing, and Grand Rapids. Ann Arbor, home to the University of Michigan, is arguably one of the liveliest towns in the state. And finally, dominating the eastern edge of the state, Detroit is an economic powerhouse, with global industrial reach.

## 1 DETROIT, MOTOR CITY  *pages 44–81*

Appropriately, there's a steady roar of honking horns, screeching brakes, and the slamming of limousine doors in the city that put our nation—and, for that matter, the world—on wheels. Greater Detroit boasts the "high" culture of museums, opera, orchestras; a setting that enables the simple pleasures of riverfront dining, strolls through woodland parks, and dancing at outdoor festivals; and a fascinating, sometimes turbulent industrial history that resulted in palatial mansions, crowded ethnic enclaves—even the chart-breaking sounds of Motown.

**2** SOUTHEAST   *pages 82–97*

Southeastern Michigan is mostly farmland and is flat as a pancake—until you get to the Irish Hills. Formed by the eroded deposits of glacial moraines, these rolling hills are distinctive for their oak openings and lakes. Lansing, the state capital, rests at the center of this largely rural land.

**3** ANN ARBOR   *pages 98–123*

A quintessential college town, Ann Arbor (or "A², " as some call it), entertains as well as educates. Museums, cinemas, and a plethora of theaters vie with Kerrytown restaurants and U of M football and basketball for the visitor's attention. Galleries and funky shops abound, and, with one of the highest concentration of used and rare bookshops in the United States, A² is a mecca for book lovers.

**4** THE THUMB   *pages 124–149*

Here, big cities give way to wide-open farmland, punctuated with silos, cider mills, and small towns. From the end of the breakwater at Port Austin, you can watch the sun rise over Lake Huron and return in the evening for the sunset over Saginaw Bay.

**5** SUNRISE SIDE *pages 150–167*
Fishing boats bob in Saginaw Bay. Marinas crowd river mouths along Lake Huron's shore, where 150-year-old lighthouses stand guard. Inland, steep wooded hills form dramatic horizons. Canoes drift on the Rifle and Au Sable Rivers, and elk roam freely through the forests.

**6** SOUTHWEST & WEST-CENTRAL *pages 168–201*
From the Indiana border to the Straits of Mackinac, you'll see ribbons of yellow sand and the blue waters of Lake Michigan, green forests, villages accented with harbors, lighthouses, vineyards, and rivers. The world's breakfast cereal capital, Battle Creek, vies for attention with the sculptures in Grand Rapids, the artist-colony feel of Saugatuck-Douglas, and the long, beckoning beaches of Warren Dunes State Park.

**7** NORTHWEST & MACKINAC ISLAND *pages 202–239*
This triangle of Michigan contains some of the best beaches, best hiking trails, best boating and canoeing opportunities, plus some of the most fascinating historic sites in the country. Take the ferry out to the Manitou Islands; or visit Mackinac Island, itself a living museum.

**8** UPPER PENINSULA
*pages 240–273*

Lakes Michigan, Huron and Superior wrap their shores around the Upper Peninsula. Country roads lead to parks, beaches, waterfalls, and trails; roadside restaurants, often furnished with communal tables, offer hikers the chance to take a satisfying coffee break: a fine

cup of java and, if you're in the mood, a friendly conversation with the local gentry. The wilderness here is unforgettable, especially on Isle Royale, with its ancient drama of wolf and moose.

*A sailboat rides a Lake Michigan wind on its approach to the
"Big Red" Lighthouse, near Holland.*

# LANDSCAPE & HISTORY

THROUGH EONS OF SCRAPING AND HEAVING, shoving and receding, the great glaciers of various ice ages sculpted North America. By the end of the most recent ice age—the Wisconsin, approximately 10,000 years ago—a great swath of continent had been leveled. Close to the center of that landmass, the glacier carved out a massive lake and deposited in its middle two 300-mile-long peninsular ridges—one running north to south, the other east to west—separating the one body of water into five. These, the Great Lakes, are easily identified on any U.S. map or satellite picture of the North American continent. Schoolchildren learn early to produce an image of these peninsulas: two hands, palms up, thumbs extended, index finger of the right hand almost touching the pinky finger of the left—the distinctive features of the state of Michigan. The right hand is Michigan's Lower Peninsula, called "the mitten" with its distinctive "Thumb." The left hand is Michigan's Upper Peninsula, or simply the "U.P." (Residents genially refer to themselves as "Yoopers.")

The state borders are washed by four of the five Great Lakes with magnificent, if sometimes treacherous, shorelines. These shoreline beaches, dunes, and sandstone cliffs stretch longer than the entire Eastern Seaboard of the United States.

Situated between the 41st and 48th parallels of latitude, Michigan is midway between the equator and the North Pole, and shares its borders with Ohio, Indiana, Wisconsin, and Ontario, Canada. The landscape is a collage of flat southern farmland and the roller-coaster hills and valleys of the north.

As the legend on the Great Seal of the State of Michigan so aptly states, "If you seek a beautiful peninsula, look about you."

## ■ GEOLOGY

On the shores and ridges of the Keweenaw Peninsula (the far northern extension of the U.P.) or on the distant Isle Royale National Park, you can kneel down and touch some of the most ancient rock on Earth: the pre-Cambrian stone is at least 2.5 billion years old. Volcanic eruptions deep beneath ancient seas deposited copper, iron, silver, gold, gypsum, and dolomite. In turn, glaciers, relentlessly grinding stone and ice, stacked the resulting sand in thick layers that eventually hardened into stone. The geologic history can be read on the multi-tinted, 200-foot sandstone cliffs of Pictured Rocks National Lakeshore along the southern shore of Lake Superior between Munising and Grand Marais.

*(opposite) Miner's Castle at Pictured Rocks National Lakeshore in autumn.*

*Keweenaw Peninsula in autumn, as seen from Brockway Mountain Drive.*

## ■ GEOGRAPHY: LAKES, PLAINS, AND FORESTS

Four of the five Great Lakes—Superior, Michigan, Huron, and Erie—define Michigan's boundaries and taken together create a shoreline over 3,200 miles long. In a straight line from the northwest tip of the Keweenaw Peninsula to the southeast corner at the Ohio border near Toledo, the state measures 456 miles. By highway, it's about 640 miles, the same as the distance from Detroit to New York City.

The topography changes from flat plains in the agricultural south to forested hills north of Saginaw Bay, with summits exceeding 600 feet up in the northwest corner. Across the Straits of Mackinac, the eastern half of the Upper Peninsula is dotted with low hills that give over, about midway across the peninsula, to the hills and ranges that we Michiganians refer to as mountains.

## ■ CLIMATE

Because of the Great Lakes, Michigan's climate is classified as semi-maritime, even though the state lies more than 600 miles from the nearest ocean. The great bodies

*The shoreline of Lake Superior freezes in winter.*

of fresh water create the famous "lake effect," cooling the westerly flow of air during the summer and warming it during the winter. This causes an average 10-degree moderation of temperature along the shore in all seasons and creates a kind of "climate-control system" near the lakes. Inland, however, temperatures reach the extremes for which the upper Midwest is known—try a record low of -51 degrees F in Vanderbilt and a record high of 112 degrees F in Mio, inland towns which lie 30 miles apart on the Lower Peninsula.

In spring, lake-effect breezes extend the growing season, ensuring bumper fruit harvests along Lake Michigan's eastern shores. The same effect in winter brings prodigious snowfalls: the average annual snowfall on the Keweenaw Peninsula is 200 inches (over 16 feet).

Climate has a dramatic effect on the people of Michigan, influencing work schedules, travel plans, education, and recreation. Those in the maritime industry are especially challenged by frozen waterways and sudden winter storms.

# ■ WATER, WATER EVERYWHERE: THE GREAT LAKES

A Michigan old-timer once told me that I "hadn't arrived" until I started towing a boat behind my car. Not surprisingly, most Michiganians do; the state's surrounded by water: 40,000 square miles of Great Lakes; laced with 37,000 miles of rivers and streams, and more than 11,000 inland lakes, along with countless bogs, fens, and marshes. These inland waters contain more than 150 named waterfalls and more than 3,000 islands, some large enough to boast lakes of their own.

Altogether, the Great Lakes hold one-fifth of the world's fresh surface water. Along Michigan's 3,200-mile coastline are 83 boating harbors; safe harbors are never more than 15 shoreline miles away. Stand anywhere in the state, and you're always within 85 miles of a Great Lake and within six miles of a lake or stream.

## ◆ LAKE SUPERIOR

Undisputed queen of the Great Lakes, Lake Superior is the Midwest's ocean and, at 31,800 square miles, the largest body of fresh water in the world. It is a lake too wide to see across, an inland sea with cliffs and sandy coves, a sea without the smell of salt but with tide-like seiches governed by the winds. Stand a thousand-foot freighter on end at Superior's deepest point, and it would disappear. Superior writes her own tales in which peaceful, glass-smooth dawns can explode into storms whose waves can ascend 200-foot cliffs to fling huge boulders like beach balls or, more dreadfully, reach up and drag huge freighters down to her depths.

## ◆ LAKE HURON

Emptying into the St. Marys River (yes, that's how it's spelled) at Sault Ste. Marie, Superior starts the waters of mid-America on a 2,000-mile journey to the Gulf of St. Lawrence. They flow first into the 223-mile-long and 183-mile-wide Lake Huron, the third largest Great Lake. Early explorers forging through the wilderness from Montreal called Huron *La Mer Douce,* the Sweet Sea. The rocky shore with long stretches of white sand hugs a lake of azure blue. But don't be fooled: Three underwater preserves mark the graves of scores of ships that met their fate in Huron's stormy embrace.

◆ LAKE MICHIGAN

Lake Michigan is the world's sixth largest lake. The 307-mile-long lake is the only Great Lake entirely within the boundaries of the United States. Its 2,730 miles of shoreline (including islands) is shared with Indiana, Illinois, and Wisconsin. Every shoreline city boasts a harbor, and this lake is liberally strewn with beaches of "singing" sand, including the world's highest freshwater dunes, towering up to 600 feet as part of Sleeping Bear Dunes National Lakeshore.

◆ LAKE ERIE

Although only 241 miles long, most of Lake Erie's coastline is claimed by New York, Pennsylvania, Ohio, and Ontario, Canada. Michigan's share of its waters are shallow and gray with cattail marshes dotted with lotus blossoms in the fall.

◆ INLAND LAKES AND RIVERS

Inland lakes tend to be serene, surrounded by green forests and sheltered bays. The largest is Houghton Lake at nearly 32 square miles. Six other lakes are 20 square miles or more. Common names range from the descriptive—such as Long, Little, Big, Round, Bass, Mud, Crooked, and Silver—to the native—such as Gogebic, Michigamme, and Ponemah. For hundreds of years, the many peoples indigenous to the Great Lakes region used Michigan rivers as water highways. The largest of these rivers—the Grand, Kalamazoo, Manistee, Muskegon, and St. Joseph—all flow into Lake Michigan.

■ FIRST MICHIGANIANS

The history of the indigenous Michigan cultures is as fascinating as it is appalling. Native American Michigan culture inspired Henry Wadsworth Longfellow to write *The Song of Hiawatha,* and two of Native America's greatest leaders, Pontiac and Tecumseh, rose to great prominence and waged their final, doomed battles against European encroachment here.

The earliest inhabitants arrived in the Great Lakes area about 11,000 years ago. These were nomadic hunter-gatherers, pursuers of mastodons, woolly mammoths, and migratory game along the edges of the receding glaciers.

Of the Old Copper Culture, whose shallow diggings can still be explored at the tip of the Keweenaw Peninsula and on Isle Royale, we know virtually nothing. Around 7,000 years ago, these early Michiganians discovered they could extract high-grade copper by heating the ore. They then fashioned the metal into tools and various utensils. Objects wrought from this exceptionally pure copper have been found as far away as New York, Illinois, Kentucky, and the Gulf of Mexico, indicating early and widespread trade with other tribes. The shallow-pit mines on Isle Royale in Lake Superior, 22 miles from the nearest mainland, further indicate that these early metalworkers were capable of safe and extended Great Lakes travel.

About 3,000 years ago, the first Mound Builders arrived, called the Adena people. They were succeeded by the Hopewell people who were architects of more complex mounds and were widely dispersed throughout the Great Lakes area.

*The above sketch, made by J. C. Tidball around 1850, shows how the artist imagined copper was mined by people of the Old Copper Culture. (Library of Congress)*

*Paul Kane painted this authentic depiction of Indians on a Lake Huron island (circa 1845) after sketches made during his travels through the Great Lakes region. (Art Gallery of Ontario)*

◆ MODERN TRIBES

In the 1600s, when French explorers first saw the lake that the local Indians called Michiganong, or Michigama, they found an indigenous population that had been in place for less than a thousand years and knew nothing of their predecessors. Michigan, like all the Ohio Valley and Great Lakes region, was a territory in flux. The Iroquois (the Five Nations to the east) had pushed the Algonquin-speaking tribes out of the eastern forests into the Ohio Valley and the Great Lakes area. These Algonquin tribes—whose language was closely related to that spoken by the Indians encountered by the first British colonists—in turn pushed the Sioux out of the Ohio Valley onto the Great Plains.

The Algonquin had formed a loose confederation called "The Three Fires," consisting of the Potawatomi, Ottawa, and Chippewa (Ojibwa) tribes. The Potawatomi resided largely in southwestern Michigan, where the rich soil promoted the cultivation of beans, corn, and squash, and there built elaborate permanent villages. Farther north, the Ottawas built semi-permanent villages where they also grew crops; but during the summer fishing season, they would move entire villages to their favorite waters. The Chippewas, a largely nomadic people of the far north country, hunted, fished, and gathered berries and nuts, which they added to ground, dried meat to make pemmican. Although these people were considered "savages" by the Europeans, their cultures were highly developed and highly competitive—a fact that the Europeans were quick to seize upon in building Indian alliances during the era of the fur trade.

The widespread and intricately interwoven nature of these tribes and sub-tribes prompted Bruce Catton, the preeminent modern Michigan chronicler, to write:

> You can study the names of the tribes until your face is blue without adding much to your knowledge, because, essentially, they were all much the same people: Chippewas (or Ojibways, Outchibous, Otchipwe, or what you choose) and Ottawas, and the blend of Potawatomis, Fox, Saux, and Massauaketon that are often lumped together as the people of the Fire; the Miamis, sometimes called the Omaumeg; and the remnants of the Hurons, driven from their Georgian Bay homeland by the cruel Iroquois, to whose family they once belonged, given now to living about Detroit, known of late as the Wyandot.

As was true for all the other indigenous peoples in the New World, contact with the Europeans spelled their doom—but in Michigan not without a long and valiant struggle. The region's two great warrior-chiefs who struck uneasy alliances with the Europeans were Pontiac (an Ottawa) and Tecumseh (a Shawnee). On one hand, Pontiac sided with the French against the British and the Iroquois, the Ottawas' ancient rivals *(see essay on page 30)*. Twenty years before the Revolutionary War, Pontiac was the figurehead for what was later called the French and Indian War. At issue were two things: the British settlers' rampant disregard of treaties and agreements over the use and occupation of Indian land; and disagreements between the British and French over the latter's long-established terms of payment for the lucrative fur trade.

On the other hand, Tecumseh, a legendary orator who during the War of 1812 built an even more powerful Confederation than had Pontiac, sided with the British against the Americans. *(See essay on page 30.)* During the early days of settlement and exploration, Indian nations held sway throughout the region, an influence that ceased only after the death of Tecumseh in 1813 at the Battle of the Thames in Canada. Tecumseh's courage and ferocity in that and earlier battles so debilitated the American troops that he is widely considered to have almost single-handedly prevented the American conquest of Canada.

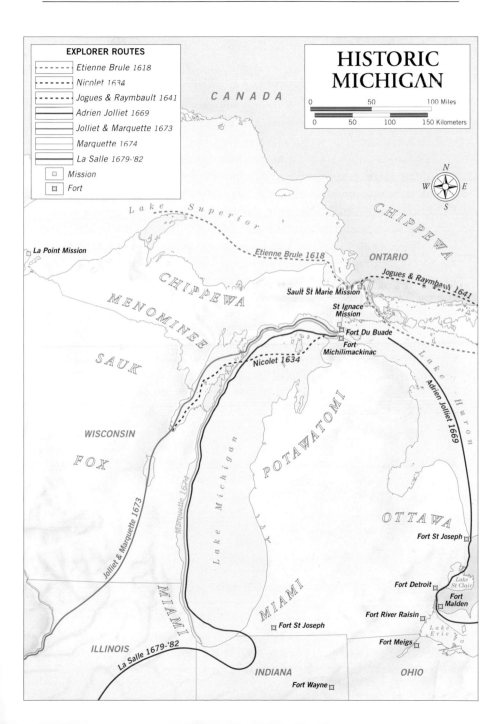

EXPLORER ROUTES

- – – – – Etienne Brule 1618
- – – – – Nicolet 1634
- – – – – Jogues & Raymbault 1641
- ——— Adrien Jolliet 1669
- ——— Jolliet & Marquette 1673
- ——— Marquette 1674
- ——— La Salle 1679-'82
- □ Mission
- ⌑ Fort

HISTORIC MICHIGAN

CANADA

0          50          100 Miles
0     50     100     150 Kilometers

La Point Mission

Lake Superior

ONTARIO

CHIPPEWA

Etienne Brule 1618

Jogues & Raymbault 1641

CHIPPEWA

MENOMINEE

Sault St Marie Mission

St Ignace Mission

Fort Du Buade

Fort Michilimackinac

Nicolet 1634

SAUK

Lake Huron

Adrien Jolliet 1669

WISCONSIN

POTAWATOMI

FOX

Lake Michigan

Marquette 1674

Jolliet & Marquette 1673

OTTAWA

Fort St Joseph

MIAMI

Fort Detroit

Lake St Clair

Fort Malden

Fort River Raisin

Fort St Joseph

ILLINOIS  La Salle 1679-'82

MIAMI

Fort Meigs

Lake Erie

INDIANA

OHIO

Fort Wayne

# ■ TRAPPERS, TRADERS, EXPLORERS, PRIESTS

In 1634, Jean Nicolet set out from Quebec on a mission ordered by Samuel de Champlain, lieutenant governor of New France, to explore the newly claimed lands to the west. Champlain, the French navigator/mapmaker-turned-politician who later became famous as the father of the fur trade, was primarily obsessed with finding a faster trade route to China—the fabled Northwest Passage.

China and her awe-inspiring riches had long captured the imagination of entrepreneurial merchants and covetous kings, thanks to the late-13th-century travels of Marco Polo and his reports of lavish silks, spices, gold, rubies, and porcelain. Great riches would reward the man who could circumvent the existing routes, then plagued by bandits, pirates, and enemy nations. In the person of Jean Nicolet, Champlain believed he had found the man to open a new water route to the Pacific. He equipped Nicolet lavishly for his mission to the Far East (which common knowledge held lay just beyond the Great Lakes), including giving him an elaborate Chinese robe of fine damask, colorfully embroidered with flowers and birds, to present as a gift for the first Chinese potentate he encountered.

*Hoping to find a water route to the Far East—then believed to lie just west of the Great Lakes—explorer Jean Nicolet landed near Green Bay in 1634 and mistakenly assumed that the Winnebago he met onshore could show him passage to Asia. (Univ. of Wisconsin Historical Society, Madison.)*

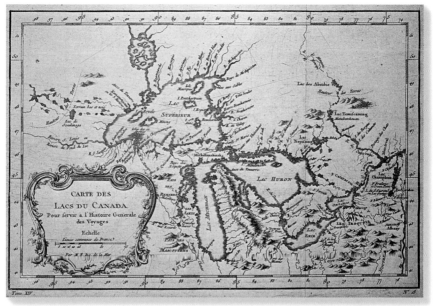

*Evidence of the high quality of French surveying techniques, this 1757 map by Jean Nicolas Bellin is remarkably accurate.*

Passing from Lake Huron through the Straits of Mackinac, Nicolet traversed Lake Michigan, hugging the shores of the Upper Peninsula until he reached Green Bay. Spotting a group of people camped on the shore, Nicolet, presuming his mission accomplished, donned his glorious robe, stood up in his canoe, fired two pistols in the air to announce his grand arrival, and stepped ashore before an astounded group of Winnebago.

While Nicolet failed to find the trade route to the Far East, he fared better than the more daring Étienne Brûlé. In 1610, at the age of 18, Brûlé was already working among the Indians for Champlain. A decade later, the group of Huron with whom Brûlé was living guided him west to St. Marys River at what is now Sault Ste. Marie, where some historians credit Brûlé with being the first European to set foot on Michigan soil. For years, Brûlé led a charmed life. Some said he became more Indian than the Indians themselves as he adopted their lifestyle and learned their language. In 1632, his luck ran out. According to legend, a violent disagreement broke out, whereupon Brûlé was beaten to death and eaten by his chosen tribe (not such an ignominious fate, as ritual cannibalism was a sign of great respect among The Three Fires peoples).

◆ THE BLACK ROBES

Hot on the heels of explorers in search of wealth and adventure came fervent and intrepid priests, whom local Indians dubbed the Black Robes. In search of souls, many settled for martyrdom. The first Jesuits came at the invitation of Champlain, and in 1641, Fathers Isaac Jogues and Charles Raymbault traveled to the present Sault Ste. Marie to conduct the first Christian religious services ever held in Michigan.

Among other Jesuit priests who left indelible marks on Michigan are Claude Jean Allouez, who established the first mission in Michigan at Sault Ste. Marie; Claude Dablon; Bishop Baraga ("The Snowshoe Priest"); and Jacques Marquette.

---

## MYSTERIOUS PAST, INCALCULABLE FUTURE

*M*ichigan has never really had a present moment. It has a mysterious past and an incalculable future, attractive and terrifying by turns, but the moment where the two meet is always a time of transition. The state is caught between yesterday and tomorrow, existing less for itself than for what it leads to; it is a road whose ends are distorted by imagination and imperfect knowledge. The great American feeling of being en route—to the unknown, to something new, to the fantastic reality that must lie beyond the mists—is perfectly represented here. If the nation is now wholly given over to the making and using of highways, here, maybe, is where the process began.

❖     ❖     ❖

So Nicolet looked for Asia west by south of Mackinac, a week away by birchbark canoe, and he failed to find it because he was half a world off the mark, a good man groping in the mysterious lake's golden twilight for something that was not there. Étienne Brûlé, who went out ahead of him, had better luck. He hunted a fantastic intangible, found it, made the most of it, and vanished at last into bloodstained legend, his final thoughts unrecorded. He wanted to get to the fabulous back-of-beyond—to discard everything he had been taught in seventeenth-century France and find out how it would go with a man who followed total loneliness into the loneliest forest on earth—and he did precisely what he had set out to do, which is more than most men ever do. The result was something he had not foreseen. Discarding civilization and making himself totally uncivilized, he nevertheless dragged civilization after him, which is why no one today can go where he went and see what he saw. By escaping into the wholly primitive, he helped to destroy it.

—Bruce Catton, *A Michigan Reader,* 1974

*Jacques Marquette discovered the portage linking the Great Lakes and the Mississippi River. (Marquette University Archives, Milwaukee, WI)*

Exploration and conversion traveled hand in glove. On May 17, 1673, fur trader, navigator, and mapmaker Louis Jolliet, along with Father Marquette and five other Frenchmen, pushed off from St. Ignace in search of the legendary "Messipi," the big river of Indian lore. A month later, their canoes were swept into the mighty Mississippi. Elated, they rode it all the way to the mouth of the Arkansas River before it became ruefully evident that they had failed to find the long-sought water route to the Pacific.

◆ FRENCH AND INDIAN TRADERS

Champlain, disappointed in his quest for the Northwest Passage, found his treasure right where he stood—and it was beaver fur. In trend-setting France, beaver hats had risen to the height of fashion. No European man of distinction was considered ready to appear in public until he had donned an elegant chapeau made from the soft inner fur of the beaver. The Three Fires nation, traders by ancient tradition, took naturally to the French, who offered knives, beads, blankets, iron kettles, trinkets, guns—and whiskey—in exchange for the prized pelts. Soon canoes full of furs were headed down the major waterways to the trading outposts.

*Wampum belts like the one shown here served as currency for the purchase of furs from Indians of the Great Lakes and Northeast regions.*

*The French-Canadian boaters of the fur trade, or "voyageurs," were hardy men, transporting furs hundreds of miles across rivers and lakes in canoes. (National Archives of Canada)*

But this traffic soon kindled another ancient tradition: raiding. The Iroquois, allies of the British and traditional enemies of The Three Fires, began plundering the convoys, striking terror into the hearts of all who were forced to run their gauntlets. The French replied by constructing forts: at the Straits of Mackinac, at Detroit, at Fort St. Joseph (near the present city of Niles), and at Sault Ste. Marie.

Even with the relative safety of the forts, the logistical problem of transferring immense quantities of furs remained, a problem solved by the colorful *voyageur* boatmen. Primarily French-Canadians, these short, muscular men, with names like Baptiste Lachapelle and Pierre Moudin, speaking a language only they could understand, traversed the lakes and rivers in large canoes, paddling them hundreds of miles a day to the cadence of their songs.

◆ BRITISH

The British, casting covetous eyes on both the fur trade and the potential for a Northwest Passage, marshaled Indian support to launch the French and Indian War. A confused enterprise at best, the French and Indian War relied on deep hatred among the various tribes that were adroitly exploited to meet either French or British ends. The true goal was domination of New France, what is now Canada. The conclusion came with Gen. James Wolfe's defeat of the Marquis de Montcalm on the Plains of Abraham outside Quebec. In 1763, France ceded all her territories to Britain, and the British assumed occupation of the forts, took over the fur trade, and began a coexistence policy with the French based on an attitude of mutual disdain that exists to this day.

*The Regent*

*The Tri-Corner*

*The French "Pope"*

*The Wellington*

■ SETTLEMENT

By the time of the treaty of the War of 1812, European styles had changed yet again. Off came the beaver hat; out went the fur trade. One effect of that trade had been the widening of the ancient Indian trails into roads—roads that now opened the land to settlement. At first it was a few log houses springing up among the wigwams surrounding the trading posts at Detroit, the Straits of Mackinac, and Sault St. Marie. Then came homesteading on a larger scale—farmers clearing the land and planting crops in ever-expanding waves from the core-city forts.

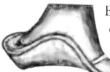

*Clerical Hat*

*The D'Orsay*

*Six examples of the stylish beaver-fur hat, in the French mode.*

## THE GREAT WARRIOR CHIEFS PONTIAC & TECUMSEH

*C*an ye not live without them? If you suffer the English among you, you are dead men. Sickness, smallpox, and their poison [whiskey] will destroy you entirely.
—Neolin, Delaware Prophet, 1761

*I*t is easy to misinterpret Pontiac's goals and ambitions. He had adopted the doctrine of the Delaware Prophet, Neolin, who called for a general attack on whites and an abandonment of white technology and trade. But Pontiac had modified Neolin's teachings; he wanted an attack on the English, not the French, some of whom fought alongside the Indians. His goal was the restoration of the French father and not a return to a pre-European past.
—Richard White, "Indian Rebellion,"
from *The Native Americans, An Illustrated History,* 1993.

### PONTIAC'S "REBELLION" AND THE FRENCH AND INDIAN WAR

By 1760, the Seven Years War (1756–63), having already engaged all the major European powers, erupted in North America as a conflict between the French and English; in the colonies, the war was known as the French and Indian War (1760–64). Frustrated by the loss of trade with the French (the English had cut off the shipping lanes) and outraged at ruthless British encroachment on Indian lands, the great Ottawa chief Pontiac formed a powerful Indian Confederation to drive out the British and return the French to power. The Confederation involved nearly every Indian tribe from Lake Superior to the lower Mississippi. Pontiac's plan called for each tribe, at roughly the same time, to attack the fort nearest to them. Intelligent and shrewd, the Indians carefully planned their attacks. In May of 1763, Pontiac initiated the rebellion with a move against Detroit. Although the commander of the fort was tipped off to Pontiac's scheme, and deflected it, Pontiac then laid siege to the fort and seized it. Emboldened, the Confederation followed Pontiac's lead, attacking 12 forts and capturing all but four. Perhaps the most striking of these was the Ojibwa-Sauk assault on Fort Michilimackinac. There, employing the ruse of an intertribal game of lacrosse (or baggatiway), the Indians lobbed a ball into the fort, rushed in after it, and slaughtered two thirds of the British Garrison. In contrast, the commander of Fort Pitt used a more insidious ruse: he pretended to placate his Indian attackers by deliberately handing out blankets that were infected with smallpox.

Although most British relief expeditions were nearly annihilated, and hundreds of pioneer settlements were plundered and burned, the Confederation dissolved with the approach of winter and the need to harvest crops. On his part, Pontiac was dismayed by the lack of French response—no one had told him that The Seven Years War had concluded in 1763 with the Franco-British Treaty of Paris whereby France ceded North America (and India!) to England. Grudgingly, the Indians retired, but won from Britain a major concession: the Proclamation of 1763 that called upon all illegal settlers to leave and that strictly limited white settlement in Indian territory. (The utter and contemptuous disregard of this treaty by white settlers would trigger decades of Indian warfare).

Pontiac's triumph was short lived. In 1769, in an act of revenge over Pontiac's stabbing of a relative during a council meeting, Pontiac was struck from behind and killed by a Peoria Indian. It was a demise Pontiac had himself foreseen.

## TECUMSEH AND THE WAR OF 1812

*T*he implicit obedience and respect which the followers of Tecumseh pay to him is really astonishing, and more than any other circumstance bespeaks him one of those uncommon geniuses which spring up occasionally to produce revolutions and overturn the established order of things. If it were not for the vicinity of the United States, he would, perhaps, be the founder of an empire that would rival in glory that of Mexico or Peru. No difficulties deter him. His activity and industry supply the want of letters. For four years he has been in constant motion. You see him today on the Wabash and in a short time you hear of him on the shores of Lake Erie or Michigan, or on the banks of the Mississippi and wherever he goes he makes an impression favorable to his purposes.

> —William Henry Harrison, letter to William Eustis, August 7, 1811,
> from *Tecumseh, A Life,* by John Sugden, 1997

*T*he War of 1812, as it was known in the United States, was merely an echo of a much larger Napoleonic War—the war of Nelson at Trafalgar and of Napolean at Waterloo—that had been raging in Europe since the 1790s. The war hawks in Washington were opposed by the Northeastern states who were benefiting from trade with England, but their tempering hand was overruled for one major reason: Indians. The Ohio Valley, stretching from the Great Lakes south almost to New Orleans, was largely barred from settlement by the many tribes residing there. The British, operating out of Quebec and Ontario, were actively inciting Indian attacks; there was little or no protection for settlers. Furthermore, the British ruled the Great Lakes. If the United States was to secure its territories and fledgling states in the west, the Indians and the British had to go.

Central to the conflict was the Michigan Territory with its two precarious Forts Detroit and River Raisin opposing a fairly well-established British presence directly across the Detroit River. Furthermore, a new force had risen in the area, the Shawnee chief Tecumseh, who had, through soul-stirring oratory and tireless travelling, formed an Indian Confederation greater than that of Pontiac's 50 years earlier. With the declaration of war, Tecumseh faced the challenge of convincing his Confederation to side with the British against the Americans. This was not an easy task because most of the tribal leaders thought the Americans would win, and given Indian tradition regarding the losing side, did not want to jeopardize their families and lands.

In terms of numbers, the odds were lopsidedly in favor of the Americans. Jefferson dispatched a Revolutionary War hero, William Hull to be governor of the Michigan Territory and to take command of Detroit. Simultaneously, he promoted William Henry Harrison, the popular governor of the Indiana Territory, to brigadier general and commander of all forces in the Northwest. Harrison took command of Fort Wayne and the forces of the Ohio Valley. Harrison knew Tecumseh, and his famous brother called The Prophet, and regarded both of them with great respect. In fact, Tecumseh and Harrison were the two sides of the same coin, mutual admirers who were destined to write history as mutual enemies.

Outraged by the continuing massacres, destruction of game, and unauthorized settlement, Tecumseh saw the looming war between Britain and America as his opportunity to avenge these crimes against his people. In 1813, he assembled his followers and joined the British at Fort Malden on the Canadian side of the Detroit River. It was the most formidable force ever commanded by a North American Indian and was instrumental in Hull's decision to surrender Fort Detroit without firing a shot, an act for which Hull, a hero of the Revolutionary War, was later court-martialed. (An ignominious historical footnote: Detroit is the only major American city ever to have been occupied by a foreign power).

Emboldened by the victories at Detroit and at River Raisin *(see essay, page 84),* Tecumseh once again reached out to gather support for the Confederacy, travelling as far south as Florida. Returning north, he joined British general Henry A. Procter in his assault upon Fort Meigs (commanded by Gen. Henry Harrison) on the Maumee River above Toledo inflicting ten American casualties to every one of his own. The Americans were faltering, but the tide turned after the remarkable victory over the British fleet on Lake Erie by Oliver Hazard Perry, which severed British lines of support. General Procter initiated a retreat to Canada, with Tecumseh, who believed the British could still attack and win, reluctantly accompanying him. General Harrison, with Kentuckian militiamen bent on revenge—"Remember the River Raisin" their rallying cry—pursued Procter and Tecumseh north through Michigan into Canada where, on October 5, 1813, Harrison routed them at the decisive battle at the Thames River in Ontario. It was here that Tecumseh fell, though by whose hand no one knows. Canada was prostrate. The British were virtually powerless to protect it, and the French citizenry more than willing to accept an American takeover. Nevertheless, the exhausted Americans quit the conflict. The credit for keeping Canada a subject of the British Crown is popularly awarded to Tecumseh whose death, however, all but ended organized Indian resistance to American settlement in the region.

William Henry Harrison went on to become the ninth President of the United States, largely because of his popularity in overcoming Tecumseh's brother Tenskwatawa, the Prophet, at the Battle of Tippecanoe in 1810, as well as the British and Tecumseh himself. "Tippecanoe and Tyler Too" was Harrison's successful campaign slogan. But it was a short-lived triumph—Harrison was the first president to die in office, after barely a month's service.

*A fictional representation of the death of Tecumseh at the Battle of the Thames in 1813. (Library of Congress)*

*This painting (circa 1820) by an unknown primitive artist portrays Mackinac Island's harbor as a bustling center for the Great Lakes fur traders.*

Early on, in 1701, the 43-year-old French army officer Antoine de la Mothe Cadillac convinced French royalty that the Great Lakes area was ready for organized settlement. With the aid of 100 soldiers and workers, Cadillac built a 12-foot-high and 200-square-foot palisade at the spot where the Detroit Civic Center now stands. For additional protection for his soldiers occupying the cabins, he enticed friendly Chippewa, Ottawa, Huron, and Miami Indians to set up villages nearby. Cadillac's wife, Marie Thérèse, soon joined her husband to become the first white woman to brave the Michigan wilderness.

Although Michigan was made part of the Northwest Territory in 1805, it yo-yoed between France, Great Britain, and the United States. All the while, homesteaders continued to make the long wagon treks across Ohio to Michigan, settling mostly in the fertile southern plains. The completion of the Erie Canal in 1825, connecting Michigan via Lake Erie to Buffalo, New York, sparked settlement in earnest. In less than five years, Michigan's population tripled to 31,639.

Hard on the heels of settlement came lumbermen who, having exhausted the forests of Maine and the Northeast, saw new fortunes in the forests of Michigan.

## ■ THE END OF THE FOREST

When settlers first arrived, deep forests stretched from the bottom of the southern edge of Saginaw Bay north to Lake Superior. Hundreds of thousands of 300-year-old white pines, towering 200 feet or more and measuring five feet in diameter, created a mixed hardwood and pine canopy that turned the hottest, brightest day of summer into cool darkness beneath it. A glimpse of this awesome forest can be found at Hartwick Pines State Park near Gaylord and Estivant Pines Sanctuary at Copper Harbor. Growing amid the white pine were Norway pine, jack pine, spruce, white cedar, hemlock, and tamarack. In groves along the southern meadows stood beech, oak, hickory, sugar maple, and ash.

*A souvenir plate commemorating the 1825 opening of the Erie Canal.*

*In 1701, Antoine de la Mothe Cadillac built a fort where the Detroit Civic Center now stands.*

## ◆ WHITE PINE TREASURE

White pine mattered most to lumbermen. Surveyors in the mid-1800s estimated standing pine at 150 billion board feet, or enough to build a floor that would cover Michigan's entire land area, with enough left over to blanket Rhode Island. French-Canadians signed on as lumberjacks, along with workers from New England, New York, Pennsylvania, and Ohio and ethnic groups from across Europe, especially the northern countries such as Finland, Norway, and Sweden.

The lumber industry began in the Saginaw River Valley, then, like a mass of slow-moving locusts, the loggers inched westward to the Grand River Valley, then along the rivers to Lake Michigan, and northward into the Upper Peninsula. The riverine system that so favored canoe travel also served as the water highway for the buoyant pine. In less than 50 years the pine was gone, the value of its timber exceeding that of the gold fields of California and Alaska combined.

Michigan trees helped build America's cities and rebuild them, as in the case of Chicago, after disastrous fires. The great cities of the treeless plains particularly benefited from the beautiful, easy-to-work lumber streaming out of Michigan.

*A stand of virgin white pine.*

*Loggers pose for a photo in Hermansville, circa 1900.*
*(Michigan State Archives)*

The introduction of the crosscut saw and railroads that could reach into the far-thest corners of the state hastened the end. Cutover land fell to unpaid taxes, re-sulting in hundreds of acres reverting to the state. Land speculators encouraged ill-fated farming on inhospitable lands. Folks failed, regrouped, made the best of it. Cherry trees flourished on the cutover land, Michigan-made furniture became world famous, and new resources such as iron and copper grew powerful new economies.

The decimation of the white pine forests had stirred national consciousness. In the 1930s, the Civilian Conservation Corps began replanting trees and working to control erosion. Today, Michigan grows twice as much timber each year as it har-vests, and prides itself on creating a sustainable forest-products industry. Its 276 sawmills, 14 veneer mills, eight pulp and paper mills, and 18 miscellaneous wood-using plants create 150,000 jobs and contribute $9 billion annually to the state's economy.

*Robert S. Duncanson painted* Cliff Mine, Lake Superior, *in 1848. The Cliff Mine was Michigan's first producing copper mine. (private collection)*

# ■ MINERALS IN THE EARTH

Great Lakes Indians had known about Michigan's copper for centuries. French and British explorers had heard the stories and had observed the crude mining pits on the Keweenaw Peninsula and at Isle Royale, but they paid them little heed. They missed other mineral troves as well: iron, gold, silver, gypsum, limestone, salt, petroleum, coal, dolomite, peat, sand, and gravel, plus natural gas and oil.

In 1844, state land surveyor William Austin Burt observed his magnetic compass swinging wildly as he travelled along Lake Superior. His curiosity led him to outcroppings of iron, but stopped there. His inventiveness did drive him to create a "solar" compass—on display at the Marquette County Historical Museum. Others were more ambitious. Enlisting the aid of Chippewa Chief Marji-Gesick, prospectors were led to hunks of iron protruding from the roots of an upturned tree on the banks of Teal Lake at the present city of Negaunee. The discovery ultimately led to the three great iron ranges of the Upper Peninsula: the Marquette, Menominee, and Gogebic.

Today the mines are largely mined out and silent. Two open-pit iron mines still operate on the Marquette Range, the Tilden and Empire, managed by the Cleveland-Cliffs Iron Company. Employing 2,100 workers, they produce about 22 percent of the nation's ore. Hundreds of thousands of bats now use the abandoned mine shafts as their winter hibernation abodes.

## ■ TRANSPORTATION AND INDUSTRY

Soldiers were the first to widen the original Indian and fur trapper trails into roads, paving them with hardwood timbers. Many of Michigan's modern roads follow these same tracks, forged by the earliest residents of this land.

After Michigan became a state in 1837, towns developed rapidly. Rails were driven into the wilderness, opening the doors even wider for more settlers, more logging, and more industrial development. On June 22, 1855, the Soo Locks at Sault Ste. Marie lifted the first steamer, the *Illinois,* up the 22 feet between Lake Huron and Lake Superior, thus bypassing a half-mile portage around St. Marys Rapids.

*Copper ingots stacked in rows await transport on this dock in Houghton, circa 1910.*
*(Michigan Department of State Archives.)*

*This 1863 painting by George B. Gardner, View of the St. Clair River, shows the Forester,
an excursion boat which made thrice-weekly trips between Port Huron and Detroit.
Bands on board provided music for dancing. (Museum of Arts and History, Port Huron)*

One of the lingering and most delightful legacies of the Great Lakes shipping boom during the lumber era is the lighthouse. Of Michigan's 116 lighthouses (more than any other state), 12 lighthouses and one light ship now house museums, each of which unfailingly captures the romance of the inland seas.

◆ THE HORSELESS CARRIAGE

In the late 1800s, Ransom "Ranse" Olds was tinkering in the gas-fired boiler engine shop of his father, Pliney Olds, comparing ideas with his friend Frank G. Clark, who had grown up working in his father's carriage shop. By 1887, they had combined the two shops and built a gas-fired horseless carriage, and they went chugging down Lansing streets. In 1897, Olds and his partners built the first Oldsmobile, producing four "carriages" that first year.

*(opposite) Point Betsie Lighthouse in late winter.*

*A Model T assembly line circa 1913. (Underwood Photo Archives, San Francisco)*

Meanwhile, Henry Ford had satisfactorily tested his invention of a self-propelled quadricycle, his first step in developing Michigan's favorite automobile of the times. In 1908, Ford was in production making Model Ts that initially sold for $850. "You can have any color Model T you want, as long as it's black," was Ford's famous quip. The public drove away with black. A year later, Michigan laid its first rural concrete highway. In 1915, the world's first traffic light was installed in Detroit. The first center stripe was painted on Dead Man's Curve at Marquette in 1917, and the first urban freeway was built in 1942.

Michigan can also boast of automotive pioneers John and Horace Dodge, David D. Buick, William C. "Billy" Durant of General Motors fame, and others. Automobiles, related industries, and the manufacture of transportation equipment continue to lead the economy.

# ■ BACK TO NATURE

Homesteaders had hardly settled into their cabins when the first tourists arrived from Chicago seeking to experience wilderness, to breathe fresh air, to fish and hunt. Tourism came early and came to stay. Mackinac Island led the way, with its Grand Hotel and fantastic Victorians, followed by Marquette, Petoskey, Sault Ste. Marie, and St. Ignace. Even during the hardest of times, people sought Michigan's sunny shores and quiet lakes. Today, it seems that one can enter a reviving and balmy quietude just steps away from almost any road, or tour a downtown humming with activity.

Welcome to Michigan.

---

## THE REAL MICHIGAN

*M*ichigan is perhaps the strangest state in the Union, a place where the past, the present and the future are all tied up together in a hard knot. It is the 20th Century incarnate, and if you look closely you can also see the twenty-first coming in; but it is also the 19th Century, the backward glance and the authentic feel and taste of a day that is gone forever. It killed the past and it is the past; it is the skyscraper, the mass-production line and the frantic rush into what the machine will some day make of all of us, and at the same time it is golden sand, blue water, green pine trees on empty hills, and a wind that comes down from the cold spaces, scented with the forests that were butchered by hard-handed men in checked flannel shirts and floppy pants. It is the North Country wedded to the force that destroyed it.

—Bruce Catton, *Michigan, A History,* 1974

# D E T R O I T
## by Bill Semion

■ HIGHLIGHTS  *page*

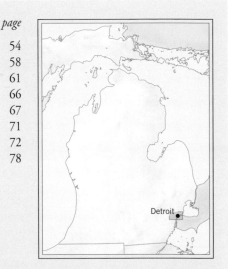

■ TRAVEL BASICS

**City Overview:** Detroit is a major urban center. Rebuilding and new construction is underway, the result of a vigorous effort to breathe life into a downtown that has in the past been the victim of neglect. As in Chicago, New York, or San Francisco, there are areas you simply want to avoid; check with your hotel or your hosts before heading out. Other areas, such as Greektown and Belle Isle, you won't want to miss. Downtown, around the RenCen and along the Riverwalk, provides some fascinating vistas from the heart of Motor City, and Detroit's museums are second to none. As such, it's important to use normal caution in venturing away from well-lit beaten paths, whether in a car or on foot.

**Getting Around:** Outside Metro Detroit, you'll need a car. But not in downtown. Park in a downtown garage and take the People Mover—an elevated trolley that makes a three-mile loop around downtown. It travels right through some hotels (on the second floor) with stops at the Renaissance Center, the Theater District, and Greektown. English-style double-decker buses are also available. Downtown is a maze of one-way streets, so be sure to pick up a good street map.

If you're driving outside the Metro area, learn the "mile" roads running east and west, beginning with 5 Mile Road up to 26 Mile at the north end of the suburbs. The

**Metropolitan Detroit International Airport,** 21 miles from downtown, is serviced mainly by limousines from the big hotels, but is easy to navigate by car.

**Weather:** Summers in Detroit are hot and humid with temperatures averaging in the mid- to high 80s Fahrenheit; yes, it can rain, so bring your umbrella. Winters are not so much cold as they are wet and mushy, so be sure to bring your galoshes. Spring and fall tend to be balmy, inviting long walks along the Detroit River.

**Food & Lodging:** Detroit is a major metropolis, so you can count on finding good restaurants and good hotels. *Please refer to our suggested list of lodgings and restaurants beginning on page 284.*

*Detroit and automobiles are inseparable in the
American imagination.*

# ■ HISTORY

Detroit is unique in the American experience. For example, it's the only major American city in which you can stand downtown and look *south* at Canada. Another curious fact—and a great bit of trivia—is that Detroit is the only major U.S. city to have been occupied by a foreign power. Yep, big D was taken over by the Brits during the War of 1812. William Hull, governor of the Michigan Territory and appointed by Thomas Jefferson to defend Detroit, turned the city over to the British without firing a shot, in part because of an ingenious trick staged by Tecumseh, the Indian leader and British ally. Leading an army of fewer than 400 warriors, Tecumseh ran them in loops out of the woods, around the fort, and back again. Already terrified of Indian warfare, Hull was given the impression that Tecumseh had about 5,000 warriors. For his action (or, rather, for his *in*action), Hull was excoriated by Congress and court-martialed by the army. Many historians point out that had Hull *not* surrendered—and if he had then pursued the decimated British after their crushing defeat at the Battle of the Thames in Canada, Canada herself would have become part of the United States. (*See essay, page 30.*)

After the War of 1812, Detroit sought more settlers from the East Coast—although letters from soldiers stationed in Michigan did little to inspire the folks back home to come west. In 1814, Gen. Duncan McArthur posted this personal letter from Detroit: "The banks of the Detroit River are handsome, but nine-tenths of the land in the Territory is unfit for cultivation."

By 1817, however, Detroit newspapers promising a more positive future made their way east. Soon the rush was on, with Detroit the major point of entry. Roads and rails were laid for travel to the interior. Steamboats such as *Walk-in-the-Water,* a popular 330-ton sail-rigged steamship, chugged across Lake Erie from Buffalo.

The Territory of Michigan received a sizeable land grant, part of which was appropriated as an endowment for schools suggested by a Judge Woodward. Today's students at the University of Michigan can be thankful that his idea for their institution was adopted, but not the name he proposed—Catholepistemiad. Former Territorial Governor Cass even stumbled over the name, calling it "Cathole... what's its name."

In 1825, completion of the Erie Canal connecting the Hudson River and Lake Erie made water travel easier. While many settlers remained near Detroit, even more unlashed their wagon wheels from the ship's masts, reassembled their gear, and headed west. A newspaper reported that a wagon was pulling out every five

*This 1820 painting depicts the steamship* Walk-in-the-Water *in Detroit Harbor.*
*(The Mariners Museum, Newport News, VA)*

minutes from dawn to dark. The first road, if the muddy trail through the wilderness can be called a road, followed the Old Sauk Trail used by Indians for generations. By 1835, two stages a week were running the Chicago Road (today's US-12) from Detroit to Fort Dearborn.

### ◆ STATEHOOD

The new state constitution of 1837 expressly forbade slavery in the state, strengthening the territorial ban that had been in place since 1787. Detroit became a focal point for the Underground Railroad for slaves of the South fleeing north where Canada and freedom lay within easy reach a mile across the Detroit River.

As settlers streamed into Michigan, shysters popped up like ticket scalpers at a sports event, with maps and land—below market value—in towns that existed only on paper, if they existed at all.

*Election Day, Detroit, November 1837: On this day, Stevens T. Mason (at left, in top hat) was re-elected to a second term as governor. (Detroit Institute of Arts, gift of Mrs. Samuel T. Carson)*

Banking institutions went up overnight, with banks boosting their reserves by borrowing from one another when inspectors were due. *(See essay on page 189.)* When the crash of 1840 came, some "wildcat" banks went on the dodge in an effort to escape note holders. In *Detroit: Dynamic City,* Arthur Pound writes:

> As banks went out of business, and those with sound money took to hoarding, there presently was not enough money left in circulation to carry on even the greatly decreased volume of trade. As a result of being cursed with too much money, Detroit was presently cursed with too little. Companies were forced to use due-bills; the city issued shin-plaster script; wooden bowls were used for small change. "Don't take any wooden money" remains in the Michigan idiom as a depression counterpart of the pithy boom phrase "land-office business."

In 1847, still mistrustful of the British nearby in Canada, legislators decided to move the capital, though Detroit fought for it. Perceiving the partisan opinions on a site for the capital, one legislator proposed a tiny town (a cluster of homes and a sawmill) on the Grand River as a neutral alternative. If *one* side couldn't win outright, then *no* side should win, he argued. The capital moved to Lansing.

D<small>ETROIT</small>

#### ◆ CIVIL WAR

By the outbreak of the Civil War, Detroit had left the fur trade and farming far behind, having turned instead to the manufacture of steam engines, wagons, buggies, ships, copper smelting, and the production of salt. Just in time. With the fall of Fort Sumter to Southern troops, President Abraham Lincoln sent out an urgent call for military support. With the state treasury empty, the city of Detroit loaned $50,000 to the war effort and called up citizens for matching funds. Within two weeks, Detroit's First Michigan Infantry was training at Fort Wayne. A month later 780 new soldiers boarded steamships, then trains for Washington, proudly reporting in as the first western regiment. Detroit's Fifth Michigan Infantry received its colors in September 1861 and fought in many battles, among them

*This 1862 broadside offered impressive incentives for those signing up with the 20th Michigan Infantry Regiment. For joining (and, of course, surviving), each volunteer would be given $100 and 160 acres of land, as well as up to $15 a month for his family. (Bentley Historical Library, University of Michigan)*

☞ **RESPOND** ☜

# TO OUR COUNTRY'S CALL!!

## WANTED!

**100 AbLE Bodied Men, to Fill up the Ranks of the**
Company being raised in this city, for the

## 20TH REGIMENT!

# $100 BOUNTY!

### 25 DOLLARS ON BEING MUSTERED INTO
Service; $13,00, the first month's pay and a premium of $2,

#### MAKING IN ALL $40

That each VOLUNTEER RECEIVES IN ADVANCE. The FAMILY of a VOLUNTEER RECEIVES $5 to $15 a month from the County.

# AT THE CLOSE OF THE WAR

100 ACRES OF LAND AND THE REMAINING 75 DOLLARS OF THE BOUNTY.

The last opportunity is now offered to patriots to volunteer in the service of their country. Men must respond speedily to the call or drafting will be resorted to for our country is in danger. The drafted man receives only his $11 per month. Our government has been liberal to us—let us be prompt to sustain it. A Regiment raised in 30 days is worth two raised in 60.

*Recruiting Office two doors West of Cook's Hotel in Donelly's new Block, Ann Arbor.*

**C. B. GRANT, CAPTAIN.**

Fredericksburg, Chancellorsville, and Gettysburg under the name of the "Fighting Fifth." Detroit alone furnished 6,000 men—one out of every eight citizens.

◆ CITY OF INDUSTRY

With the war over, soldiers returned. Their wounds and diseases attracted the attention of medical men, pharmacists, and chemists. In 1867, a company started manufacturing drugs to address the soldiers' problems. Four years later, the company changed its name to Parke, Davis & Co. Soon other firms followed suit, and Detroit became a center for the manufacture of quality pharmaceuticals.

Detroit was still a major shipping port, manufacturing products for the Great Lakes maritime industry, both for building and repairs. At the end of the 19th century, factories were producing railroad cars, horse-drawn streetcars, stoves, furnaces, engines, and other products based on raw materials such as lumber, copper, and iron. Products ranged from beer to paint to cigars to shoes. The popular Governor Cass had called Detroit the City of Muscle, and it was flexing it with factories. Under the pall of factory smoke, citizens built libraries, colleges, theaters, a fine opera house, and grand estates along the river.

*A 1900 panoramic photochrome print of Detroit, then known as "the most beautiful city in America." (Library of Congress)*

Subsequently, Henry Ford and his use of assembly lines made Detroit the world's first truly modern industrial city, and, more importantly, vaulted it into prominence as Motor City. The only Motor City. While it is true that by 1904, Detroit had already established itself as the world's leading auto producer, it was not until 1908 that Henry Ford propelled the city into unassailable dominance when he utilized assembly lines to produce an *affordable* Model T.

In revolutionizing personal transportation, Ford also revolutionized labor, offering a five-dollar minimum wage for an eight-hour day, thereby launching the largest economic immigration the world had yet seen and creating the ethnic mix that remains Detroit's essential strength today.

By 1913, 43 auto companies were operating in Detroit, plus all their attendant parts manufacturers. The following year, 26 new auto firms were in production. By 1933, there were only seven left, led by Ford, General Motors, and Chrysler, creating a web of manufacturing that spread from the riverfront across Detroit to the suburbs and nearby towns.

Along its 300-year-old history Detroit has become both hard-bitten and sophisticated. It is a town of dirty fingernails where assembly line workers and executives alike bring their families to the Art Institute to admire Monet's paintings, Rodin sculptures, and the worker-oriented murals of Diego Rivera.

So take off those myopic, greener-pastures lenses we all tend to use, and put this city into proper focus. Come along on a trip through time to the place that is still the world's motor capital, despite its smudges and black eyes—a city that has, over the years, had as profound an effect on American culture as any other U.S. city.

## DETROIT GOES TO WORK

*In 1946, the* WPA *guide to Michigan described Detroit as being "not so long ago a quiet tree-shaded city, unobtrusively going about its business of brewing beer and making carriages and stoves."*

*B*ulky Georgian mansions frowned over iron fences on Woodward and Jefferson Avenues and Detroiters took modest pride in calling theirs "the most beautiful city in America." Then came Ford. Not only Ford, but Buick, Durant, R.E. Olds, the Fisher brothers and numerous others whose names survive in present and past motorcars. The automobile, which was to change all America, wrought its first profound changes in Detroit. The city grew at an unprecedented pace, its pulse beat quickening to the staccato rhythm of the riveters, as steel swung into place and grimly functional factories reared up almost overnight. Here was a new America: a new frontier coming into existence long after the physical frontier had been conquered. Detroit grew as mining towns grow—fast, impulsive, and indifferent to the superficial niceties of life. Niceties could wait. Meanwhile, there were automobiles to be made.

Detroit rolled up its sleeves and went to work. The old Georgian mansions were converted into rooming houses. Trees were chopped down so that the streets could be widened. The title of "most beautiful city" became hollow. But who cared? Go-getters thought up snappier slogans: "Dynamic Detroit"; "In Detroit Life Is Worth Living"; "Watch Detroit Grow; Better Still, Grow with It!" And Detroit grew. It absorbed suburbs and, when it could not absorb them, grew around them. Young fellows flocked in from the farms of Michigan, Tennessee, Georgia, Poland, Italy, Hungary, Greece—from all over the old and the new world.

Detroit had a special need for young men. The high-speed machines, in which auto parts were cut and shaped, and the throbbing converyor belts, on which the finished cars were assembled, needed the suppleness of youthful fingers, the nervous alertness of youthful brains, and the stamina of youthful bodies. Detroit needed young men and the young men came.

—Michigan Writers' Project, *Michigan,* 1941

## ■ DETROIT TODAY

There is a saying in this one-industry city: "When the nation catches a cold, Detroit gets pneumonia; when the nation prospers, Detroit is on a boom." Thus it weathered booms and recessions, depressions, race riots, wars, and strikes that led to the formation of the United Automobile Workers of America and other unions.

Today, Detroit is at a crossroads. After the race riots of the late 1960s, industrial flight from downtown, and the impact of foreign competition from Japan and Germany, the city seemed caught in an endless downward spiral. Now, there are hints and glints of an upturn. In the background, however, there lurks the dread of yet another downturn in the automobile industry. Remember when it laughed at those "unsellable" VW bugs, Honda Civics, and early BMWs?

Still, there is a vibrancy to the city that has not been felt in at least 40 years. After decades of talk, new building is finally returning. The side-by-side **Comerica Park**, new home of the Detroit Tigers, and **Ford Field**, where the Detroit Lions will play, have spurred some companies to re-enter the city. Burned out hulks of homes from another era are being razed, and new housing and other developments are appearing. The venerable Eastern Market area, where many metro residents shop for fresh vegetables on Saturday mornings, winter and summer, is getting a face-lift. There is talk of refurbishing more of the movie palaces that circle the area surrounding the elegantly restored Fox Theater, and commercial developers are dangling a toe into the water, giving hope that eventually they can build a solid downtown commercial base.

A dearth of shops and other retail businesses still throws a shadow over downtown. In the 1950s and '60s, the streets filled with movie-goers and diners on weekend nights. Stores like Hudson's, the largest department store in the world—brought down under a cloud of dust by demolition a few years ago—bustled with shoppers. Today, the small shops that replaced the large department and clothing stores along Woodward Avenue close at dusk, and sidewalks quickly empty after business hours. There are a few pockets of entertainment, particularly the new, brightly lit temporary casinos and the principal dining districts of Greektown and Rivertown. On summer weekends, Hart Plaza regularly hosts a series of festivals.

And, as in any other big city, there are places to avoid, such as the east side, but there is nevertheless plenty to see and do in this city that can be enjoyed in safety.

By American standards, Detroit is a very old community—300 years old in 2001—and in places it shows its age. But the city of Antoine de la Mothe Cadillac the explorer, and Edison and Ford the inventors, is very much alive and well, feeling better, thank you, and waiting for you to explore it.

◆ RENAISSANCE CENTER    *map page 55–see inset*

For a view of Detroit's future, stroll from downtown onto one of the city's principal thoroughfares, Jefferson Avenue, to the building where Detroit's reinvention began.

In 1974, in the midst of an oil embargo and economic recession, the late Henry Ford II announced the building of a multitowered complex and 73-story skyscraper that would soar above the Detroit River and the city like a phoenix rising out of its ashes—the Renaissance Center.

When it was completed, pedestrians along Jefferson Avenue stared up at walls designed to hide air conditioning systems—and saw battlements instead. Despite the architects' attempts to give it a friendly appearance, "RenCen" looked like a fort, a walled-off safe zone in the middle of a hostile city. Inside, the center wasn't much more successful. The maze of towers was nearly impossible to navigate. Developers tried everything from color-coded painted lines on the floor to information booths where people could get directions.

*Evening skyline view of downtown Detroit as seen from the Canadian side of the Detroit River. The Renaissance Center rises at right.*

# DETROIT

0    .25    .5 Miles

0    .25    .5    .75 Kilometers

## Inset map (downtown detail)

New Hellas Macomb
Cafe
Greektown
Trappers
Alley
Pegasus
Taverna
People
Mover
Courtyard
by Marriott
US Customs

Comerica Park

Atheneum
Suite Hotel

Mariners'
Church

Ford
Renaissance
Center

Ford
Auditorium

Fox Theater

Grand Circus
Park

Joe Louis
Statue

Woodward

Cobo
Center

Dossin Great
Lake Museum

Belle Isle Aquarium
& Whitcomb
Conservatory

Gabriel
Richard
Park

Douglas MacArthur
Bridge

Belle Isle
Zoo

Belle Isle Park

BELLE ISLE

Fountain

Waterworks
Park

Stockton
Park

Memorial
Park

Owen
Park

## Main map

Cadillac

Mack

Charlevoix

East Grand

Ketcheval

Blvd

Blvd

East

Mt Elliott

Avenue

McDougal

St Aubin

Forest

Warren

East

Ave

To
Hamtramck

Russell

Mack

St Aubin

Gratiot

Chene
Park

Lafayette
Park

375

Lafayette

Jefferson

River

Detroit-Windsor Tunnel (toll)

Gladstone

St E

St E

St

St

Louis

Wyandotte

Riverside

Erie

WINDSOR

Canadian
Customs

Ouellette

Avenue

Dieppe
Park

Ave W

Janette

St

St W

Drive

University

Riverside

Wyandotte

Detroit River

United States
Canada

Museum of
African-American
History

Detroit
Science Center &
Omnimax Theater

DETROIT

Brush

Woodward

Brush

Elizabeth

Woodward

Michigan

Fort

Cass
Park

Avenue

Stinson

Warren

Lincoln

Trumbull

Harrison

14th
St

West

Forest

Ave

Trumbull

Grand River

Warren

St

14th

To
Dearborn,
Ann Arbor

Michigan

Hitsville USA

W Grand
Blvd

To
Dearborn,
Ann Arbor

Bagley

14th

21st St

US
Customs

Street W

Fort

Ambassador
Bridge (toll)

Vernor

Clark

Blvd

Detroit
Historical
Museum

Institute of Arts

Woodward

Ave

Harrison

Trumbull
St

14th

Grand

Blvd

See map
at right

With the 1996 announcement that General Motors had purchased the complex in a $75 million deal to move its headquarters from its 1930s New Center area GM Building, changes were announced to make the RenCen into what its original designers had intended. *Jefferson Ave. between Brush St. and Beaubien; 313-568-5600.*

◆ RIVERWALK    *map page 55–see inset*

Overlooking the river on the RenCen first floor is a model of plans almost too immense to imagine. With the help of a guide, I could almost see the new entrances and towers pulsing with renewed vitality, and allowed myself to dream about the lighted riverfront promenade stretching from Joe Louis Arena to the RenCen. Eventually it will extend all the way to Belle Isle to the north, with miniparks and viewing areas for watching the passing parade of boats and ships. Right now it's a shadow of what it will be, but when it's eventually finished (some skeptical citizens say "if"), this four-mile pathway will top my list as the city's outstanding park resource.

◆ MARINER'S CHURCH    *map page 55–see inset*

Remember the line in Canadian singer Gordon Lightfoot's ballad "Wreck of the *Edmund Fitzgerald,"* in which he sings about the "maritime sailor's cathedral"? This is it. Nestled amid the noise and hubbub of downtown near the Renaissance Center, this Gothic-style limestone church holds regular Anglican services. Once a year, the Great Lakes fleet is blessed and the *Fitzgerald* remembered. As the song describes, the church's bells echo 29 times along the busy Detroit River, one for each man who went down aboard the ore freighter in 1975. *170 E. Jefferson; 313-259-2206.*

◆ JOE LOUIS FIST AND STATUE    *map page 55–see inset*

This is quite a sight. Hanging from a black triangle on the Jefferson Avenue median immediately east of Woodward across from Hart Plaza is a huge black fist directed horizontally towards the river. It's the fist of Joe Louis, former heavyweight boxing champ, who grew up in Detroit. Some say it is a fist of anger; others, a fist of power and pride. Whatever the interpretation, it depicts the Brown Bomber's legendary devastating power. A standing Joe Louis in his prime, ready to take on any challenger, is inside the lobby of Cobo Center. *One Washington Blvd.*

*(opposite) The Renaissance Center and the Detroit People Mover.*

DETROIT

◆ GREEKTOWN    *map page 55–see inset*

When looking for fun downtown, I inevitably head for Greektown. So named when Greek immigrants laid claim to that part of the city as the nucleus of their community in the 1880s, the city's most popular entertainment district is alive both day and night with tourists as well as city residents.

I feel the same vibrancy here as found in faraway Athens, with small cafes where elderly gentlemen meet for morning coffee, and grocers who sell hard-crusted Greek bread, feta cheese, and Greek wines. Storekeepers stand on the sidewalk hawking the wares that wait inside.

**Trapper's Alley**

A Greektown centerpiece, the four-level marketplace is housed in a late-19th-century tannery with shops, boutiques, and restaurants, with exposed brick walls part of the decor. From balconies and cross-walks diners and shoppers can be seen in the courtyard below, with banners and lush foliage adding splashes of color.

There's a favorite two-block stretch of Monroe Street where you hear "Ooopa!" shouted continually from the numerous Greek restaurants as waiters light *saganaki* (flaming cheese appetizers) to the delight of diners. Take your pick of restaurants here; you can hardly go wrong. Other recommendations are included in the lodging and dining section of this book, but since

*The Joe Louis Fist in downtown Detroit.*

Greektown and Detroit's Coney Islands are an attraction unto themselves, they both deserve a visit. They're all good, but here are a few of my favorites:

*New Hellas Café.*

### New Hellas Café

Walk through the glass and wood doors and step into the soul of Greektown. Opened in 1901, New Hellas is one of the original Greek restaurants and has been continuously owned by the same family. All the Greek dishes are great, from braised lamb shanks and rice pilaf, to the appetizers. And don't let the idea of marinated squid scare you from trying it. It's great.

The saganaki here is a must. *583 Monroe Ave.; 313-961-5544.*

### Pegasus Taverna

More epic Greek meals await. Try the combo platter of lamb, shrimp, gyros sandwiches, stuffed grape leaves, artichokes, and eggplant. *558 Monroe St.; 313-964-6800.*

### Fishbone's Rhythm Kitchen Café

Okay, so it's not Greek. But this relative newcomer to Greektown fits right in with the fun, offering up spicy authentic New Orleans–style meals, including jambalaya and alligator appetizers on tables festooned with several types of hot sauce, from mild to wild. If you're looking for a quiet, romantic spot, go elsewhere, as it can get a bit loud. *400 Monroe St. at Brush; 313-965-4600.*

### ◆ DETROIT'S CONEY ISLANDS

About half a dozen blocks from Greektown and west of Woodward, it's coney central for Detroit's hometown meal. I can still remember my family heading for our favorite coney place after attending anything from the symphony to the auto show downtown. We'd sit at tables with scenes straight out of Edward Hopper's classic painting *Nighthawks,* and listen as waiters in white paper caps and white aprons delivered coneys and bowls of steaming, cumin-laced, meaty chili to our table, accompanied by my favorite drink of choice, Orange Crush, thick with orange flavor, with bits of orange dancing in the bubbles.

The original Coney Island hot dog normally just comes with mustard, say the Coney Island folks, who should know. When it arrived in Detroit, residents made it into what it is today, so ours is a Detroit original.

There are two restaurants that have been serving 'em up for more than 70 years. Don't be surprised if you're the subject of some friendly competition for business by waiters who often step outside these two neighboring establishments looking to nab the hungry in search of a quick, inexpensive, and tasty meal that has Detroit written all over it. Operating round the clock since the 1920s, these two places were originally started by the same Greek family. The only difference is that the **Lafayette Coney Island** does not serve beer and the **American Coney Island** does. The American also has a bit more elbowroom.

Inside at a counter stool or table, you may rub elbows with prominent lawyers, judges, a cop just off the beat, or a visiting celebrity. It's about as an eclectic mix of clients as you'll find anywhere.

There are only three things to order. The first is a tube steak fixed with onions and mustard—never, never ketchup—but always slathered with chili dolloped on with such dexterity by the counter cook you'd think he'd done it nearly all his life (which some of them have). Next is a streak of yellow mustard, topped by a spoonful of onions, if you wish. It's done so fast you must pay attention or you'll miss the show. Or, third, try a combo of a coney and a bowl of chili, thick and spicy, in a meaty sauce you can chew.

Waiters have a unique way of placing your order. They shout out to the front in their own unique dialect of the coney dog. It sounds something like "six on four, two no onions, two chilis, and a burger." In coney-ese, that means six coneys on four plates, two without onions, with two bowls of chili and a hamburger—but not an ordinary pressed burger. Coney burgers are made with loose beef, topped again with chili and then served traditionally on a hot dog bun or, with a nod to more modern tastes, sometimes a burger bun. All finished? Now you have tasted "down-home" Detroit. *Lafayette at 118 W. Lafayette; 313-964-8198; American at 114 W. Lafayette; 313-961-7758.*

■ BELLE ISLE    *map page 55, F-3*

Floating high like an emerald yacht in the middle of the Detroit River a few miles north of the RenCen, Belle Isle has been in the hearts of Detroiters almost since Cadillac arrived, but at first not with the intention of making it a park.

Settlers let pigs loose on the island (ostensibly to eat the rattlesnakes there). Then they had to contend with the pigs until city fathers came along and recognized what the city had here. In the late 19th century, Frederick Law Olmsted, the designer of Central Park, transformed Hog Island into Belle Isle. It quickly became a 985-acre playground for the city, where deer hid in its interior woods.

The park still is a summer playground for Detroit residents who want to picnic, play baseball, or veg out watching the ships and water go by. And yes, the deer are still there. Keep an eye out for them if you elect to take a drive around the island on its 5.5-mile loop.

On the island's south side, the **Dossin Great Lakes Museum** pays homage to the city's nautical past. Two cannons from the War of 1812's Battle of Lake Erie guard the entrance. Inside, you can listen to the communications from passing ships on the radio in the wheelhouse of a former Ford Motor Company ore carrier. *100 Strand Dr.; 313-852-4051.*

*(above) The Dossin Great Lakes Museum.*

*(opposite) Fireworks explode above the harbor during the Freedom Festival, behind the head of the* Spirit of Detroit *statue.*

DETROIT

### ◆ BELLE ISLE ZOO

Belle Isle's 13-acre zoo used to be called the children's zoo, but it has grown to become a favorite park fixture featuring more than 130 animals from kangaroos to Sumatran tigers, all viewed from a three- to four-mile-long elevated walkway. The zoo's past isn't forgotten. There are lots of farm animals for children to pet, as well as a unique spider exhibit that will either fascinate them or send 'em squealing. *Central Ave.; 313-852-4083.*

### ◆ FISH AND FLOWERS

It may not be the largest aquarium on the Great Lakes, but the **Belle Isle Aquarium** is one of my favorites. Perhaps I feel that way because I am a fisherman. Focus is on freshwater fish found in Michigan and others imported from around the world. It also features a coral reef exhibit with stingrays, electric eels, and saltwater species, *(313-852-4141)*. Next door is the domed **Whitcomb Conservatory,** which houses more than 2,000 species of blooming tropical plants. Clumps of orchids dot the pathways. *Conservatory and Inselruhe Aves.; 313-852-4064.*

*Scott Fountain in Belle Isle Park.*

*A hydroplane races in the APBA Gold Cup.*

## ◆ APBA GOLD CUP

Watching a boat speed past at 200 m.p.h. down this stretch of the river in early July raises my heartbeat to almost the same speed. Now sponsored by Jeep, the race is one of the city's biggest events, drawing close to a half-million fans who watch as a dozen unlimited hydroplanes test the waters and themselves.

Hydroplanes are built to literally skip across the water's surface. Most are powered by jet turbine engines and send rooster-tail sprays high into the sky. They run at around 225 m.p.h. in the straights, but the course is trickier than most on the circuit due to waves that kick up along portions of Belle Isle and cause the craft to bobble and bounce. The races can be viewed for free from a limited stretch of Belle Isle or for a fee from stands and the grass on the mainland.

## ◆ DETROIT GRAND PRIX

The location of the future Detroit Grand Prix featuring Indy-style CART open-wheel race cars is up in the air. Plans call for moving the race from the island's southern end, possibly to the Michigan State Fairgrounds on the city's northern edge. However, this is uncertain due to concerns by residents over noise.

Regardless, there will be a race somewhere in early June, when some of the best in racing come to the city and compete over a tight road course. *313-222-0024.*

## ■ CANADIAN NEIGHBOR

Perhaps it's partly the lure of another country with different customs and different currency, *eh?* Whatever it is, **Windsor, Ontario,** draws me over and under the mile-wide Detroit River time after time. The **Detroit Windsor Tunnel** was a marvel when it opened in 1930, and it remains so. It's billed as the first and only vehicular subway built between two nations (the "chunnel" between England and France is for trains only). Proper identification is required at both ends. *100 E. Jefferson Ave., next to the Renaissance Center; 313-567-4422.*

While browsing the shops with their fine British linens and woolens, remember the duty tax at customs. (Check customs rules on refundable VAT tax and tax

*This 1941 aerial photo shows the Detroit River, with Canada in the foreground and Detroit in the background. The Ambassador Bridge can be seen in the distance.*
*(Underwood Photo Archives, San Francisco)*

*Children's Day at the Children's Museum in the Detroit Cultural Center.*

breaks for longer stays.) Or check out the duty-free shops at both ends of the bridge. I recommend the fine restaurants. Windsor dotes on its riverfront parks, especially **Dieppe Park** with its gardens and promenade along the river.

Return via the **Ambassador Bridge**, completed one year after the tunnel, from which you can see freighters and other traffic coursing up and down the river, and the skyline of Detroit stretches as far as the eye can see. *Porter St. and I-75; 313-849-5244.*

■ CULTURAL CENTER    *map page 55, B-1*

Many of Detroit's cultural attractions are conveniently located four miles north of downtown, where Wayne State University and the sprawling Detroit Medical Center campus create a mini-downtown we call the Cultural Center.

Not many think of Detroit as an arts community, but the **Detroit Institute of Arts** is the nation's fifth largest fine arts museum, with more than 100 galleries from ancient Egypt and Greece, through the Renaissance and Impressionism, and up to contemporary masters. The collections of auto tycoons like the Ford family stock the walls, as do traveling exhibits from museums around the world. *5200 Woodward Ave.; 313-833-7900.*

The Detroit Science Center, one of the top draws for families with children, is located just behind the DIA. *5020 John R St.; 313-577-8400.*

Sunlight streams through the multifaceted glass-domed ceiling, painting rainbows across the terrazzo floor of the Charles H. Wright Museum of African-American History. A three-part multimedia display orients us to eight "historical stations," with images, quotes, facts, statistics, and artifacts that bring to life the centuries-long plight of African Americans in American history.

Some exhibits are painful to examine, such as the re-created slave ships, where lifelike human figures are chained in cramped quarters, with anguish and sorrow carved on their faces. Or the replica of Dr. Martin Luther King's Birmingham jail door and a ballot box used by "colored" people. Others are victorious, such as the flight suit of NASA astronaut Mae Jemison. *315 E. Warren Ave., behind the Science Center; 313-494-5800.*

The Detroit Historical Museum captures the breadth and scope of the city's history, from Cadillac's landing on the river's banks to the city's role in industry. There's even an exhibit on the old downtown Hudson's department store. My favorite is the "Streets of Old Detroit," a cobblestone walk through history past replica 17th- and 18th-century shops. Upstairs is the interactive "Motor City" display that showcases an assembly line section where a car body drops onto a chassis. *detroithistorical.org; 5401 Woodward Ave.; 313-833-1805.*

◆ THEATER

Believe it or not, Detroit is a great city for live theater. From large houses and college repertories to neighborhood companies and comedy troupes, Detroit's stages glitter with everything from opera to Shakespeare.

The Fox Theater was one of the grandest movie palaces of the era when movie studios owned theaters. Opening in 1928, the Fox was rescued from sure self-destruction by Little Caesar's Pizza mogul Mike Ilitch and now echoes with the sounds of musicals, concerts, and other programs. The interior looks like a stage set for a Cecil B. DeMille epic, with faux marble columns, gilt, and elaborate gargoyles staring down at the immense 5,000-seat house. *2211 Woodward Ave.; 313-471-3200.*

*The lobby of the Fox Theater.*

### ◆ Sports

From a field that once held the shells of long-neglected 19th-century mansions rises an entertainment complex. For decades, both the Detroit Tigers and the Lions played in one stadium, the old Tiger Stadium on Michigan Avenue. Now, two new stadiums provide cheek-by-jowl entertainment from April to December.

**Comerica Park,** the newest addition to major league baseball diamonds, is more like a mini-amusement park than a venue for baseball. The 40,000-seat open-air stadium features the league's largest scoreboard, street-level viewing (even sidewalk umpires can call the game), a Ferris wheel, a carousel, and statues of famous players who wore the Olde English "D." *2100 Woodward Ave.; 313-962-4000.*

**Ford Field,** meanwhile, is the newest domed stadium in the Nation Football League. The Detroit Lions will abandon Pontiac's Silverdome and return to downtown, where the new stadium will seat up to 65,000 of their screaming fans. (Guess which famous Detroit family owns the team.) *Adams and Brush Sts. at St. Antoine; 800-616-ROAR, or 313-965-8450.*

AMERICAN LEAGUE CHAMPIONS 1907

| | | | | | | | | |
|---|---|---|---|---|---|---|---|---|
| Eubanks, p. | Rossman, 1st b. | Crawford, r.f. | Donovan, p. | Mullins, p. | Willett, p. | Payne, c. | Killian, p. |
| | D. Jones, l.f. | Downs, 2nd b. | Ty Cobb, c.f. | Coughlin, 3rd b. | Schaefer, 2nd b. | B. Jones, p. |
| Stever, p. | | Archer, c. | | Jennings, mngr. | | Schmidt, c. | O'Leary, s.s. |

*Detroit boasts a long, illustrious sports tradition. In 1907, the Detroit Base Ball Club won the American League Championship. Ty Cobb is seated in the middle row, third from the left.*

*A replica of Thomas Edison's laboratory stands in Greenfield Village.*

## ■ METRO DETROIT *map page 87*

Detroit is ringed by successful, vibrant suburban communities that stretch for miles. Here are highlights of the best:

### ◆ DEARBORN *map page 87, C-4*

Perhaps nowhere else is there such a collection of Americana—historically significant art, artifacts, architecture—than here in **Greenfield Village**. Founder Henry Ford was friend to moguls and inventors and brought to this 93-acre complex more than 100 historic homes, laboratories, businesses, and examples of inventions of the 19th and early 20th centuries.

Costumed characters now roam the grounds to present old-time medicine shows or other depictions of how life was, or at least how present-day residents imagine it. An authentic steam train circles the complex with an introductory overview, passing reassembled farms including the Firestone complex, where tire inventor Harvey Firestone grew up. In another spot stands a replica of Thomas

Edison's Menlo Park laboratory. Ford so revered his camping friends Edison and Firestone—they practically invented the pastime, including what might have been the first recreational vehicle—that during the celebration of the 50th anniversary of the invention of the lightbulb, Ford ordered the chair that Edison had sat in nailed to the floor of Edison's studio to exhibit it for all eternity.

Down the street stands **The Wright Cycle Co.**, where the first practical airplane was conceived and built. (The building was imported from Ohio.) Other exhibits include the **Suwanee** Steamboat, an antique carousel (that still wheezes out a merry tune), and at the **Eagle Tavern** guests are greeted by employees in period costume who treat you as if you had just stepped off the stage at this former stage-coach inn on the old route between Detroit and Chicago. African-American contributions are remembered with a replica log cabin of inventor **George Washington Carver**, along with a cabin depicting how slaves lived.

◆ HENRY FORD MUSEUM     *map page 87, C-4*

A replica of Philadelphia's Independence Hall, this museum is dedicated to American life. "The Automobile in American Life" exhibit is a wonder of 20th-century design and rolling sculpture. A ramp guides visitors along a moving caravan of the development of the automobile through more than 100 classic models, including the only remaining 1896 Duryea—the first mass-produced vehicle made in the nation—to the Ford GT cars that swept Le Mans, as well as present-day models. A replica drive-in, an old service station, a classic gleaming chrome roadside diner, an example of one of the first Holiday Inns, and some early camping gear are in this building, which features the largest teakwood floor in existence (at 405,000 square feet, or 9.2 acres). The world's largest indoor-outdoor museum includes some of the equipment used by Ford and his cronies. A separate display includes the Lincoln in which John F. Kennedy was riding when he was assassinated, as well as the rocking chair in which Abraham Lincoln was siting when he was shot.

Attached to the museum's west side is the complex's newest offering, the an IMAX theater. Thirteen stories tall, it features a 60- by 80-foot screen, and seats 400 persons. *From downtown Detroit, take Jefferson Ave. east and merge onto John C. Lodge Freeway north, then west on I-94 to Dearborn Ave. and Oakwood Blvd. 20900 Oakwood Blvd.; 313-271-1620.*

Across the street from the museum is the gleaming white, oval-shaped **Spirit of Ford** and its auto-oriented exhibits and shows. Hey, it's Detroit; we love cars! Inside, while you wait in the large main display hall for a turn inside one of the

## THE HENRY FORD MUSEUM

*I*walked through the museum in a state of sudden, deep admiration for Henry Ford and his acquisitive instincts. He may have been a bully and an anti-Semite, but he sure could build a nifty museum. I could happily have spent hours picking around among the memorabilia. But the hangar is only a fractional part of it. Outside there is a whole village—a little town—containing eighty homes of famous Americans. These are the actual homes, not replicas. Ford crisscrossed the country acquiring the residences and workshops of the people he most admired—Thomas Edison, Harvey Firestone, Luther Burbank, the Wright brothers, and of course himself. All these he crated up and shipped back to Dearborn where he used them to build this 250-acre fantasyland—the quintessential American small town, a picturesque and timeless community where every structure houses a man of genius (almost invariably a white, Christian man of genius from the Middle West). Here in this perfect place, with its broad greens and pleasing shops and churches, the lucky resident could call on Orville and Wilbur Wright for a bicycle inner tube, go to the Firestone farm for milk and eggs (but not for rubber yet—Harvey's still working on it!), borrow a book from Noah Webster and call on Abraham Lincoln for legal advice, always assuming he's not too busy with patent applications for Charles Steinmetz or emancipating George Washington Carver, who lives in a tiny cabin just across the street.

It is really quite entrancing. For a start, places like Edison's workshop and the boardinghouse where his employees lodged have been scrupulously preserved. You can really see how these people worked and lived. And there is a certain undeniable convenience in having the houses all brought together. Who in a million years would go to Columbiana, Ohio, to see the Harvey Firestone birthplace, or to Dayton to see where the Wright brothers lived? Not me, brother. Above all, bringing these places together makes you realize just how incredibly inventive America has been in its time, what a genius it has had for practical commercial innovation, often leading to unspeakable wealth, and how many of the comforts and pleasures of modern life have their roots in the small towns of the American Middle West. It made me feel proud.

—Bill Bryson, *The Lost Continent, Travels in Small-Town America,* 1989

*A line of 1899 horseless carriage designs is unveiled in front of the Olds Motor Works factory, which once stood near the Belle Isle Bridge.*

three theaters, you can ogle the latest in race or concept cars. My favorite show is the simulator ride. All strapped in? You're about to enter a NASCAR race. Hold on! No need, really, but I feel that way as the seats begin to move, rocking and rolling to the rhythm and the roar of the speeding car. Next, you become an automobile running through a Ford assembly line. Such bouncing and tilting and rocking, metal grinding against metal, misters adding the smells of paint and rubber as new Fords near the assembly finish line. Aha, my motor is revved and I'm rarin' to go!

Once, after watching a youngster "ride it out," I saw her tugging at her mother's hand, calling, "More, more." So, you can figure it's safe for kids. I even watched from the bleachers as preteens formed teams to change tires against the clock during a simulated NASCAR pit stop. It's easy to let the inner child out to enjoy the computers where you can design your own cars or mold your own accessories into the big clay model. There's also a gift shop. The admission fee is a bit high, but it's worth it. *1151 Village Rd.; 313-31-SPIRIT.*

*A 1999 "concept car" design is unveiled at the International Auto Show, held at the Cobo Center in Dearborn.*

◆ FAIR LANE    *map page 87, C-4*

Henry Ford grew up in Dearborn. After he'd made his vast fortune, he came home again, building this estate beside the Rouge River a few miles upstream of the Ford Rouge complex. Tours of the 1914 mansion and grounds include the restored and working river powerhouse that provides electricity to the mansion. The 1920s camper Ford used with friends Edison and Firestone is on display, as is a prototype electric car Ford built with Edison, and a Fordson tractor, which helped mechanize the American farm. A walking tour meanders through the restored gardens created by renowned designer Jens Jensen. *4901 Evergreen Rd. at the southern end of the University of Michigan-Dearborn campus; 313-593-5590.*

◆ ROYAL OAK    *map page 87, D-4*

Opened in 1928, the **Detroit Zoo** was nationally acclaimed and copied for its bar-free animal exhibits using dry or water moats to keep animals confined and thus providing better views. Make reservations in advance for the trackless train and a narrated tour around the 125-acre grounds. A great ride.

*continues on page 78*

# HENRY FORD

*I*n every sense of the word, Henry Ford was a complex man. On one hand, he may have contributed more than any other individual besides his friend and mentor Thomas Edison to the reality of the modern world. On the other hand, he fought to suppress and control a society that would remain forever at arm's length. He could be talkative and entertaining, but could suddenly stop in mid-sentence and blurt out, "That's not what I was thinking at all," excusing himself to disappear into his laboratory, sometimes for days, until he emerged with a new engine element, new car design, factory layout, rail locomotive, or other pioneering idea.

*Henry Ford, circa 1925. (Bentley Historical Library, University of Michigan)*

Born on July 30, 1863, in Dearborn, he was the oldest of six children born to first-generation Irish farmers William and Mary Litogot O'Hern Ford. Not rich but far from poor, the family fared well. Ford's legendary curiosity was demonstrated at an early age. Fascinated by the vapors rising from the boiling water in the tea kettle on the kitchen stove, Henry plugged up the spout. With no outlet for the steam, the kettle exploded, shooting hot water in all directions. His practical side began as he tinkered with farm tools. He was fond of recounting the July day in 1876 when he saw his first self-propelled steam engine working a farmer's field.

Fifty years later, Ford was producing 57percent of the automobiles sold in America and around half the cars sold worldwide. As an adult, Ford allowed no one to use his first name, but he was proud to affix his last name on the affordable Model T and Model A automobiles. The slender five-foot, nine-inch, long-legged industrialist baffled even those who knew him best. When he set the industrial world on edge with his production line for the Model T and $5 for an eight-hour workday, he built nearby housing complexes where workers lived to keep his factories moving. Workers grumbled at Ford rules that came with living there. Inspectors knocked at regular intervals, inquiring into lifestyles with questions that some took as intrusive. As in other matters, it was Ford's way or no way.

In 1915, as World War I dragged on, Ford's pacifist leanings led him to lease the sailing ship *Oscar II* which he proclaimed the Peace Ship. On December 4, he boarded her and set sail for Norway on a self-proclaimed mission to end the war, pledging to be "home by Christmas." The effort failed, but Ford later said, "At least I tried." Years later, with the advent of World War II, his pacifism took a back seat to full-out, one-an-hour factory production of B-24 "Liberator" bombers at Willow Run.

In 1916, the *Chicago Tribune* attributed to Ford the incorrect information that employees who left their jobs to serve in the National Guard would lose their jobs. The following day a *Tribune* editorial followed up by calling Ford an "ignorant idealist." Ford sued, and the trial—staged in Mount Clemens—made headlines around the world. Well aware of Ford's lack of interest beyond the inventive, experts drilled him for hours about his general knowledge of the day. He saw little value in the drills, since he said he could pay workers to locate such information for him in five minutes. Badgered by lawyers, with journalists frantically taking notes, Ford calmly sat in the witness chair, his long legs crossed as he sharpened his pocket knife absently on the bottom of his leather shoe. When asked what this nation was before its discovery by the Europeans, he kept sharpening his knife and without a glance upward, said, "Dirt, I guess." The jury settled against the *Tribune,* but awarded Ford only six cents in damages.

The common people loved his folksy responses—and bought more Fords. After the trial, Ford seemed more conscious of education and history. He built schools, experimental farms, small-town factories, and hospitals. He developed an obsessive collection of historical memorabilia, and housed it in the Henry Ford Museum and Greenfield Village at Dearborn. An avid camper, Ford took long auto trips—in Model Ts, with a Japanese chef—with Thomas Edison, Harvey Firestone, and naturalist John Burroughs. An avid hiker, he would be out morning and afternoon, ending the day around a campfire telling rambling stories and tall tales.

Exasperated with the newspapers of the day, he published his own *Dearborn Independent* where he aired his own anti-Semitic and anti-labor views. In 1933, Ford led the fight against the fledgling United Auto Workers (UAW) unionization efforts led by Walter Reuther. Hiring an army (some claim it numbered up to 2,000) ironically called the "Service Department," Ford took on the union organizers. In 1937, the conflict erupted in the "Battle of the Overpass," where Ford's goons viciously attacked Reuther and other UAW officials handing out union flyers near a Ford plant gate. Photojournalists captured the incident, and it outraged the nation. Courts ordered Ford to cease interfering with union activities, and the UAW contract was signed in 1941.

Ford was notorious for avoiding his office, preferring instead the noise and clatter of his assembly line. To escape the social whirl of Detroit, he built his Fair Lane estate at Dearborn. Then, prompted by his love of dancing, he organized grand balls that were the rage of society. In 1945, Ford's grandson Henry II took him to Greenfield Village, and watched his 81-year-old grandfather climb aboard his original "quadricycle" horseless carriage for a ride along the streets of the man-made colonial America. In 1947, the man who idolized Thomas Edison and his electric lightbulb, the man who did the most to create the world on wheels, died quietly by candlelight.

DETROIT

At **Prairie Dog Town,** I enjoy watching the kids as much as the critters. Kids enter an underground tunnel to pop up in a plastic bubble in the middle of the town, with the burrowing animals all around them.

The newest exhibit to open is the **National Amphibian Conservation Center.** It showcases frogs and other amphibians from across the planet and will be used to study why these animals are disappearing so quickly. Other favorites include the **Penguinarium** and the **Chimps of Harambee.** Visitors can view chimpanzees in natural settings and even up close from blinds. Another new gallery includes an aquarium with Pacific Ocean fish, plus a butterfly-and-hummingbird garden.

*From downtown, take I-75 north to I-696 and watch for the zoo signs near the Woodward Avenue exit. Ten Mile Rd. and Woodward Ave; 248-398-0900.*

**Cranbrook** in suburban Bloomfield Hills boasts an extraordinary institute of science, an art museum, and gardens. *39211 Woodward Ave.; 877-GO-CRAN-BROOK.* Wake with the dawn to join farmers for breakfast at restaurants in **Eastern Market** as they set up their stalls of tomatoes, potatoes, petunias, live chickens, and other market goods fresh from local farms. Then wander through shops of nose-tingling spices, freshly ground coffee beans, and baskets hanging from the rafters. *On Russell St. between Mack Ave. and Gratiot; 313-833-1560.*

*Produce stalls at the Eastern Market, shown here in full swing on a Sunday morning.*

## MOTOWN: MORE THAN MUSIC

For a particular group of Americans—many of them born between 1955 and 1968, in or near a Northeastern or Midwestern city, Detroit's most significant product was not a Chevrolet, or a Ford, or any car. For us, "Motown"—a contraction of "Motor City"—calls up visions of scratched-up 45s, little faded blue maps, and faded blue, sequined gowns, and subtle, stylish dance moves. A Motown hit is likely to be as etched in our memory as our first crush. (Likelier still for those such as myself, whose first crush *was* a Motown star—in my case, Michael, youngest of the foxy Jackson 5.) Clearly, our fandom is strong, but our opinions are not monolithic. For instance, I believe that a life without Stevie Wonder is not a life worth living, while others say the same of sultry Marvin Gaye. Some prefer Smokey Robinson's vulnerable, sweet falsetto; others, Edwin Starr's angry, percussive bass. Energetic and earthy types work it out to the Vandellas; the fashionably fabulous swoon over the Supremes.

For most of us, hearing these songs today inspires fond, sweet recollections; it's hard to resist singing along or mimicking the slick moves of, say, the Temptations, the Four Tops, or Gladys Knight's Pips. Witness how the Motown-heavy soundtrack for *The Big Chill*—1983's Target-the-Baby Boomer film about a dozen upper-middle-class 30-somethings and their New England y college reunion—made for extra nostalgia in every soundbite.

The setting in which Motown the Company came to be, however—the turbulent, racially charged Detroit of the 1960s—reads a little different from the upbeat memories most of us acquired as children. From its 1958 founding until the 1973 relocation to Los Angeles, Motown was deeply intertwined with both the changing automobile industry and the Civil Rights Movement in Detroit.

The African-American community in which Motown founder Berry Gordy Jr. grew up was one long established in Detroit, largely because of the auto industry. In 1914, Henry Ford announced a five-dollar daily wage, drawing many black Americans from the South. (The Model T was also the first car black Americans could afford). "I'm goin' to Detroit, get myself a good job / I'm goin' to get me a job, up there in Mr. Ford's place," went one frequently played blues tune. The migration resulted in a large black community whose members shared similar backgrounds and musical traditions; they could also commiserate about their dreary jobs—as in Joe L. Carter's lyric, "Please, Mr. Foreman, slow down your assembly line. No, I don't mind workin', but I do mind dyin'." Blues singer/Chrysler assembler Bobo Jenkins drew rhythmic inspiration, "That whirlin' machinery gives me the beat. Every song I ever wrote that's any good has come to me standin' on that line."

DETROIT

*The fabulous Supremes.*

Likewise, when Berry Gordy, Jr., worked a short stint on the line at the Ford Wayne Assembly plant, he found himself composing songs to fight the oppressive machine beat. He learned about something else, too: mass production. After seeing shiny new cars rolling off the line, one after the other, Gordy realized that the concept could be applied at the record company he hoped to start. And apply it he did. With a loan of $800 from his family, in 1959 he and songwriter partner Raynoma Mayberry Liles rented a converted house on West Grand Boulevard. The highly talented musicians they'd attracted—Gordy, already manager for the Miracles, had a gift for pulling talent—went with them, and optimistically dubbed the barebones studio "Hitsville, USA."

Their nickname came true two weeks after moving in, when their song "Money (That's What I Want)"—an appropriate tune for the ambitious company—hit Number 2 on the charts. While Detroit could claim many African-American owned-and-operated companies, Berry Gordy's company was the first to aim for and achiecve great crossover success. One key to his success was the attention he paid to "packaging" his acts, especially in the case of the Supremes, for whom choreographers, hair and makeup stylists, fashion consultants, even elocutionists were hired to give them the right polish. And befitting a Detroit company, Motown used the auto industry to sell product. Marvin Gaye posed next to his Cadillac. Martha and the Vandellas were filmed riding in the new Ford Mustang, itself specifically marketed to the vast numbers of young drivers. Groups were filmed in automobile assembly plants for local appeal. And finally, song writers paid special attention to the advent of the car radio, writing short songs more likely to be played by radio stations—especially by white radio stations. Of all Mustang purchasers in 1963, 80 percent asked for radios in them—proof, perhaps, of Motown's marketing savvy.

Meanwhile, ironically, increasing automation in the auto industry was leaving a disproportionate number of African Americans out of work in this one-industry town: black Americans were still denied access to the executive ranks, and were discriminated against on the job. The Civil Rights Movement, gaining momentum in the South, had different issues to wrestle with than in the industrial north. Since 1953, urban renewal projects had demolished

*The foxy Jackson 5.*

*The slick Temptations.*

10,000 buildings in the city; 70 percent of the occupants displaced were black. By the early 1960s, Detroit's black political action groups were prominent, staging protests over job discrimination and segregation.

As Motown's economic strength increased, activists looked to Gordy and Motown for support. In 1963, Martin Luther King visited Detroit and led the Great March for Freedom. Berry Gordy recorded King's Detroit speech, and released it on Motown's pioneering spoken-word label—Black Forum—just in time the Great March on Washington. But the words of Detroiter Malcolm X, who spoke in Detroit just a few months later, were too controversial for Black Forum: Malcolm advocated separatism and nationalism, while Motown's political line was integrationist—its financial gains were dependent upon crossover. Nonetheless, in the years that followed, Motown became the sound of Detroit of the '60s. Martha and the Vandellas' 1967 hit "Dancing in the Street," became a rallying cry for urban protests, even though its singers insisted it was just a "party song." Later in the decade, Stevie Wonder and Marvin Gaye challenged the Motown standard of lightweight Motown hits and created albums of social protest; Edwin Starr's version of "War," contrary to executive predictions, was a smash hit. While Motown was truly of Detroit, by the end of the 1960s, internal differences at Motown put the company at odds with its community. While the assassination of Martin Luther King had inspired Gordy and his executives to participate in civil rights causes again, for many this was not enough. Artists wanted more songwriting freedom as well as more equitable royalty payments. The Dodge Revolutionary Union Movement (DRUM) was challenging the status quo in the auto industry and inspiring worker movements all over town. And Berry Gordy began pursuing the acquisition of small Detroit-born-and-raised record labels. Motown decamped to Los Angeles in 1973; no longer in spirit or place in Motown City, the company was never the family it had been. You can even tell by the record label: after the relocation, the map on the label was faded back, with the star marking Detroit barely visible.

*Marvin Gaye's landmark album* What's Going On?

Still, you *can* visit the Motown Museum, on the site of the original Hitsville USA, where The Sound was born. *2648 West Grand at Rosa Parks; 313-875-2264.*

—Julia Dillon

# S O U T H E A S T

## ■ HIGHLIGHTS

*(for DETROIT, see pages 44–80)*

## ■ TRAVEL BASICS

**Area Overview:** The landscape of southeast Michigan is flat as a pancake—until you get to the Irish Hills. Formed by the eroded deposits of glacial moraines, these rolling hills are distinctive for their oak openings and lakes. The state capital, Lansing, rests at the center of the crossroads of Interstates 96 and 69, in the middle of farmland and forest—a patchwork pattern that continues north all the way to Bay City. The best time to visit is from late March to November.

**Getting There:** The highways of this part of Michigan are a rough grid of interstates with the long, lazy diagonal of US-12 (the old Chicago Road) stretching from Michiana at the Indiana-Michigan border to downtown Detroit. Major airports are located at Detroit, Flint, and Lansing.

**Climate:** Summers average between 85 to 90 degrees and are humid and warm. Fall and spring are similar in temperature ranging from 65 to 75 with lows in the 50s. Winters average in the upper 30s and drop to the 20s, but rarely fall below zero, even on winter nights.

**Food & Lodging:** Cuisine in these parts is mostly "fast." However, many small town diners and B&B breakfasts can be pleasantly surprising. *Please refer to the listings beginning on page 274 .*

# ■ HISTORY

Attracted by the flat terrain and rich soil, homesteaders began arriving in Southeast Michigan in the early 1800s They were soon followed by timbermen who, having exhausted the forests of the northeast, were attracted to the vast tracts of Michigan white pine.

In 1837, as it sought statehood, Michigan claimed a piece of land on its southern border that Ohio (admitted in 1803) claimed as well. A bit of saber-rattling ensued revolving around an eight-mile-wide slice of land at the mouth of the Maumee River *(see map page 87)*. Known as The Toledo Strip, this stretch of land formed the northern edge of the Black Swamp—a daunting, virtually impassable morass about 40 miles wide and 100 miles long (long since drained and built over). However, both Michigan and Ohio believed it would become the launching point for future inland development. (When you consider that I-80, the nation's great bilateral highway, cuts right through it, you can see how right they were.)

Seeking to resolve the conflict, Congress offered up a shotgun marriage— Michigan and Arkansas were to be admitted simultaneously on the condition that

*A contemporary drawing allegedly depicting the River Raisin massacre in 1813.*
*(William M. Clements Library, Univ. of Michigan, Ann Arbor)*

## "REMEMBER THE RIVER RAISIN"

*I*n 1812, Britain, France, and the Americans were fighting head-to-head, with Tecumseh and his great Indian Confederation siding with the British. In that same year, the British held two strategic and critical forts: River Raisin, in French-town (now Monroe) on the River Raisin; and Detroit—which had been surrendered by William Hull, governor of the Michigan Territory, "without a shot"—an act for which he was court-martialed. *(See essay, page 30.)* In January 1813, Col. William Lewis led 700 men, mostly Kentuckians, against the British at River Raisin. Crossing from Toledo under heavy fire over frozen Lake Erie, he captured the fort.

Fearing British reprisal, Lewis sent for reinforcements from his superior, Gen. James Winchester, who crossed over with 300 additional troops. Winchester, howev-er, chose to billet them and himself on the opposite side of the river from the fort in order to stay in the comfortable house of a well-to-do Frenchman. So comfortable was he, in fact, that he failed to leave his warm house after receiving word that the British were about to attack the fort. Early on January 22, before daylight, the British did so, and before Lewis's Kentuckians had time to form, they were set upon by the British and their Tecumseh-led Indian allies with devastating results. The tardy Win-chester was turned back, many of his troops killed and scalped, and Winchester him-self captured. But the deadly fire of the Kentuckians from within the stockade forced the British to retreat.

It was a standoff, with many dead and wounded on both sides. The British com-mander, Col. Henry Procter, convinced the Americans to surrender on the pretense that he could not prevent "his" Indian allies from wreaking havoc on civilians, even though Tecumseh was famous for his compassion toward prisoners and the wounded. Promised that the wounded would be protected by British soldiers and placed in the care of the Frenchtown civilians, Lewis capitulated, and Procter marched his prison-ers north toward Fort Malden in Canada. Early in the morning of January 23, how-ever, about 200 whiskey-inflamed Indians—who historians believe were "opportunists" and not an integral part of Tecumseh's Confederation—swept through the village, murdering and scalping the wounded. Finding most of the wounded in two houses, they set the houses afire, hurling those who tried to escape back into the flames. The display of cruelty stunned the American forces, especially the Kentuck-ians, whose rallying cry "Remember the River Raisin" ignited battlefield hatred for the British until the end of the war.

Michigan recognized Ohio's claim to the Toledo Strip. To to compensate Michigan for the loss of the Strip, Congress tossed in the Upper Peninsula—then part of the Wisconsin Territory. *Quel Insult!* Appalled by what would ultimately become the most lucrative concession ever granted to an individual state, one Michigan senator scoffed that the Upper Peninsula "could furnish the people of Michigan with Indians for all time and now and then a little bear meat for delicacy."

The rush to statehood was also spurred by a congressional decree that all states admitted to the Union by January 1, 1837, would receive a launch grant of $400,000. While most Michigan politicians decried the proposal, a small group of Michigan delegates snuck off to Ann Arbor and grudgingly acceded to it (illegally, some declared later)—in the nick of time to collect the bonus.

What Wisconsin thought of the loss of the Upper Peninsula, as colossal fortunes were garnered from its mineral riches, is not in the record.

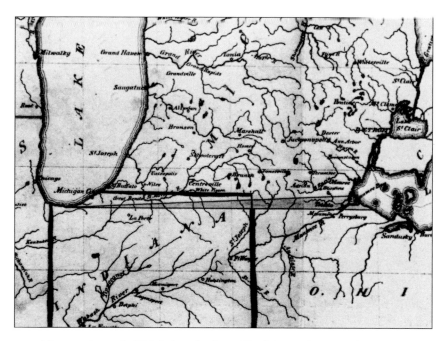

*This map depicts the "Toledo Strip," a sliver of land that Michigan was forced to cede to Ohio in order to gain statehood for itself. (Michigan State Archives)*

SOUTHEAST

# ■ MONROE   *map page 87, C-5*

In 1780, the French set up a trading post along the stream they named River Raisin after the heavy clusters of grapes that hung over the banks. A few French settlers built log cabins here, a community dubbed Frenchtown by the British. In 1835, the city of Frenchtown changed its name to Monroe in anticipation of a visit by President James Monroe (1817–25). The town of Monroe today, alas, could be Any City, with its service turnoffs and strip malls. However, there are places of interest. *For information contact: Monroe County Convention & Visitors Bureau; 106 West Front Street; 800-252-3011.*

## Custer Statue and Museum

At the Monroe Street Bridge (over the Raisin in downtown Monroe) stands a bronze equestrian statue of Lt. Col. George Armstrong Custer of Little Big Horn fame. Monroe was Custer's home town, and the **Monroe County Historical Museum** contains more Custer memorabilia than you can shake a stick at. *126 S. Monroe St.; 734-240-7780.*

## Fort River Raisin Battlefield

In 1813, when the British were challenging the fledgling United States, a regiment of Kentuckians came here at the behest of the Union and took the British fort at River Raisin. What ensued was a battle and a massacre. *(See essay, page 84)*

Today, at the River Raisin Visitors Center in Monroe you can study, on two large wall maps, the ebb and flow of the battle through recorded narrative and the clever use of fiberoptic lights embedded in the maps that pinpoint the critical events of this battle. *Weekends only, Memorial Day to Labor Day; take Exit 14 off I-75 to 1403 East Elm St.; 734-243-7136.*

## Shores of Lake Erie

The River Raisin is a twisting, turning river with reeds along its banks and low sand dunes where families picnic. Beyond the river, Lake Erie's gray-green waters beckon. Once declared dead, these waters have rebounded to the point that they now contain some of the best walleye fishing in the country. "It's walleyes from May through July," explains Capt. J. M. Ulrich, owner of a three-boat operation, "then perch from mid-August through early November. Great eating." *Trade Winds Sportfishing, Erie Party Store and Dock; 6838 La Plaisance Rd.; 734-243-2319.*

## Sterling State Park

East from Exit 17 on Dixie Highway North, follow the signs to Sterling State Park. Although smokestacks are visible both north and south, the marshes are splendid, especially when you're armed (and legged!) with bug repellent. Occasional lotus blossoms raise their snowy faces to the passersby, just as they did for the explorers who paddled past these sands 300 years ago.

## ■ STICKY MUD AND PLANK ROADS

Settlers heading west from Monroe in the 1820s and 30s faced more than 20 miles of tough going across the ancient beds of Lake Erie. Although not as bad as the Black Swamp around Toledo, the road was full of wheel-shattering potholes and wagon-miring mud. Travelers formed small trains, affording them enough horses and men to drag wagons from the mire.

### Oak Openings

The erstwhile farmers' goal was the higher ground west of Adrian, and the Oak Openings that reminded early Irish settlers of the hills back home. The Irish Hills around Cambridge Junction south of Jackson, lush green in spring and ablaze with all the glory of autumn in October, are blessed with the rich soil that marks the southern edge of the glacial drift from the last ice age.

### Walker Tavern    *map page 87, B-5*

At the junction of US-12 and M-50 near Cambridge Junction stands the 1836 Walker Tavern, which served as a stage-coach stop along the Chicago Road until 1855. While the stage driver changed horses, travelers taking the five-day journey got out, enjoyed a meal, or spent a night in the two-story farmhouse. *Walker Tavern Historic Complex; 13220 M-50; 517-467-4401.*

*Lake Erie Beach at Sterling State Park south of Detroit.*

## ■ JACKSON

*map page 87, A-4*

In 1854, a much-bally-hooed new political party convened in Jackson with a fundamental goal: elimi-nating slavery in the terri-tories. Several thousand men showed up (remem-ber, this is 70 years before women's suffrage). The overflow crowd spilled into the street and, with tem-peratures skyrocketing in the meeting hall, the con-vention was hastily recon-vened "under the oaks" at **Morgan's Forty** just out-side town. Before the sun had set, a party platform was drafted, a statewide slate of candidates was named, and the Republi-can party was born. *Second and Franklin Sts.*

*The Walker Tavern served as a rest stop for stagecoach passengers on the Chicago Road.*

### ◆ JACKSON AREA HIGHLIGHTS

**Cascade Fountain**
The 465-acre **Sparks Foundation County Park** features the Cascade Fountain, a stair-step series of 18 waterfalls in six varying heights and patterns built into the 500-foot hillside. Especially attractive at night: the fountain becomes a light show with a musi-cal background. *Follow brown Cascades Park signs; May–Sept.; 517-788-4320.*

**Michigan Space and Science Center**
Beneath its geodesic dome reside the Apol-lo 9 command module, a memorial to the astronauts on the shuttle *Challenger,* and other reminders of our first steps into space. *2111 Emmons Rd.; 517-787-4425.*

### Ella Sharp Museum

In contrast to the Space and Science Center is this evocative reminder of 19th-century farm life with its pioneer log cabin, Victorian house and barn with 1800s carriages and sleighs, and three art galleries. *3225 Fourth St.; 517-787-2320.*

### Mann House

Twelve miles west of Jackson on M-60 in the village of Concord, is another historic farm. Daniel and Ellen Mann built this two-story Victorian house in 1883. The eight rooms, all with period furniture, date back to the 1840s. Visit the herb gardens and the restored Victorian Rose Garden. *205 Hanover St.; 517-524-8743.*

## ■ LANSING    *map page 87, A-3*

When visiting Lansing, look for the capitol on the skyline, with its spiral dome and spire rising 267 feet. Adjacent is East Lansing, home to Michigan State University. Together, these two towns are beehives of state offices, restaurants, taverns, shops, and museums.

### ◆ LOOKING BACK

From the beginning Michigan politicians seem to have been cast from a different mold. When the Michigan Territory was formed in 1805, Lewis Cass was appointed governor. He got along well with the Indians (his whiskey barrel had no bottom), appointed capable men to conduct a state survey, spread the word to would-be settlers, and set Michigan on the way to settlement.

When President Andrew Jackson named Cass his Secretary of War, he appointed John T. Mason as his successor, with Mason's son Steven T. as territorial secretary. The elder Mason retired and young Mason found himself governor of the Michigan Territory at the ripe young age of 20. For a kid, he didn't do badly. He maneuvered around the Toledo War and negotiated the rush of railroad problems, but lost a bid for a second term over the first efforts to construct the Soo Canal at Sault Ste. Marie.

There were other hot and divisive issues. For example, which city would be its capital? Since its beginnings, the capital of the Michigan Territory had been Detroit. But Detroit's distance from much of the state—as well as its proximity to the potentially hostile British and their Indian allies just across the river in Canada—prompted legislators to seek a more central site. Such a wrangle! Almost every town and village from Calumet to Marshall vied for the honor. Marshall probably tried the hardest. As legislators argued, Marshall's city fathers built mansions they believed fitting for a state capital—including some on wannabe Capitol Hill that are historic treasures today.

When Ingham County representative Joseph H. Kilbourne proposed that the capital be sited in the Township of Lansing—still just a cluster of houses and a sawmill along the Grand River rapids—legislators hooted at the idea. What was there? In 1837, German tailor, Jacob Frederick Cooley, had claimed a plot of ground on the south bank of the Grand River. He liked the river, especially at the rapids, had cleared some land and built a cabin for his family. A few other pioneers settled nearby and they built a sawmill at the rapids to cut lumber for their homes. Ten years later, 88 souls were living in a 36-square-mile area around Cooley's cabin. That was Lansing.

Yet with the pressing deadline—a capital had to be declared by 1847—Lansing won the honor, largely because it was favored by no particular party.

State workers, politicians, lawyers, and storekeepers arrived together to construct the new town, and hastily built a wooden statehouse. Legislators trudged to the capital amid stumps, fallen trees, and mud. They found lodging either with local residents or on the capitol floor. Within a few years, in 1855, Michigan Agricultural College (now Michigan State University) was founded. A brick capitol building replaced the wooden structure and was dedicated in 1879.

◆ SEEING LANSING

**Convention and Visitors Bureau**
Drop by for an update on the exhibits, festivals, and other special events being staged in Lansing and on the MSU campus. *1223 Turner St.; 800-968-8474.*

**Old Town**
Somewhat off the beaten path in the north part of town, Old Town is a mix of art galleries, gift shops, and restaurants; festivals are held here year-round.

**State Capitol**
Restored in 1992, this dome-and-wing–style building was constructed of slate, white pine, and copper. The rotunda rises three stories, with balconies on its perimeter. Woodwork in the Senate chamber gleams when sunbeams stream through the skylight. Now a national landmark, Michigan's capitol was one of the first state capitols to follow the design of the U.S. Capitol in Washington, D.C. *Mon.-Sat.; Capitol and Michigan Aves.; 517-373-2353.*

**Michigan Historical Center**
This architecturally elegant complex houses the **Michigan Library,** the **Michigan Archives,** the **Michigan Historical Center** proper, and the open-air **Rotunda,** with its three-story living white pine. The Historical Center features 26 permanent galleries

on four levels that capture the state's history from early Native American times up through the late 20th century. A meandering tour guides you through an Upper Peninsula copper mine, 1920s village streets, and a re-created lumber camp. *717 West Allegan St.; www.sos.state.mi.us/history; 517-373-3559.*

### Michigan Museum of Surveying

This fine small museum presents the history of Michigan's surveyors who, with a minimum of supplies, spent months on end forging order through the wilderness. They fought black flies, deer flies, mosquitoes, and swarming no-see-ums whose bites stung like nettles. A favorite display is the famous "solar compass" invented by U.S. Deputy Surveyor William Austin Burt to circumvent the magnetic effect of the iron mountains of the Upper Peninsula. *220 South Museum Dr.; 517-484-6605.*

### Oldsmobile Heritage Center

Ransom E. Olds was making cars in Lansing well before Henry Ford constructed his first Model T in Detroit. Olds would haul his horseless carriage out of the shop for testing only at night, lest he be laughed off the streets. Nevertheless, by 1897 he was mass-producing Oldsmobiles, and the rest, as they say, is history, and you can find it here. *The Oldsmobile Heritage Center; 414 East Michigan; 517-482-0717.*

### R. E. Olds Transportation Museum

Displays antique vehicles, including the first 1897 Oldsmobile. *240 Museum Dr.; 517-372-0422.*

*The Michigan State Capitol in winter.*

## Impression 5
## Science Center

Reminiscent of a mad scientist's lab, this museum offers more than 200 hands-on science exhibits. With its original wood floors and brick walls, the century-old building is the perfect setting for kids of all ages to touch, feel, hear, smell, and watch to their hearts' content. *200 Museum Dr.; 517-485-8116.*

## Michigan State University

In 1855, the first land-grant college in the nation was created, with the stipulation that it be located within 10 miles of Lansing. Originally called the Michigan Agricultural College, the school had an enrollment of 81 students its first year; they began classes in May 1857 and also worked four hours each day on the college farm! Today students at Michigan State University at East Lansing number over 43,000, many of whom study hotel, restaurant, and institutional management.

*A dormitory on the Michigan State University campus in springtime.*

exhibits inside. Tours are available, or you can wander by yourself among the dinosaur skeletons and the audiovisual presentations. *On W. Circle Dr.; 517-355-7474.*

## University Museums

The MSU Museum is a quintessential university museum, housed in an ivy-draped building that seems right for the three floors of natural and cultural history

## Kresge Art Museum

Exhibits here span more than 5,000 years of art history, from prehistoric art objects to modern displays. *On the MSU campus in the Kresge Art Center; 517-355-7631.*

SOUTHEAST

■ FLINT    *map page 87, C-2*

In 1830, John Todd found trader Jacob Smith living at the rapids where the Pontiac Trail intersects the Flint River. Todd built a tavern and started a ferry for traffic crossing the river, and the transportation business was up and running. In 1837, when Michigan became a state, a land office was added to the growing community, and more settlers moved in. Lumbering came first. Logs were floated down the river network to Saginaw. For overland transportation, a plank road of three-inch-thick white pine was laid for 30 miles north to Saginaw.

With logging came the need for big-wheel, horse-pulled, log-hauling equipment. Flint was soon manufacturing big wheels, wagons, and road carts. In 1868, as lumber declined, Flint turned toward the manufacture of carriages. Eighteen years later, William ("Billy") C. Durant with partner J. Dallas Dort founded the Durant-Dort Carriage Company, the precursor to General Motors. GM set Flint on the road to becoming the second largest manufacturer of automobiles in the world, after Detroit.

*Flint, as photographed circa 1900, boasted the title "The Vehicle City."*
*(Genessee County Historical Society)*

*Crossroads Village and Huckleberry Railroad is a restored village, circa 1900.*

### Alfred P. Sloan Museum

This museum traces the history of Flint and the birth of General Motors (founded by Alfred P. Sloan) to the present day. Over 600 artifacts are displayed in addition to the many antique automobiles. *1221 E. Kearsley St.; 810-760-1169.*

### Crossroads Village and Huckleberry Railroad

Wandering through the 30 historic buildings and shops of this restored village on the shores of Lake Mott is a time-warp back to the early 1900s. Michigan's oldest operating gristmill creaks and groans. The steam-powered Huckleberry Railroad blasts its whistle at crossings as it winds through the village. *6140 Bray Rd.; 800-648-PARK.*

### Genesee Belle

The perfect way to conclude your visit to Flint is a lazy, water-slapping cruise on Mott Lake on this paddle-wheel riverboat. (The Mott family, and its non-profit foundation, are GM's largest shareholders). *6140 Bray Rd.; 800-648-PARK.*

### Flint Area Visitors Bureau

General information. *519 S. Saginaw St.; 800-25-FLINT.*

## A MICHIGAN AUTOMOBILE TIMELINE

1890 A young Henry Ford builds a Silent Otto Engine from scratch.

1895 Ransom E. Olds patents a "gas or vapor engine" and changes the name of his father's Lansing carriage shop to the Olds Gasoline Engine Works.

1896 Henry Ford knocks out bricks to widen the door for his "quadricycle" in which he toodles around his Detroit home on Bagley Avenue.

1899 Ransom Olds establishes the Olds Motor Works in Lansing.

1899 Henry Ford finds investors and creates the Detroit Automobile Company.

1899 David Dunbar Buick invests the profits from the sale of his plumbing company in a new venture: the Buick Auto-Vim and Power Company in Flint.

1900 Ford collapses the Detroit Automobile Company blaming the failure on his investors whose "main idea seemed to be to get money."

1900 The Olds Motor Works relocates to Detroit and calls its products Oldsmobiles.

1901 The Olds Motor Works burns to the ground forcing Olds back to Lansing where he employs subcontractors who, in turn, are inspired to manufacture their own vehicles, among them: Cadillac, Maxwell and Dodge.

1903 Ford gathers other investors for his new enterprise: the Ford Motor Company.

1904 The first production Buick leaves the plant in Flint. William C. Durant takes control of the company leaving David Buick with one share of common stock.

1904 Ransom Olds sells his stock in the Olds Motor Works and founds Reo Motor Company, naming it after himself.

1905 Vincent Bryan and Gus Edwards compose "In My Merry Oldsmobile" in honor of the immensely popular one-cylinder Curved-Dash Runabout.

1908 At 1,400 cars per month, Buick's Flint plant is heralded as the world's largest.

1908 William C. Durant sells the Buick Motor Company to his own new enterprise, the General Motors Company; he then buys the Olds Motor Works and the Cadillac Motor Company.

1909 Henry Ford produces the Model T, the "Tin Lizzie" that puts America on wheels—changing America, and the world, forever.

1914 The first Dodge is manufactured by brothers John and Horace Dodge.

1924 Walter P. Chrysler creates The Chrysler Corporation and buys the Dodge Brothers Motor Co.

1937 Invoking "Unionism, Not Fordism," a 30-year-old Walter Reuther is assaulted by Ford-employed goons in full view of press photographers. Called the "Battle of the Overpass," it marks the birth of the UAW.

1941   The Willys Jeep (short for GP or General Purpose vehicle) is launched. Developed for war, it becomes an icon for fun and adventure.

1949   The Volkswagen Beetle arrives in America.

1952   A prototype fiberglass-bodied Chevrolet "Corvette" is accidentally rolled during a test run. Undamaged, fiberglass is chosen for the new sports car's body.

1954   The American Motors Corporation (AMC) is formed by combining the Nash Motor Company and the Hudson Motor Car Company.

1955   Poet Marianne Moore is hired by Ford to name its new mid-size car. Her suggestions include: "Resilient Bullet," "Varsity Stroke," and "Utopian Turtletop."

1956   Ford launches the new mid-size car—the Edsel.

1957   The Edsel Show, a one-hour special hosted by Frank Sinatra, Bing Crosby, Louis Armstrong and Rosemary Clooney airs on CBS in place of The Ed Sullivan Show to enormous ratings.

1959   Faced with near-total public rejection, Ford discontinues the Edsel

1964   Pontiac releases the first "muscle car," the 389 cubic inch, 325 hp V-8 GTO

1964   Ford introduces the Mustang, making Lee A. Iacocca a household name.

1965   Ralph Nader publishes *Unsafe At Any Speed* targeting General Motors who admits to wrongdoing and leads to congressional enactment of safety standards.

1973   The VW bug becomes the most popular car ever produced, outselling Henry Ford's Model T.

1978   Lee A. Iacocca leaves the Ford Motor Co. to become head of Chrysler.

1984   The Jeep Cherokee is introduced—the nation's first SUV.

1998   Daimler-Benz of Germany, purchases Chrysler Corp. for $92 billion.

1998   Ford introduces the Lincoln Navigator SUV—5,470 lbs curbweight, 75.2 in. tall, 79.9 in. wide, 204.8 in. long. It gets 12 mpg city, 20.7 mpg highway.

1998   The California Air Resources Board (CARB) designates SUVs as automobiles and requires that they be held to the same emission standards as cars.

2000   Amid record profits, GM admits that SUV sales have exceeded car sales, but argues that CAFE (Corporate Average Fuel Economy) standards should remain frozen at 20.7 mpg for SUVs and 27.5 mpg for cars.

2000   Ford and UAW announce ambitious plans to establish day care, teen programs, computer classes, and book clubs for retirees.

2000   General Motors announces that it will no longer produce Oldsmobiles.

# ANN ARBOR

*by Dan Stivers*

■ HIGHLIGHTS

Ann Arbor●

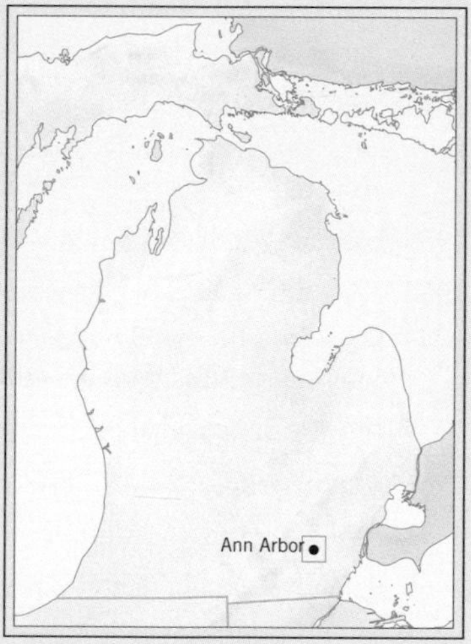

■ TRAVEL BASICS

**City Overview:** Ann Arbor is perhaps the quintessential college *city*. The university extends outwards in all directions from the campus hub to embrace different neighborhoods. The university's touch is gentle, even exciting, and the neighborhoods are resilient, charming, and authentic. All in all, one of the nicer American cities to get lost in.

**Getting Around:** Parking can be difficult during the school term, but there are many convenient parking structures. In terms of mass transit, think of Chicago without the subway system, the el, or Metro trains. Ann Arbor has an impressive bus system—one that stretches to neighboring small towns such as Dexter and Chelsea. **Metropolitan Detroit International Airport** is about 20 miles east of Ann Arbor on I-94 and easy to navigate, with the customary rental car, taxicab, and limousine services available. Ann Arbor Municipal Airport and Ypsilanti's Willow Run Airport have no major commercial passenger services. The Amtrak station is just north of downtown Ann Arbor. The train makes for an enjoyable way to get to Ann Arbor by way of small town Main Streets and everyone else's backyards, and is highly recommended.

**Weather:** Summer is a mixed bag. Could be sunny and more perfect than anything this side of San Diego; could be cold, wet, and absolutely wretched; may even spice things up with life–threatening lightning storms, tornadoes, or heat waves. Likewise, winters can cheerily live up to Michigan's former motto of Water Winter Wonderland, or be marked by week after week of single-digits and howling winds—a sunless horror, devoid of joy or hope. Halloween night can greet trick-or-treaters with anything from 60 degrees to 20 degrees, maybe even the winter's first blizzard. TV weathermen out of Lansing or Detroit, who spend years in college and should understand Michigan's weather as well as anyone, are generally no more accurate or informed than a chimp flipping a coin.

**Food & Lodging:** Ann Arbor offers more lively bars, trendy nightclubs, and sophisticated restaurants than most college-related environments. And with the large number of parents, friends, and faculty—not to mention *il studentii*—lodging is plentiful and relatively inexpensive. *For our suggestions, please see listings beginning on page 276.*

ANN ARBOR

## ■ OVERVIEW

Ann Arbor, since 1837 the home of the University of Michigan, is a pleasant, sprawling city. Less than an hour west of Detroit along I-94, 30 minutes or so east of Jackson, and about a half hour north of Ohio along US-23, "A-Squared" (or "A²" as it's known to the locals) is seen by some Michigan residents as hip and energetic. Others see it as pretentious and galling. A head football coach at Michigan's other Big Ten school, East Lansing's Michigan State University (eternally battling an inferiority complex with regard to its sister to the south) once referred to University of Michigan adherents as "those arrogant asses."

Whatever others think, Ann Arborites obviously enjoy living in one of Michigan's most comfortable, cosmopolitan, and intellectually stimulating atmospheres. Over a quarter-million permanent residents call Washtenaw County (and Ann Arbor) home—a home that consistently ranks among *Money* magazine's listings of the nation's most livable, and realtors' listings show A² to be one of Michigan's priciest cities. Partially through its proximity to the think-tank atmosphere of the U of M, partially through a recent growth spurt that left it unburdened by the outmoded business and manufacturing processes that haunt many firms, Ann Arbor is one of the Midwest's leading centers of high technology and research.

Once an isolated world amid the cornfields of Michigan—and still seen that way by many—Ann Arbor has begun spreading its influence throughout neighboring small towns. Saline, Dexter, Chelsea, even tiny Hell, Michigan, are finding themselves little more than satellites to dynamic A$^2$.

Is this welcome? Feelings are divided. As a teenager growing up in Dexter, the first small town northeast of Ann Arbor and home of the fearsome Dexter Dreadnaughts, I welcomed the film societies, student parties, and general larger-town feel that existed just eight miles up Dexter–Ann Arbor Road (named because it links Dexter and Ann Arbor; the other imaginatively named roads leading out of Dexter are Dexter-Pinckney, Dexter-Chelsea, and Mast Road—each one honoring a local farmer because it really didn't lead much of anywhere).

Other residents, however, decry the "Ann Arborization" of such towns. As acre upon acre of farm fields leading to Ann Arbor become subdivisions, and as auto parts stores in the hearts of small towns morph into quirky little galleries and coffee houses, many longtime residents smell something noxious seeping under the door: progress, that very same devil they moved here to escape. And they don't like it one bit.

Should they? Many of these proud little towns trace their lineages back further than even Ann Arbor itself. Tractors pulling wagons of fresh-cut corn still creep down Main Street. Homecoming queens are still crowned at halftime. Weekly newspapers discuss whose sheds were broken into, and volunteer firemen risk their lives for their neighbors.

■ HISTORY

In the fall of 1823, a "well-proportioned and physically grand specimen of a man," John Allen, rode out of Virginia with a herd of cattle and a hunger for fortune. Left behind were a new wife, Ann, and a pile of unpaid debts. No record of the cattle survives, but Allen's ambitious wanderings over the next few months led him to Detroit. There, in January 1824, he met fellow New Englander and fortune hunter Elisha Rumsey.

*The Ann Arbor Art Fair on State Street.*

Deciding their best chance at wealth lay a few miles west of already-bustling Detroit, Allen and Rumsey rode a one-horse sleigh on a scouting trip deep into the newly minted county of Washtenaw. Little more than a month after shaking hands, the two entrepreneurs strode into the U.S. Land Office in Detroit, stomped the snow from their boots, and purchased 640 acres along the Huron River.

Luck appears to have been on their side, as territorial governor Lewis Cass quickly anointed their tract as the county seat. On May 25, 1824, the town plot was registered as "Annarbour"—in honor of Allen's and Rumsey's wives, both named Ann, who would meet under a grape arbour, hence Ann's Arbor.

The village grew quickly. In early June, Allen and Rumsey placed advertisements for their new town in Detroit's main newspaper. Before long several houses were under construction, two sawmills were operating, and a grist mill was on the drawing board. In autumn, Ann Allen left her beloved Virginia behind and made the two-month journey to her namesake town, grudgingly moving with her husband into a two-room blockhouse.

*(above) This lithograph shows the University of Michigan at Ann Arbor in 1874, about 30 years after it opened for classes. (Bentley Historical Library, University of Michigan)*

*(opposite) The Huron River runs through Gallup Park.*

*John Allen. (Bentley Historical Library, Univ. of Michigan)*

As increasing numbers of settlers arrived, Ann Arbor's social, religious, political, and economic foundations developed around them. In 1825, John Allen built a crude log building at the northwest corner of Main and Ann Streets and opened Ann Arbor's first school, funded by assessments levied only to parents who chose to have their children educated. Also in 1825, the civic-minded Allen—one can't help but wonder if it was with Ann's blessing—opened his home for Methodist services held by itinerant clergyman John Boughman. This was followed in 1826 by a Presbyterian congregation whose organizers usurped the log schoolhouse. Thomas Simpson founded Ann Arbor's first newspaper, the *Western Emigrant,* in 1829, largely supported at first through notices placed by the village's doctors and lawyers.

By 1837, with John Allen's little village thriving and having been named the county seat, Michigan's legislature named Ann Arbor the new home of the University of Michigan. A land company was formed, and the fledgling university was given 40 acres east of State Street. The university opened with five buildings in 1841, and its first graduates received their diplomas in 1845.

John Allen—and Ann Arbor—never looked back.

## ■ ANN ARBOR TODAY

Today, you can find virtually anything you want in or near Ann Arbor—generally within a 20-minute drive.

Are you looking for a cosmopolitan-yet-comfortable atmosphere? Ann Arbor's square mile or so of downtown, lazily meandering east until it dissolves into the University of Michigan's world-class campus, will fill that bill.

Theater? Any city that's cleared a space for the likes of U of M will, of course, have cleared space for theater. Traditional? Try the **Performance Network** or the **Ann Arbor Civic Theater.** Inventive? Try the U **of** M **Basement Arts Theater.**

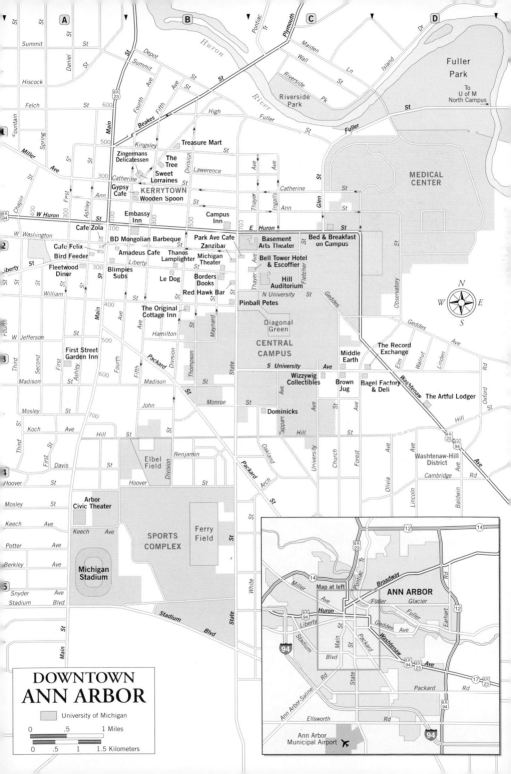

# DOWNTOWN
# ANN ARBOR

University of Michigan

0        .5        1 Miles

0     .5      1     1.5 Kilometers

**A** **B** **C** **D**

Summit St
Daniel St
Hiscock
Felch St
Fountain
Miller Ave
Spring St
Chapin

Depot
Summit
Beakes Fifth
Kingsley
Zingermans Delicatessen
Catherine
300
First
Ann
Ashley St
500
W Huron
300
Cafe Zola
Embassy Inn
BD Mongolian Barbeque
Cafe Felix
Bird Feeder
Fleetwood Diner
Liberty
Blimpies Subs
William St
Main
400
The Original Cottage Inn
Hamilton
W Jefferson
First Street Garden Inn
Third Second
First
Ashley
600
Madison
Mosley St
Koch Ave
Hill
First St
Davis
Hoover St
Mosley St
Keech Ave
Potter Ave
Berkley Ave
Snyder Ave
Stadium Blvd

Huron River
Riverside Park
Riverside Pk
Fuller
High
Fuller
Treasure Mart
The Tree
Sweet Lorraines
Gypsy Cafe
Wooden Spoon
KERRYTOWN
Lawrence
Division
Campus Inn
Park Ave Cafe
Zanzibar
Amadeus Cafe
Thanos Lamplighter
Michigan Theater
Le Dog
Borders Books
Red Hawk Bar
Maynard
Thompson
State St
Packard
Division St
Fourth
Fifth
Madison
John
Monroe St
Benjamin
Elbel Field
Hoover
Arbor Civic Theater
Keech Ave
SPORTS COMPLEX
Ferry Field
Michigan Stadium
State St

Pontiac
Plymouth
Maiden Ln
Wall St
Island Dr
Fuller Park
To U of M North Campus
Riverside Park
Catherine St
Ann St
Glen St
E Huron St
Basement Arts Theater
Bed & Breakfast on Campus
Bell Tower Hotel & Escoffier
Hill Auditorium
Thayer
Ingalls
Fletcher
N University
Pinball Petes
Diagonal Green
CENTRAL CAMPUS
S University Ave
Geddes
Observatory
The Record Exchange
Middle Earth
Wizzywig Collectibles
Brown Jug
Bagel Factory & Deli
Dominicks
Tappan
Hill
Washtenaw
The Artful Lodger
Washtenaw-Hill District
Cambridge Rd
Geddes Ave
Elm Walnut Linden Rd
Oxford St
Oakland
University
Church
Forest
Olivia
Lincoln
Baldwin
Hill
MEDICAL CENTER

N
W · E
S

## ANN ARBOR (inset map)

Map at left
Miller Ave
Huron
Liberty
94
BR 23
14
Pontiac Tr
Broadway
ANN ARBOR
Fuller
Glacier
Fuller Ave
Geddes Ave
Washtenaw
Ave
12
14
Earhart Rd
12
17
BR 23
Stadium Rd
Main St
Packard
Blvd
BR 94 23
State St
Ann Arbor-Saline Rd
Packard Rd
BR 94
Ellsworth Rd
94
Ann Arbor Municipal Airport

Music? Leon Redbone cut his chops at folk institution **The Ark** in the '70s; Bob Seger was born and banged out his first chords here. Rock bars abound—this is, after all, a college town through and through—where, for a small cover charge, you can listen to the raucous dreams of starry-eyed local kids.

Art? If you haven't heard of the **Ann Arbor Art Fair,** drop in around mid-July and fasten your seat belt.

Shopping? Downtown is thriving with art galleries, boutiques, thrift shops, clothing emporia, drive-thru convenience stores, and other types of retail fun.

Let's take a closer look.

*(opposite) Main Street is lined with cafes and restaurants, many of which offer outdoor dining in warm-weather months.*

*A trolley used to run down the middle of Main Street, as shown in this wintertime photo, taken around 1890. (Bentley Historical Library, University of Michigan)*

### ◆ MAIN STREET
*map page 105, A–2*

The Main Street area (at most six blocks long) has few chain retailers and an abundance of art galleries and shops, many of them open well into the evening for the dining crowd.

**Galleries on Main Street**
**16 Hands** carries interesting pieces, from crafts to furniture to fine arts; **Gallery 212** keeps more specialized hours to match its specialized juried shows and occasional performance art; **Gallery Von Glahn** falls somewhere in between the two in terms of what's available; **Overmyer's Gallery** features lithographs, photographs, posters, and limited editions. Our descriptions don't do these establishments (nor the

many who aren't listed here) the justice they deserve. You must follow your own visual and aesthetic tastes.

**Peaceable Kingdom**
This is a toy store with nary a GI Joe in sight. The highlight for me is this narrow store's middle aisle: bin after bin of cheap geegaws, windup shuffling frogs, pencil sharpeners in the shape of a nose—guess where the pencil goes—and the like.

On the glass counter by the door, I spy something I haven't seen or thought of for over 20 years: an "I brake for Jake" bumper sticker. "Is Jake still around?" I ask the clerk behind the counter. "Oh yeah, he's still rompin' and stompin' out there somewhere," she says with a laugh. *210 S. Main St.; 734-668-7886.*

*The Ann Arbor Bicycle Club, circa 1887.*

◆ KERRYTOWN   *map page 105, A–2*

Ann Arbor's hot **Kerrytown Historic Market District** is located just steps north of Huron and east of Main at the northeast corner of the campus. Though just a few blocks in total area, it could well be a little city in itself.

**Ann Arbor Farmer's Market**

Kerrytown's anchor and hub, this market sells produce and other farmer's market–type goods year-round on Saturdays, and Wednesdays from May to December. On Sundays, May to December, local artisans take over the space to peddle their own unique, affordable goods (my wife and I bought a huge, not-very-portable garden bench made from an old headboard and some barn timbers, carefully tied it to the roof of our car, and made our slow way home).

**Kerrytown Shopping Center**

Here you'll find fine food markets, including **Monahan's Seafood Market** and **Sparrow Meats** as well as **Partners in Wine and Cheese** and T. T. Durham's Smokery.

Nearby, shoppers can find top-quality cookware at **Kitchen Port** and top-quality furniture at **Workbench.** Cool kiddy delights you won't find at Toys-R-Us are featured at the fun, eclectic **Mudpuddles.**

ANN ARBOR

*The Tour De Kios Bicycle Race takes place in Ann Arbor.*

**Reusables**

If you truly want to take home a memento of Ann Arbor, then choose something that's lived in Ann Arbor for a while. Detroit Street secondhand shops **Treasure Mart** and **The Tree** sells cast-off flotsam and jetsam, from used corduroys to $12 ceramic mallards. When the fascinating Treasure Mart's warehouse-like space can't hold all the stuff they've collected, it spills out into the driveway. The Tree will set you back eight bucks for a nice pair of used Dockers.

**North Fourth Avenue**

Just across a small plaza from the Farmer's Market is a mini-mecca of one-of-a-kind shops. In the **Wooden Spoon**, one of Ann Arbor's most chaotic used book stores, a jumble of rooms packed floor to ceiling with previously owned reading materials fans out in all directions. A hand-lettered sign (Kerrytown's most common form of commercial communication) in the entryway requests, "Don't set stuff here"—right beside, of course, a couple of piles of stuff.

Next door, **Dreamer's Nook** is filled with a fascinating hodgepodge of pillbox hats, quirky decorative doodads like a combination hanging planter/wind chime, and dream-related aphorisms painted on the walls, seeming at times more of a Manhattan art installation than a retail emporium.

**Gypsy Café** offers up art, poetry, coffee, and atmosphere, atmosphere, atmosphere.

ANN ARBOR

**Eating Out**

*See Food & Lodging, page 276 for addresses, phone numbers, and more detail.*

Two dining establishments in Kerrytown come particularly recommended. **Sweet Lorraine's**, also just off the Farmer's Market, serves a wide-ranging menu of inventive sandwiches and meals, all from a basement-level outdoor café that provides an intriguing subterranean viewpoint of shoppers strolling by. Feel free to ask for an additional plate of fresh muffins as you wait for your order; you won't be disappointed. **Zingerman's** deli, almost every bit as renowned locally as the Fleetwood, is Ann Arbor's home of the stacked meat deli sandwich. Packed all day long, it promises a little taste of the New York deli experience—down to the Brooklyn Egg Cream ("It contains neither eggs nor cream," explains the hand-lettered sign) you can find in Zingerman's Next Door. Seating is haphazard and minimal, so grab the first open table you see and hold on for dear life.

◆ STATE/LIBERTY STREETS
*map page 105, B–2*

The State/Liberty area, about five or six blocks east of Main Street, has a character all its own—a character shaped by its proximity to the U of M campus.

*The Michigan Theater is Ann Arbor's most famous art-house cinema.*

## Fun and Games

New and used record stores and the legendary brain drain **Pinball Pete's** share sidewalk with the still-lively **Michigan Theater**, the formerly cavernous State Theater, now subdivided into two screens and restored to 1927 glory by the city; the original **Border's Books**, original model for today's national chain; along with used- and rare-book havens such as **West Side Books** reward the curious browser.

One interesting retail feature of this interesting area is **Nickels Arcade**. This glass-covered passage between State and Maynard offers a unique landscape and a hit-or-miss hodgepodge of shops

## Eating Spots

*See Food & Lodging, page 276 for addresses, phone numbers, and more detail.*

While numerous pizza places speak to the proximity of students, you still can't look past **The Original Cottage Inn**. And don't be fooled by recent renovations—this is the same classic deep-dish pizza that mom and dad washed down in their undergrad days.

**Thano's Lamplighter** comes close to Cottage Inn's landmark status, serving a wide-ranging late-night menu from Greek specialties to, of course, deep-dish pizza. If you worry about pounds of delicious cheese clogging your arteries, slip into vegetarian sandwich shop **Park Avenue Café**.

**Le Dog** may be the only hot dog stand this side of LA that serves bouillabaisse and lobster bisque alongside its franks.

At **Red Hawk Bar and Grill,** half-pound burgers and varietal microbrews go great with the roasted red pepper bisque du jour, inexpensive enough for students yet satisfactory for just about anyone.

The two-story "pantropical bistro" **Zanzibar**—medium on the price scale, high on the spice scale—blends Thai, African, Indian, and South American flavors into an eclectic mix.

**Escoffier**, arguably Ann Arbor's most elegant restaurant, in the equally elegant **Bell Tower Hotel** (on the U of M campus) can be viewed as either delightfully European or elitist, depending on your politics and tailor; nobody questions the originality and excellence of its seasonal classic French menus.

Finally, for the more traditional palate, **Victors**—located in the **Campus Inn**—offers up meat and potatoes, seafood, and other favorites, just the way Dad likes 'em.

## Lodging

*See Food & Lodging, page 276 for addresses and phone numbers.*

Which is a perfect segue into the subject of where to spend the night. The aforementioned Campus Inn vies with the Bell Tower Hotel for the title of "most centrally located luxury hotel," and you'll pay around $150 a night in either for the convenience. The Campus's outdoor pool will ease the pain during the summer months, though you can't imagine many parents of

*The main quad on the University of Michigan campus.*

undergrads lounging around poolside. The Bell Tower trades the pool for warmth and charm. I'd take the charm. For a little bit less, you can cool your heels in the nearby Bed & Breakfast on Campus.

◆ SOUTH UNIVERSITY
*map page 105, D-3*

**Burns Park**
You've hit campus, folks. Surrounded by frats, sororities, and faculty members living in gracious Burns Park, this area seems torn between appealing to the student crowd and the tourists and fun-seekers.

**The Galleria**
This small mall lures shoppers with a typically outsized **Tower Records**. The **Record Exchange** across the street sells used CDs to students who aren't yet downloading their music for free off the web. For your textbook and/or maize and blue toilet seat fix, there's **Ulrich's**.

Middle Earth—where it appears dependence on the bong trade has gone down considerably since it was considered the premier local head shop in the mid-'70s—stocks a wide variety of stuff, from witty trinkets and jewelry of every taste and size to high-quality imported African crafts.

Pokémon addicts can feed their joneses and pick up a video or two at **Wizzywig Collectibles,** while an assortment of obscure shoe, sportswear, and jewelry shops share the rest of the strip with drugstores and restaurants.

### Eating Out

*See Food & Lodging, page 276 for addresses, phone numbers, and more detail.*

**The Brown Jug** has been a favorite of students, faculty, townies, and anybody looking for good food and drink since 1928. It's one of the few places where you can get a homemade hot turkey sandwich and coffee while your friend orders chili cheese fries and tequila. The walls are covered with decades of random snapshots and menus complete the scene.

Around the block is **Dominick's,** where outdoor seating has been raised to an art form. Whether you sit packed along the sidewalk or in the quieter, oddly charming courtyard, complete with fountain constructed out of an unused (we hope) headstone, you'll have to wade gingerly through the self-serve menu. Try one of the time-honored sandwiches, or perhaps the pizza. Chances are that what brings you back will be the atmosphere. And with any time around here, you'll be back.

ANN ARBOR

*The Asian collection at the University of Michigan Museum of Art.*

**Lodging**

*See Food & Lodging, page 276 for addresses and phone numbers.*

Lodging is also distinctive in these parts. **Vitosha Guest Haus** is a chalet-style home dating from 1917. Its 10 restored guest rooms offer private baths, fireplaces, and a healthy dose of arts-and-crafts charm.

**The Artful Lodger** is a breathtaking 1859 Italianate Victorian home, topped with a pretty cool cupola, sporting four guest rooms with private baths, off-street parking, and an eclectic theatrical decorating theme. You can spend the night in most rooms for about a hundred bucks. Both establishments are within shouting distance of each other on busy Washtenaw Avenue.

◆ **MUSEUMS AND GARDENS**

**Ann Arbor Hands-On Museum**

Among the more frenetic museums in town, the Hands-On is located in a historic redbrick firehouse in the midst of downtown. Kids up to twelve or so can wander around looking, learning, experimenting, and just having fun with well over 100 interactive science and nature exhibits. Kids who love to learn will go nuts; those who would rather be watching TV will wish they were home, watching TV. *220 E. Ann St.; 734-995-5437.*

**U of M Museum of Art**

This is one of the better university art museums you'll come across. The wide-ranging permanent collection covers Western and Asian art, and the special exhibitions are themselves worth the price of admission—considering admission is free. (If you appreciate the art and work involved and still don't make a donation of even a buck or two, then shame on you.)

**U of M Exhibit Museum of Natural History**

Essentially a smaller version of its Chicago counterpart. While you won't find a world-famous T Rex skeleton here, you will find other dinosaur and mastodon skeletons and special exhibits on Native American life. Again, *technically* free and, again, give them something! *525 South St.; 734-764-0395.*

**Neighborhood Gardens**

In summer, a stroll through the neighborhoods is a rewarding garden walk in itself. These folks pride themselves on turning tiny city lots into blasts of color and pollen.

**Matthaei Botanical Gardens**

A good-sized indoor conservatory blooms year-round, divided by climactic regions. In the warmer months, the grounds feature 350 acres of woodlands, wetlands, ponds, and theme gardens. If quiet beauty is your thing, a few hours here are well spent. *1800 N. Dixboro; 734-7060.*

ANN ARBOR

## ANN ARBOR ART FAIR

*T*his annual fine art free-for-all, held in closed-to-traffic downtown Ann Arbor, is Ann Arbor's hugest party. Huge in reputation, huge in numbers of attending art lovers and likers, huge in the amount of annual budgetary requirements met by many of the artists, huge in frustration and disappointment for those artists who watch streams of viewers glance at their works and quickly, wordlessly move on—just trust me; stick with huge.

Actually three art fairs—the original juried Ann Arbor Street Art Fair (recently selected by members of the National Association of Independent Artists as the top-ranking arts festival in the nation), the State Street Area Art Fair, and the Summer Art Fair—this annual four-day ode to art covers about 25 city blocks and attracts over 500,000 visitors. Street musicians abound, demonstrations of technique are around every corner, and you are dared to leave without buying *something*.

Traffic in the area of the fair would no doubt leave Mother Teresa pounding the steering wheel and screaming bloody vengeance, but parking is still generally available for a price. Shuttles run from local mall parking lots, but I've always taken my chances and driven straight in. Going through the madness of the art fair only to end the day waiting in line for a shuttle bus just never made much sense to me, not when a $10 spot within easy walking distance could always be found.

Expect crowds, expect "no vacancy" signs, and expect to be overwhelmed.

*The University of Michigan Football Stadium is the largest college-owned stadium in the United States: it can seat over 107,000 Wolverine fans.*

◆ FOOTBALL

You wanna talk football? 'Scuse me, you wanna talk *football?* On a crisp, sunny autumn afternoon, the **University of Michigan Football Stadium** *(map page 105, A–5)* is the place to be. Built in 1927 to hold 72,000 fans, the nation's largest college-owned stadium now seats over 107,000, from shy three-year-olds taking in the spectacle to lunatic, screaming face painters looking to shine on national TV. Consistently sold out and leading the nation in attendance virtually every season, this

place hasn't seen a football crowd of less than 100,000 in at least 25 years. Deceptively small and looking like nothing more than another college building with another stately, brick-facade exterior, the building becomes a sunken-bowl spectacle once you step through the gates. Surrounded by lawns and houses instead of asphalt, and within walking distance from many of the venues featured in this chapter, it is one of a kind.

## ◆ FAIRS AND FESTIVALS

### Ann Arbor Antiques Market
The third Sunday of every month brings more than 350 booths featuring every imaginable old thing, some priced quite reasonably, some quite ludicrously. It's fun to look and the food is good.

### Ann Arbor Blues and Jazz Festival
Sometime after Labor Day, the town likes to toss its Ann Arbor Blues and Jazz Festival. Launched in 1969, shelved in '74, then rekindled in '92, the festival is a two-day outdoor affair that in the past has featured Miles Davis, Muddy Waters, Ray Charles, Bonnie Raitt, and hundreds of other artists.

### Ann Arbor Film Festival
Generally helps usher in spring with its collection of 16-mm labors of love. Held in the **Michigan Theater**, on Liberty just east of State, it can be both damned entertaining and marvelously stupid. A lot of it is strictly for film buffs, but even casual viewers can enjoy seeing films they won't see at the local googolplex.

### Ann Arbor Folk Festival
This celebrates folk music, and, as it benefits the nationally venerated Ark, it can generally bring out some big names. Arlo Guthrie and Shawn Colvin headlined the 2000 show, held in comfortable Hill Auditorium in the heart of campus.

### Ann Arbor Antiquarian Book Fair
Since 1976, book dealers from throughout the midwest have flocked to this mid-May William L. Clements Library benefit.

*Cruise Night takes place on Thursday nights in Ypsilanti's Depot Town.*

# ■ YPSILANTI   *map page 87, C-4*

No guide to Ann Arbor would be complete without mentioning Ypsilanti, its smaller sister city directly to the east. Often mispronounced as "Yipsilanti" by everybody but its residents—and even some of them stubbornly refuse to say it correctly, that is, "Ipsilanti"—Ypsi officially began its life as the settlement of Woodruff's Grove in 1823. Over the years it became the home of Eastern Michigan University, the birthplace of S&H Green Stamps, the site of the nation's first triple-decker highway bridge, and the spot selected by the Monahan brothers to open their first Domino's Pizza store.

## Depot Town and Cross Street

**Silver Spoon** is filled with antique furniture, glassware, and other odd old things, while **Apple Annie's Vintage Clothing** concentrates on items of clothing and jewelry that, for whatever reasons, were never given to the Salvation Army by their original owners.

## Ypsilanti Automotive Heritage Collection

Anchoring the east end of Depot Town. Here you can see antique cars, learn about Ypsi's role in the development of the auto industry, and learn more about the "other guys": Hudson, Tucker, Kaiser, and Frazier.

## Cruise Night

Thursday nights have become Cruise Night in Depot Town, when dozens of old MoPars and other gas slurpers roll onto Cross Street for 50/50 drawings, ogling, and general camaraderie.

## Eating Out

For food, wander in to **Aubree's Saloon** for sandwiches and Mexican food (plus a mean shepherd's pie on St. Patrick's Day).

In **Sticks**, the pool hall above Aubree's, you can work up a hunger or have an "Ypsi aperitif" (over 100 beers on the menu).

The nearby **Cady's Grill** is a bit more Ann Arborish, with memorabilia, fish and pasta, and good burgers can be had at the **Sidetrack Bar & Grill**—legendary home of Frog Island Beer.

*See Food & Lodging page 312 for addresses and phone numbers of places listed below.*

## Frog Island Music Festival

Speaking of Frog Island, the annual early summer Frog Island Music Festival has developed quite a name for itself. Pushing two decades of existence, it showcases newer talents of blues, jazz, and zydeco with legends like Son Seals and Larry Coryell, all on the banks of the Huron River in Frog Island Park. You could do a helluva lot worse than a side trip—if not a weekend—at the Frog Island Festival. For year-round music in a temperature controlled atmosphere, cross the river to **Cross Street Station** or **The Tap Room**.

ANN ARBOR

ANN ARBOR

# ■ DAY TRIPS

If it's a nice spring or summer day, take Main Street north out of Ann Arbor, veer left on Huron River Drive just before you climb onto the M-14 expressway, and settle in for a winding, slow-speed, extraordinarily pretty drive. Watch for bicyclists who seem emboldened by the beauty, riding three abreast and risking their limbs in their private pursuit of washboard abs.

## Huron-Clinton Metroparks: Delhi, Dexter-Huron, and Hudson Mills
*map page 87, B-4*

The parks themselves are clean and open if you feel like being mellow and tossing a Frisbee, but, dammit, you're here to canoe. Check at the front gate for instructions, but you should be able to inexpensively rent a canoe and spend the afternoon ambling down the leisurely Huron River.

Trips begin either from the Dexter-Huron Park for the (too) short trip, or from Hudson Mills for the longer (about right) trip. If you start upriver at Hudson Mills, stop at the Mast Road bridge just short of Dexter-Huron and walk over to the party store for a cupcake and a cold one. Either way, you'll end up at Delhi, where Skip the canoe man or one of his kids will haul you back to get your car. Easy and painless.

If lazy canoeing seems too, well, pedestrian, who in their right mind would turn down the chance to ride a horse in Hell?

## Hell, Michigan
*map page 87, B-4*

A half-hour or so out of Ann Arbor, just southwest of the international hotspot of Pinckney, sits lovely Hell, Michigan, at the corner of Patterson Lake Road and Silver Hill Road.

*A postcard from Hell. The crossroads village got its name from its reputation as a haven for whiskey distillers—and for whiskey drinkers.*

Visitors to Hell can drink with bikers at the **Dam Site Inn,** then sidle next door to the **Hell Party Store** to buy every kind of play-on-words trinket imaginable and send postcards to out-of-favor uncles and in-laws inviting them to Hell. The other local industry seems to be **Hell Creek Ranch.**

With a couple of days' notice, a riding hand from Hell—though they probably live in Gregory, which is nowhere near as much fun to say—will show you the finer points of riding and squire you around the ranch.

---

## A WINTER NIGHT

*I* remember, forty years ago, a January night when the thermometer registered five below and there was a brilliant full moon, and I went to the front door, late at night, to lock up. I stood in the doorway for a moment looking out at the moonlit landscape, the little grove of trees across the street and the three feet of snow that covered everything. There is not in all America today anything quite as still and quiet as a Michigan small town could be, late on a moon-swept night, in January, in the days before World War I. Nobody in all the earth was making a sound, nothing was moving, there was only the white snow, the black trees, the blue shadows lying on the whiteness, and the big moon in a cloudless sky; and to stand there and look out at it was, inexplicably, to be in touch with the Infinite—and, somehow, the Infinite was good, it was lonely and friendly, it meant something you did not have to be afraid of if you understood it. So Michigan means that to me—along with much else—and coldness and loneliness and shattering loveliness go hand in hand, so that while you will always be awed and abashed when you come up against the Infinite you do not really need to be afraid. And maybe that is a fairly good idea to get and take with you.

—Bruce Catton, *The Land of Long Horizons,* 1957

*(following pages) Sunset over Port Austin.*

# T H E       T H U M B

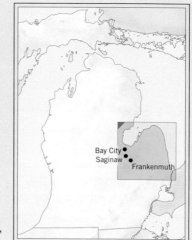

■ TRAVEL BASICS

**Area Overview:** Farmlands, small towns, long, leisurely drives past the beaches, harbors, lighthouses, and wetlands along Lake Huron's shore—this is The Thumb. Not heavily populated and not thronging with tourists, even in summer, this is Michigan's nearest faraway place.

**When to come:** The best time to visit The Thumb is from Memorial Day through October. From mid-June to Labor Day the beaches along Saginaw Bay and small lakeside towns on the eastern side beckon weary city dwellers. Bird watchers and hunters return in autumn when migratory fowl visit the wetlands.

**Weather:** Summer temperatures are in the 80s and all along Lake Huron the beaches are at their most inviting. Fall brings highs of 65-degree days. Winter days usually stay above freezing; nights drop into the high 20s—enough to keep about three inches of snow on the ground through February. Spring and fall bring rain, so don't forget your umbrella.

**Food & Lodging:** This is not great restaurant country, but the small-town cafes and diners offer a lot in the way of personality. Some of the B&Bs are wonderful. *Please see listings beginning on page 274.*

*(previous pages) A vivid sunset highlights a pier in Port Austin, one of The Thumb's popular lakeside resorts.*

## ■ FARMLAND AND FORESTS

The "Thumb" of Michigan's "mitten" is dominated by farmland and small towns. Highway M-25 traces the outline of Lake Huron's shore from Port Huron to Bay City, while M-46 bisects its middle like a rifle shot from Port Sanilac to Saginaw. The land is comparatively flat, a bucolic countryside with weathered barns and cows peering placidly over fences at passersby. It is the "Closer Up North" (the countryside resembling "up north," only "closer" to the urban areas in the southern part of the state), rimmed with blue water and scattered green forests. With few tourists, entertainment is for the locals: farm festivals, fishing tournaments, auctions, parks, and main streets where folks jaywalk against traffic lights. It's where farms in summertime offer "U-pick" orchards as well as vegetable and berry patches, and bring U back in the fall with fields full of pumpkins.

From the head of the St. Clair River looking north across Lake Huron, it's easy to see why early explorers called it *La Mer Douce*—the Sweet Sea. The lake and its shore provide endless entertainment—swimming, boating, fishing, sightseeing charters, and scuba diving. A walk along the beach provides time for contemplation, for listening to the sea's sweet song.

THE THUMB

*A dairy farm along Highway M-25, near Harbor Beach.*

Weather, however, can transform that song into a howl with unexpected suddenness. Two underwater preserves mark graveyards for the ships that met their fate on *La Mer Douce:* **The Thumb Area Great Lakes State Bottomland Preserve** at Port Hope, and **Sanilac Shores Underwater Preserve** off Port Sanilac and Lexington.

# ■ HISTORY

In 1686, to stymie English traders trying to reach the upper lakes, Governor Denonville ordered Daniel Greysolon, Sieur Du Luth to build a fort between Lake Huron and Lake Erie. Du Luth named it Fort St. Joseph and placed it at what is now the north end of Port Huron. Governor Denonville (who in 1689 built another Fort St. Joseph at present-day Niles) planned an all-out war against the Iroquois to punish them for leading the English into French territory. Fort St. Joseph was the mobilization center, bringing together about two hundred *coureurs de bois* and nearly five hundred Indians—Chippewa, Huron, Menominee, Winnebago, Potawatomi, Illinois, Fox, Kickapoo, and Mascouten. The campaign fizzled, but the force gathered demonstrated that a large body of *coureurs de bois* and Indians could be quickly assembled to defend the French fur trade. Two years later Du Luth's replacement, Louis Armand de Lom d'Arce, Baron de Lahontan, an ardent sportsman, excellent wit, and articulate observer of New France, anticipating a winter of intolerable boredom, burned the fort to the ground and returned to the relative civility of Fort Michilimackinac. Regional authority then moved to Fort Ponchartrain du Detroit, which became the focal point of French, British, and American conflict in Michigan.

## ◆ LUMBER INDUSTRY

The Thumb was once a magnificent and seemingly limitless forest of white pine and hardwood, with trees so tall and a canopy so dense that sunlight seldom reached the forest floor. As a prime source for white pine, The Thumb was where lumbering really took off after Detroit was destroyed by fire and sawmills on the St. Clair River were set whirling to rebuild it. Thus began Michigan's initial industrial boom, laying the pattern for what was to come. In 1834, the first steam sawmill was erected on the Saginaw River, and by 1854, there were 558 mills in operation. In 1876, with the timber business entering a decline, a sawmill between Harbor Beach and Bad Axe sent a plank to the World's Fair in Philadelphia. Cut

*Michigan lumbermen often entertained themselves by seeing how many massive old-growth logs they could stack on a single sled. Above is a winning load, stacked and photographed for posterity in 1890. (Michigan State Archives)*

from a single tree and measuring 16 feet long by four feet wide, it became known as the Centennial Plank and symbolized the rapidly vanishing grandeur of Michigan's forest treasure.

## ◆ THE FIRST PLANK ROAD

Fort Gratiot was built by the Americans during the War of 1812 as a supply post just below the outlet of Lake Huron. In 1829, funding was provided for the Fort Gratiot Turnpike—connecting Fort Gratiot to Detroit—the first "plank road" in Michigan. The Turnpike, the St. Clair River, and later the Erie Canal channeled settlers from Canada and the eastern U.S. to the four bourgeoning settlements of Huron, Gratiot, Desmond, and Peru. Some homesteaders continued westward; others settled around Port Huron to engage in shipbuilding. Still others moved up The Thumb to grub out small farms on the logged-over "stumpland."

## ◆ FOREST FIRES

Fires in The Thumb were always a hazard, as they were throughout Michigan. In the early days before logging, the settlers had simply burned the "useless" logs that piled up as they cleared the land. Sometimes fires would be deliberately set—in order, it was claimed, to increase the harvest of blueberries. However, in 1871 and 1881, two great fires changed the ecology of The Thumb forever. Fueled by heaps of slash from reckless logging, these fires roared across The Thumb, destroying cities and obliterating the landscape.

While both fires were disastrous, the 1881 fire was the more devastating of the two. All through August of that year, small wildfires burned out of control, hopping and skipping through the countryside, changing directions unpredictably with each shift of the wind. Then, on September 3, an extraordinary weather phenomenon occurred. Darkness covered the land. By noon, housewives were lighting lamps. By 3 P.M., lanterns were lit along village streets throughout The Thumb. Newspapers recorded the bizarre event as "an Egyptian darkness like the darkness of an eclipse." Wind increased to a gale, howling and coursing through The Thumb at tornado force. The small fires converged. It was, by all accounts, the perfect firestorm. Around 4 P.M., fireballs began soaring through the sky like meteors, dropping down to explode and devour everything in their paths. Then, picking up oxygen created by their own draft, they would shoot back into the air again. Sergeant William O. Bailey with the Michigan Department of Conservation later reported that "even the earth sometimes took fire." People sought refuge in Lake Huron; others crawled into wells, where many suffocated.

The fire raged for 48 hours. At its conclusion 282 lives were reported lost, 15,000 people were rendered homeless, and over 3,400 buildings were destroyed. Perhaps the only positive note was that the 1881 Thumb fire initiated the first relief effort by Clara Barton and her newly formed American Red Cross.

◆ THE THUMB TODAY

After the "endless" forest was reduced to sawdust and ashes, the land beneath it was plowed, and farming became a major factor in the economy of The Thumb, and it remains so today. In some places, the replanting of trees has enabled a small resurgence in the timber industry, but the largest sector of The Thumb's economy is tourism. With its long lakefront beaches, hidden lagoons, canoeable rivers, fishing, and hunting, The Thumb remains (as it has for over a century) the favored vacationland for working folks from Detroit, Toledo, and other cities nearby.

THE THUMB

*Long beaches on The Thumb, such as those at Albert Sleeper State Park on Saginaw Bay, are favorite vacation spots for many Michiganians.*

Alas, farmland in the southern part of The Thumb and along I-75 is rapidly being gobbled up by suburbs. Writer Tom Carney has lived his life in what he terms the "bottom knuckle of The Thumb" around Shelby Township, now Greater Pontiac. Whenever he drives north on M-53, which cuts through the middle of The Thumb, he says he never feels that he's in farm country "until I'm north of Imlay City and I can see, sometimes smell, the rich, dark loam on either side."

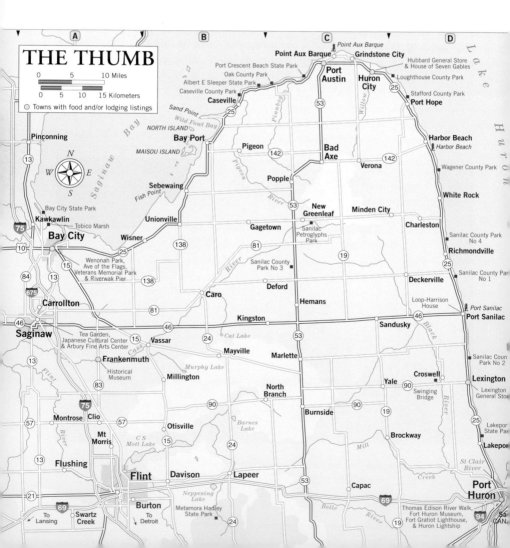

# ■ UP THE ST. CLAIR RIVER AND THE THUMB

Interstate 94, having split from I-90 at Billings, Montana, charts a high, arching path across the high plains. It then travels down through Wisconsin to Chicago and loops around the bottom of Lake Michigan before crossing Michigan diagonally to Detroit, finally coming to rest at Port Huron. It's definitely the fastest way from Detroit to Port Huron. The slower, prettier state highway M-29 skirts the international waterway shared with Canada and saunters through the quaint little river towns of Algonac,

*An ore freighter enters the St. Clair River at Port Huron.*

Marine City, and St. Clair (with its 1,500-foot-long river boardwalk). Car ferries here can shuttle you from St. Clair to Ontario, Canada. Ontario Highway 33 hugs the river from Fort Lambton to the south edge of Sarnia, and makes for an appealing drive that passes through several small towns. Parks along the way open to the river, affording great views of ships moving to and fro.

◆ **PORT HURON** *map page 130, D-4*

Port Huron boasts a Great Lake, a river, a lighthouse, a trolley, two 8,021-foot-long bridges, an international neighbor, and a history as one of the oldest settlements in the state.

### Thomas Edison Drive

From M-25, access Thomas Edison Drive and follow it north along the St. Clair. When you see the Blue Water Bridge, pull into the parking area next to the statue of a young Thomas Alva Edison. This is where Alva, so-called by his family, spent his boyhood and conducted his first experiments.

### Thomas Edison River Walk

One of the nicest things to do in Port Huron is to stroll along the city's two-mile-long History Trail Walking Tour that begins under the Blue Water Bridge and follows the river south. The twin spans of the Blue Water Bridge (connecting to Sarnia, Ontario) rise 152 feet to afford passage to the thousand-foot-long "salties" that ply the river.

### Fort Gratiot Lighthouse

At Lighthouse Park and U.S. Coast Guard Station (Omar and Garfield Streets just north of the Blue Water Bridge) is the 86-foot white brick **1925 Fort Gratiot Lighthouse** with its 1874 lightkeeper's home. *May–October; 810-982-3659.*

### Huron Lightship

Downriver, the Huron Lightship is moored permanently in Pine Grove Park. Now a museum, the 97-foot ship with its 52-foot lantern mast was the last lightship on the Great Lakes, guiding ships through shallows and treacherous shoals. *810-982-0891.*

*(above) The Blue Water Bridge forms a backdrop for the Huron Lightship.*

*(opposite) Visitors tour the Huron Lightship Museum.*

Old-timers call Port Huron the sailor's nursery: young lads come here to watch the big ships on the river, dreaming of faraway places, and later learn to throw ships lines instead of lassos. In 1679, French explorer La Salle's ill-fated *Griffin* became stuck here, and 12 crewmen had to haul her across the shallow rapids into Lake Huron.

water parade of nearly 300 racing craft down the Black River, up the St. Clair, under the Blue Water Bridge, and into Lake Huron to reach the starting line near the Fort Gratiot Light.

Then, 259 unpredictable miles later, competitors lay anchor in the Mackinac Island Marina, and the winner is declared.

**Port Huron Waterfront**
Banners fly along the waterfront during the annual Blue Water Festival and the Port Huron to Mackinac yacht race in mid-July. The highlight is the Mardi Gras–style

**Fort Huron Museum**
Other good stops include the Fort Huron Museum, which includes Indian artifacts, maritime history, and Thomas Edison memorabilia. *1115 Sixth St.; 810-982-0891.*

■ Towns and Sights along the Huron Shore

Lakeside towns ring The Thumb like small beads on a string. Short main streets line M-25, with side streets leading to Lake Huron. *See map page 130.*

◆ Lexington    *map page 130, D-3*

The village of Lexington preserves a touch of New England in its architecture, with steepled churches and a tidy downtown of false storefronts on the slope above the marina. The 130-year-old **Lexington General Store** offers a cornucopia of country wares, replete with creaky floors and glass bins filled with penny candy. *7272 Huron Ave.; 810-359-8900.*

◆ Croswell    *map page 130, D-3*

Detour west on M-90 five miles to Croswell for the fruit and berry farms. At harvest, **Croswell Berry Farm** bakes "Berry-Berry-Cherry" pies, a juicy mix of their own black and red raspberries with cherries. *33 Black River Rd.; 810-679-3273.*

Walk off the calories at the "Be Good to Your Mother-in-Law Bridge." The 139-foot swinging bridge over the Black River was built in 1905 without railings or handrails. Safety rails were installed later, but the name stuck.

◆ PORT SANILAC  *map page 130, D-3*

Eleven miles north of Lexington, M-25 reaches Port Sanilac, another shore village and 1886 brick lighthouse. The lighthouse is on private property, but there are great views of it from the marina. When the first settlers arrived in 1844, the only sign of settlement was a shack thrown together by tanners who distilled tannin from the evergreen trees. To spread news around the area, the postmaster and storekeeper in the growing community laid a pile of newsprint on the counter along with a stack of pencils. Whoever had news to print wrote his or her own. Called the *Bark Shanty Times*, this was the only newspaper in Michigan without editors, reporters, or a printing press. Most everybody stopped in to read the news.

The town's 1875 **Loop-Harrison House,** now the Sanilac County Historical Museum and Village, is staffed by ladies in hoopskirts and wide picture hats who will lead you through exhibits spanning three centuries. Builder Dr. Joseph Loop's family were avid collectors. Exhibits include maritime antiques, souvenirs from four wars, and natural history objects. Dr. Loop's own medicines are still on the shelves. The building is part of a reconstituted village that includes a log cabin, a country store, and a dairy museum. *228 S. Ridge Rd. (M-25); 810-622-9946.*

◆ WHITE ROCK  *map page 130, D-2*

Nineteen miles north of Port Sanilac on M-25, a road sign indicates the location of White Rock. During 1835–36, when the Michigan Territory was clamoring for statehood, banking laws fell lax and land speculation ran wild. When the first land office opened in Detroit, the city became a beehive of shysters pushing bogus real estate. It all looked fine on paper: supposed cities complete with streets with hotels, stores, and homes. Alas, most buyers found only wilderness or swamp. White Rock was a classic. Named for a boulder at the mouth of a river on Lake Huron, its virtues were posted in Detroit's hotel lobbies and on barroom walls. Naturally, there was nothing at all in the "town" of White Rock, and today it remains merely a curiosity along the road.

*The Port Sanilac Marina at dawn.*

◆ HARBOR BEACH     *map page 130, D-1*

During Prohibition, Harbor Beach was used as point of entry for illegal liquor smuggled across the water from Canada. Local historian Leonard DeFrain relates a singular confrontation between bootleggers and G-men when a boat loaded with 24,000 bottles of beer and wine was headed for Port Hope, eight miles north of Harbor Beach, where trucks were ready to speed the goods to Chicago. Word spread that federal agents were waiting for them, so the boat pulled into Harbor Beach. Agents were tipped off, surprised the smugglers, and tried to set the boat afire. As flames licked at the wooden deck, the bottles started exploding, but because of their low alcohol content, the beer and wine spewing from the bottles doused the flames as fast as the agents could start them. The agents finally gave up, resorting to axes to scuttle the offending craft.

About a mile south of the fishing and tourist town of Harbor Beach, Crane Point juts from a woodland into Lake Huron. The point was named after an amiable hermit who one year admitted to a farmer neighbor that he was coining and engraving illegal currency including Mexican dollars and Canadian and German banknotes, a skill he had learned while working at the U.S. Mint. He hid his presses in shanties scattered through the forest in order to evade federal agents.

◆ HURON CITY   *map page 130, C-1*

On the northeast tip of The Thumb on M-25 sits the ghost town of Huron City, preserved as a 19th-century museum town. It has a visitors center, **Hubbard Lake General Store**, a boarding house, lifesaving station, and a chapel. Lumberman Langdon Hubbard built the 16-room Victorian **House of Seven Gables** in 1881, when lumbering in The Thumb was at its peak. Later, the Gables became the summer home of Hubbard's son-in-law William Lyon Phelps, one of the nation's most popular professors and syndicated columnists. His remarkable Sunday services in the little white chapel regularly drew overflow crowds that stood outside in the dirt street to listen to his inspiring sermons.

◆ PORT AUSTIN
*map page 130, C-1*

Located at the tip of The Thumb, Port Austin is a friendly town with wide streets. Residents and visitors gather along the half-mile break wall to observe the first blush of morning streak across Lake Huron. They return in the evening as the sunset casts long purple shadows over Charity and Little Charity Islands in Saginaw Bay.

*Huron City is a Victorian-era ghost town with many architecturally significant structures under preservation, such as this log cabin.*

THE THUMB

The red **Garfield Inn** bed and breakfast is rich in stories of the nation's 19th president, James A. Garfield, and the raven-haired wife of a Michigan lumber baron. The President met Maria Learned when she and her husband, Charles, lived in the state of New York. In 1857, Learned followed the harvest of tall timber to Michigan and purchased a stately home and carriage house at the tip of The Thumb. Garfield was a regular visitor. *8544 Lake St.; 517-738-5254.*

In 1868, Garfield delivered a stirring political speech from the Learneds' third-floor balcony in the inn that now bears his name. Back home in Washington, word reached him that Maria was gravely ill. He caught a train and headed back to Michigan. In a swaying railroad car, he penned these words in his diary: "As I drew near to Troy, my heart began to ache afresh. All my hopes, fears, doubts, concerning Maria came into my heart afresh. The thought that in a few moments I might hear 'she's dead' or 'she's dying' was so terrible that it seemed as though I could not meet it."

Maria recovered, but in 1881 Maria Learned and James Garfield died within months of each other, Maria of tuberculosis and the President by an assassin's bullet.

*Fishing off the city pier in Port Austin.*

*Pointe aux Barques Lighthouse rests on the tip of The Thumb.*

THE THUMB

## ■ SAGINAW BAY NATURAL AREAS

From Port Austin Highway, M-25 follows west side of The Thumb along the shore of Saginaw Bay. Lakeside cottages stand back modestly from shore. Sandbars reach long fingers into the bay; idle watercraft sway in stilted boat hoists where the water is too shallow to make the shore. The area is dotted with marshes and wetlands that attract ducks, geese, and hunters.

### ◆ PORT CRESCENT STATE PARK    *map page 130, C-1*
   ### ALBERT E. SLEEPER STATE PARK    *map page 130, B-1*

Four miles southwest of Port Austin are the twin state parks of Port Crescent and Albert E. Sleeper, separated by **Rush Lake State Game Area.** Boardwalks lead across the dunes to decks fine for picnicking. Children take to the low dunes with relish, building sandcastles or leapfrogging into Mother Nature's sandbox, while adults loll about in the sun or dash into the water for a cooling plunge. Virtually the whole western shoreline of The Thumb is parkland. After Albert E. Sleeper,

*An elevated boardwalk crosses through Port Crescent State Park.*

there is **Wildfowl Bay State Wildlife Area** and **Fish Point State Wildlife Area,** both of which are extraordinary sites for viewing waterfowl (hunting is allowed in both of these parks). *Port Crescent State Park; 517-738-8663. Albert E. Sleeper State Park; 517-856-4411.*

At Port Crescent, check out the **Sanilac Petroglyphs Park.** Here, along the north bank of the Cass River 1,000 years ago or so, Woodland Indians lightly etched over a hundred carvings in the sandstone. Of special interest is a Native American archer stalking game. *Follow M-53 south from Port Austin to New Greenleaf, then take the Bay City–Forestville Rd. east four miles to Germania Rd.*

◆ BAY PORT    *map page 130, B-1*

Slow down, or you'll miss this fishing village in the curve of Wild Fowl Bay. Fifty years ago the city was home to the largest freshwater fishing fleet in the world. During those busy days when fleets docked here, fish were so big and plentiful that they threatened to break the nets. Overfishing and pollution exhausted the resource and today only the 1895 Bay Port Fish Company remains in operation. *For information contact the Huron County Visitors Bureau; 800-358-4862.*

## ■ BAY CITY    *map page 130, A-2*

Bay City is a thriving city of 39,000 straddling the Saginaw River about 10 miles upstream from where the river empties into Saginaw Bay at the crook of Michigan's Thumb and Mitten.

### ◆ HISTORY OF BAY CITY AND SAGINAW

Between 1850 and 1900, Bay City and Saginaw were twin brawling lumbertowns, literally and figuratively duking it out over which town was number one in timber production. At the climax of the white pine craze in 1882, sawmills lined the banks from town to town. Mills sliced and whined their way through the logs, engines squealing and grinding, while other mills sawed through some of the best oak in the world. The bulk of the oak went to build ships, adding to the ever-growing fleet of timber ships that ferried the pine along Lake Huron, down the Detroit River, and across Lake Erie to Buffalo. Many a captain claimed he could steer his ship up the Saginaw River by sawdust smell alone.

By 1900, the timber was gone, and the once-roaring mills lining the banks of the Saginaw had fallen silent: rusting monuments to greed surrounded by

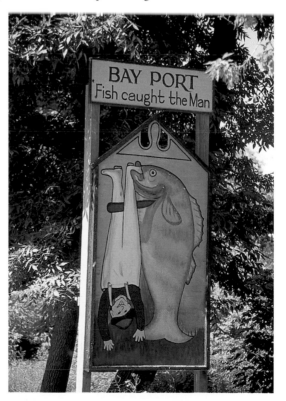

*The sign for the Bay Port Fish Company. The outfit was founded by Henry Engehardt, who claimed that his fish stand offered the state's first (and best) fast food.*

acres of trim-slabs and sawdust. Bay City hung on briefly as a shipping supply and repair yard, but by 1908, that, too had followed the trail of the tall pines and beautiful oaks. All that remained were the barons' mansions and elegant churches that remain today the most graceful elements of the city.

◆ VISITING BAY CITY

Parks and river walks line the banks; restaurants offer dockside service; marinas offer boat rentals and launches. The river teems with pleasure craft and huge ocean-going freighters, making Bay City the second busiest Michigan port on Lake Huron.

The city's heart beats in **Wenonah Park,** a riverside park named for the mother of Hiawatha. The **Avenue of Flags** represents ships from around the world that regularly call here. The path through the flags leads to a fountain and **World Friendship Arts Shell,** where summer concerts and performances are held. I always find time to claim a bench in Wenonah Park to sit and watch the river traffic and families out for a stroll.

Across the Saginaw River, **Veterans Memorial Park** offers picnic areas, tennis courts, a music pavilion, a boat launch, and a marina. Hikers and bicyclers take to the path along the waterfront on the way to the 700-foot **Riverwalk Pier,** my favorite pier. This is not just a straight shot into the river. It's a zigzag with balconies where fishermen can cast their lines and a gazebo where wanderers can pause to gaze at the islands up the river.

Fascinating trolley-bus tours of Bay City's old mansions, or "painted ladies," begin each Saturday at 2 P.M. at the **Historical Museum of Bay County.** *321 Washington Ave.; 517-893-5733.*

Next door, the 1894 Romanesque-style **City Hall** features a dramatic free-standing staircase with wrought-iron railings winding from the foyer to the fourth floor. A 31-foot tapestry depicting Bay City's history, woven in 1977 by Monika Chmielewska, hangs in the council chambers. *301 Washington Ave.; 517-894-8147.*

For a fishing charter, Captain Dave DeGrow is always ready with the 27-foot *SeaRay Amberjack. 517-692-0255.*

The 65-foot topsail schooner *Appledore* is a striking feature on the waters of Saginaw Bay. It sails from Wenonah Park most weekends. *901 Saginaw St.; 888-229-8696.*

*(above) A red-bellied woodpecker.*
*(below) Swans migrating from the far north stop to rest in Michigan's lakes.*

◆ BAY PORT WETLANDS

Walk to the observation tower over the wetland and marsh of **Tobico Lagoon**, a favorite perch from which to follow the comings and goings of hundreds of birds. The 1,700-acre Tobico Marsh refuge attracts more than 100 species of birds and migratory waterfowl. *Three miles north of Bay City at 3582 State Park Dr.; 517-667-0717.*

■ SAGINAW  *map page 130, A-3*

◆ SAGINAW AND ITS INDIAN HISTORY

The Cass, Flint, Bad, Shiawassee, and Tittabawassee Rivers all cut across wide marshes before draining into the short, deep Saginaw River, which then flows into Saginaw Bay. In 1819, Washington forwarded $10,000 to Michigan's Territorial Governor, Lewis Cass, with instructions to negotiate a treaty with the Indians for a pie-shaped heart of Michigan along Lake Huron. Cass sent word to the Ottawa and Chippewa occupying the land to meet at the junction of the rivers flowing into the Saginaw River during the full moon of September. Two ships were loaded and dispatched from Detroit with supplies and liquor to be distributed at the proper time.

Louis Campau was instructed to build a council house for the meeting. Cass arrived on September 10, flanked by assistants and instructors. Cass was a good negotiator. Indians called him "Big Belly" for his portly figure. Over the next two weeks, up to 4,000 Indians wandered in and out of the encampment. The proposed treaty encompassed one-sixth of Michigan's total land area from the tip of The Thumb, deeper south beyond the Saginaw Valley, and north to Thunder Bay up the Lake Huron shore. When the treaty seemed stalled, Cass suspected it was the subversive work of trapper Jacob Smith. Cass offered Smith a buy-off of 11 sections of land and $3,000 in silver coins. Smith accepted, and the Indians swung their vote to accept the trade.

Campau was furious, claiming part of the silver was rightly his, to pay off the past debt the Indians already owed his post. To celebrate the signing, Cass ordered five barrels of whiskey to be distributed among the Indians. In the book *Michigan*, Willis F. Dunbar and George S. May give the following account:

Campau now had his revenge. He opened ten barrels of his own whiskey, and began passing it out. The Indians became roaring drunk, and their violence alarmed Cass. "Louis! Louis!" he cried. "Stop the liquor." Campau replied, "General, you commenced it; you let Smith plunder me and rob me." But after another plea, Campau restrained the Indians, saying, "I lost my money; I lost my fight; I lost my liquor; but I got good satisfaction."

◆ TIMBERING AND TAILORING
IN THE SAGINAW VALLEY

The Saginaw Valley held dense forests of some of the best timber in the world: white pine that was strong and durable, did not warp, crack, shrink, or splinter, and floated like a cork. Soon a line of sawmills stood on the river from Saginaw to Bay City.

With the April thaw, the swaggering "red-sash brigade" was on: French-Canadian lumberjacks with red sashes tied at their waists, bright mackinaws, and tasseled caps worn at a jaunty angle. Add to that an ethnic mix of many nationalities, and the men from the woods presented a dramatic picture. All winter they worked hard, and when spring came, they played even harder, drinking and carousing on an epic scale.

Lumbering towns pushed to out-boast the next with tall tales of their orgies, and most were true. Saginaw's Potter Street offered 32 saloons within nine blocks. The town hired its own Wyatt Earp, ex-cavalryman Marshall Charles Meyer. When fighting turned mean, Meyer rode his horse into the barroom and clubbed away in all directions with his nightstick.

Little Joe "Jake" Seligman, a diminutive 4-foot-11-inch haberdasher, counted on his size, or lack of it, to pocket his share of lumberjack cash. Having established a reputation for outlandish self-promotion in Pontiac, he moved to Saginaw and established "Little Jake's." Popular with the lumberjacks, who appreciated his sense of humor, Jake became a huge success. Among his many jocular self promotions was the construction a large tower atop which he mounted a giant copper statue of himself, thereby proving his motto: "The largest retail clothier in Michigan."

*Saginaw's prosperity allowed for the pursuit of costly leisure activities.*
*This print shows a race held at the East Saginaw track in 1874. In this particular race,*
*Goldsmith Maid, here shown in the lead, set a record time for trotters.*
*(Museum of American History, Smithsonian Institution)*

One fondly recounted legend has him tossing vests from his store's second-story window to a crowd of lumberjacks, promising a free coat and trousers to every man who caught a vest. Most of the time, the vests were torn to shreds before they made it back through the door. But Jake was allegedly as good as his word: The victor received a new $12 suit for free—but had to remunerate Jake $12 for the ruined vest.

## ◆ SAGINAW SIGHTS

### Friendship Garden and Japanese Cultural Center

The Friendship Garden and Japanese Cultural Center, a gift from Saginaw's sister city Tokushima, Japan, is a treasure. A walking path along the Flint River cuts through a tree-shaded garden with bridges over small streams to the sculptured garden surrounding the **Tea Garden**. Watching the ritual of the Japanese tea ceremony makes for a memorable afternoon. *West on M-46, then north on M-13 to Ezra Rust Dr. and South Washington Ave.; 517-759-1648.*

### Saginaw County Visitors Bureau

General information. *One Tuscola St., Suite 101, 800-444-9979.*

### Shiawassee National Wildlife Refuge

This 18,000-acre refuge includes wetlands that spread along creeks and bayous, cut by dikes. Will Hufton operates his **Johnny Panther Quests**—three- to five-hour treks into what he calls Michigan's Everglades, maneuvering his 16-foot flatbottom motorized boat in and out of creeks and bayous he's prowled since childhood.

"This has been my playground since I came here with my father when I was three," Hufton says. *Johnny Panther Quests 810-653-3859. Shiawassee NWR; 6975 Mower Rd.; 517-777-5930.*

### Marshall M. Fredericks Sculpture Museum

Here you can wander among the outdoor and indoor displays of monumental sculpture (models, casts, and finished pieces) by Michigan artist Marshall M. Fredericks, whose works grace many civic venues in the state. *Exit 160, then left on M-84. Follow the signs; 7400 Bay Rd.; 517-790-5667.*

*A plaster for the statue Freedom of the Human Spirit at Marhsall M. Fredericks Sculpture Museum. (photo by Molly Barth)*

### ◆ U-Pick Farms

Throughout Saginaw County, numerous small towns have attractions worthy of a stop. Around the villages of Freeland, Hemlock, and Merrill are nine or more "U-pick" farms of strawberries, raspberries, and blueberries. At **Bayne's Apple Valley Farm** northwest of Freeland, aromas are tantalizing in the autumn air, with fresh juice squeezed at the cider mill. From the bakery come the spicy smells of apple cookies, muffins and homemade pies. I certainly can't resist a take-along caramel apple and a bushel of fresh fruit. *North on Midland Rd. (M-47) to 5395 Midland Rd.; 517-695-9139.*

### ■ FRANKENMUTH *map page 130, A-3*

One August day in 1845, with four grueling months of travel behind them, a small group of Bavarian colonists loaded their belongings and two church bells from their homeland onto an oxcart at Saginaw and pushed their way southeast 12 miles through dense wilderness and swamps to carve out a settlement at the Cass River. Impassioned by a new beginning and zeal to convert the resident Indians, their St. Lorenz Church and mission were built and bells ready to ring by Christmas Day. The Indians quickly headed west while the group, soon joined by other family members and neighbors, established themselves as Bavarian Lutherans, a heritage that is preserved today. A replica of the old log church stands near the present St. Lorenz with the original bells displayed nearby.

The 1856 Exchange Hotel evolved into **Zehnder's Restaurant** *at 730 S. Main St.; 517-652-0450.* Across Main Street, the 1880 Fischer Hotel evolved into the **Bavarian Inn Restaurant,** famous for Mrs. Kern's all-you-can-eat chicken dinner, first served in 1895, a family-style tradition that now keeps both restaurants accommodating more than a thousand people a day. *(See page 286.)*

The **Frankenmuth Historical Museum** highlights the area's German ancestry with permanent and changing exhibits. *613 S. Main St.; 517-652-9701.*

THE THUMB

Frankenmuth is known for its Bavarian style of architecture, glockenspiel towers, and festivals with plenty of sausages, beer, and polka music. The 239-foot-long 19th-century replica Holz Brucke (covered bridge) spans the lazy Cass River. *Frankenmuth Convention & Visitors Bureau; 635 S. Main St.; 800-386-8696.*

**Bronner's Christmas Wonderland,** the world's largest Christmas store, might best be described as four football fields of glittering baubles, with sparkling garlands chasing rings around the Christmas trees. Wally Bronner opened the fairyland Christmas store in 1945; he still stands at the door wearing his contagious grin 361 days of the year. *25 Christmas Lane; 517-652-9931.*

*The Bavarian Inn Restaurant in Frankenmuth.*

# S U N R I S E   S I D E

■ HIGHLIGHTS

■ TRAVEL BASICS

**Area Overview:** The rolling hills along Michigan's Lake Huron shore are dotted with small towns that beckon tourists, campers, boaters, and picnickers. Most dutifully travel along US-23 as it curves gently northward following the lakeshore from Bay City to the top of Michigan's mitten at Mackinaw City. Several highways cut across the section to connect with the major north-south trucker highway I-75, many of which offer marvelous side trips into Michigan's past and into its special beauty.

**Weather:** Like the rest of Michigan, water tempers the climate along the lakeshore throughout the year. Alpena profits in particular from its lake position, offering some of the mildest temperatures in the state. Summer is T-shirt-and-shorts weather. Daytime temperatures average in the 80s, dropping into the 60s at night for good sleeping weather. Spring and fall temperatures drop to 60, and the nights are cool. Winter temperature are sometimes the coldest in the lower peninsula, creating ideal weather for snowmobiling and ice fishing. Daytime winter days can climb into the 40s.

**Food & Lodging:** Small cafes and local-favorite restaurants can be surprisingly good; B&Bs abound and lakeside cottages can often be rented, but be sure to plan ahead! *Please see listings beginning on page 274.*

# ■ OVERVIEW

First comes a soft morning glow across the eastern sky. Then dawn leaps out of Lake Huron, spreading glitter on the waves and casting the lighthouses guarding the shore in sharp silhouette. So begins the day on Michigan's "Sunrise Side," where the flatlands of the south roll into the hills of the north, creased with rivers that invite canoeing, kayaking, tubing, and fishing.

Highway US-23 hugs the shoreline as it follows the green and white "Circle Lake Huron" signs from Bay City to Mackinaw City at the top of Michigan's mitten. I-75 marks the western boundary of this section, while between the two highways, M-33 zigzags through the forested heartland from the village of Alger (on I-75 between Standish and West Branch) north to Cheboygan. I savor driving these Sunrise Side highways: a 90-degree summer day with car windows down and wind blowing free, the thrill of the elements on an icy February morning when snowflakes speckle my windshield and Lake Huron claws at the beach over my shoulder. Along the way are 19th-century lumbering and fishing towns, small villages such as Wooden Shoe and Red Oak, as well as the major towns of Bay City and Alpena.

Other than on I-75, the major north-south truck route, traffic moves slowly, without horns or squealing brakes. There are no shopping malls or crowded tourist attractions. "We can fancy up, but plain just suits us better," says longtime Rogers City resident Harry Whiteley. Inland, folks tend to work hard through the week, "eat out" on Friday night, attend church on Sunday, and line up for parades on holidays; on weekends, they'll likely tow their boats out to one of the myriad lakes for a day of fishing, picnicking, and swimming.

# ■ HISTORY

The first European to trace the length of the Sunrise Side in a craft larger than a canoe was French explorer Robert Cavelier, Sieur de La Salle. In 1679, he built a 45-ton schooner above Niagara Falls, the *Griffin,* and sailed her across Lake Erie, up the Detroit River, and into Lake Huron.

After his ship nearly capsized in rough seas, he dropped her anchor at St. Ignace for a few days of rest before sailing on to Green Bay. There, La Salle loaded the *Griffin* with furs and ordered her back to Niagara for more supplies. She never made it. (The remains of this long-lost craft are believed to lie at the top of Lake Huron near Tobermory, Ontario.) It would be a hundred years before a ship the likes of the *Griffin* would again hoist sails on the lower Great Lakes.

*This painting by George Catlin depicts the expedition of Robert Cavelier, Sieur de La Salle, leaving Fort Frontenac in 1679. (National Gallerty of Art, Washington, D.C.)*

During the 1700s, eastern Michigan was largely ignored by settlers. The population consisted of small Indian villages of approximately 30 people clustered around the river mouths. Occasionally a fur trapper or lone fisherman built a crude shelter and stayed awhile. Surrounding these villages, a great forest of white pine and hardwood covered the land, the canopy of intertwining branches so dense it blocked the sun from reaching the forest floor. Lakes and rivers teemed with whitefish, sturgeon, and the trout-like grayling.

Then came timber fever—first leveling the forests around Saginaw and the Thumb and then, its appetite unsatiated, turning north for yet more timber. Logging camps sprang up—rungs on a ladder of rivers—climbing from the Rifle River to the Au Sable, Black, Thunder Bay and Cheboygan, leaving in their wake the rubble and slash of clear-cut forests, decimated spawning grounds, and towns

suddenly forced to figure out ways to survive: Tawas City, Oscoda, Harrisville, Ossineke, Alpena, Rogers City, and Cheboygan.

By the end of the 19th century, the white pine on the morning side of Michigan had been felled, their canopies pulled down, their whisper silenced. Fishermen came for the grayling with the same zeal as the lumberjacks had for timber—with the same results. It has taken nearly 50 years of careful management to restore a significant timber harvest, but the legendary grayling, like the blue pike, no longer brightens the Au Sable. Pioneers scratched farms from the poor soils of the cutover land, and industries slowly evolved catch as catch can. Today, a century after the timber fever burned its way across the land, eastern Michigan's economy is based on a carefully resuscitated timber industry, light industry, limited farming, and tourism—for it remains a beautiful place to come to restore one's depleted spirits.

### ■ UP THE SUNRISE SIDE

◆ RIFLE RIVER RECREATION AREA    *map page 155, C-6*

The meandering Rifle River, which empties into Saginaw Bay near the village of Omer on US-23 east of Standish, is the core of the 4,300-acre Rifle River Recreation Area. To begin a 90-mile canoe float trip from RRRA headquarters at Devoe Lake, drive I-75 north to Alger, north on M-33 to Rose City, then east on Rose City Road, following the RRRA signs. Rustic campgrounds, coveted by fishermen, are scattered along this slow-moving, sparkling river. *Information; 517-473-2258.*

If a 90-mile canoe trek seems a tad daunting, stop off in Sterling and put in along a very pleasant mile of maintained river. **River View Campground and Canoe Livery** will set you up with the canoe or kayak of your choice. *5755 Towline Rd., Sterling; 517-654-2447.*

◆ TAWAS CITY AND EAST TAWAS   *map page 155, C-5*

From the Rifle River at Omer, follow M-23 northeast along the coast for 35 miles to the twin cities of Tawas City and East Tawas, which hug the wide sweep of Lake Huron's Tawas Bay. (You say "Tawas" a lot while visiting here.) The main street, Newman Street, is lined with shops, and on lazy afternoons folks stroll the marina boardwalk licking ice cream cones.

For 50 cents (a bargain) hop the green-topped Old Number 9 trolley to **Tawas Point State Park** (a treasure). Curving like a comma into Lake Huron, the park offers a few campsites directly on the powdery sand and another 200 sites only steps from the water's edge. In the evenings, as if on cue, campers by the dozens gather on the bay beach to watch the sun reflecting on the water before it drops behind the distant hills. *Tawas Point State Park; 800-447-2757.*

The **Sandy Hook Nature Trail** is a fine place to look for shorebirds along the water's edge and to listen for the musical *o-kaleee!* song of red-winged blackbirds atop the cattails. In spring and fall, Tawas is a regular migratory stop for numerous songbirds; in mid-August, Monarch butterflies stop here for brief rests before fluttering on. The trail leads past the white brick **1876 Tawas Point Light** with its 70-foot conical tower over the redbrick keeper's quarters. It is a working light that is seldom open to the public. *Tawas Bay Tourist & Convention Bureau; 402 Lake St. (US-23); 800-558-2927.*

■ AU SABLE AND OSCODA   *map page 155, D-5*

When you arrive at the Au Sable Bridge, you know you're in paddling country. Outfitters stack canoes high along the riverbanks. The spiderweb headwaters of the shallow, fast-flowing Au Sable converge at Grayling, about 70 miles west of here as the crow flies. Designated a State Natural River, the Au Sable twists and turns for 120 miles before reaching the twin towns of Au Sable and Oscoda on the Lake Huron shore. Deeper waters lie in "ponds" (actually small lakes) created by power dams. During the annual World Championship Au Sable River Canoe Marathon, the challenging course includes at least 14 hours of full-bore paddling and leg-straining portages over the river dam support banks that reach higher than a three-story building. A crowds come to cheer on participants. *Last weekend of July. For information: The Oscoda Area Convention & Visitors Bureau; oscoda.com; 4440 North US-23; 800-235-4625.*

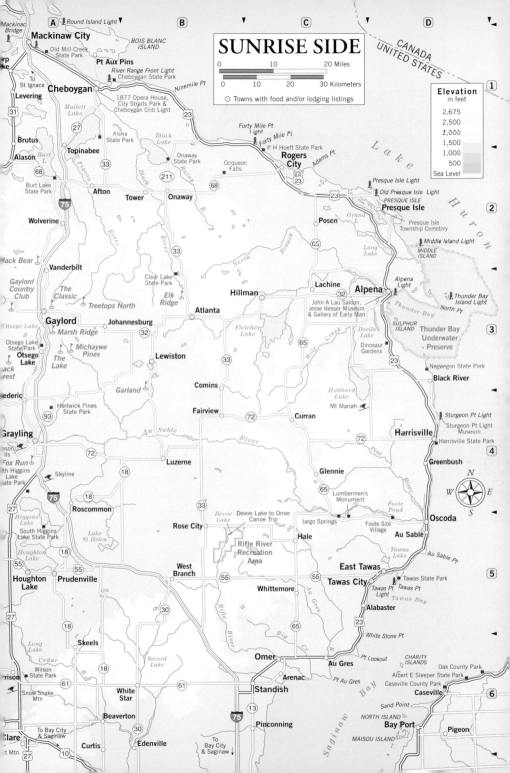

*Canoeing the Au Sable River.*

Before the arrival of the marathoners and power dams, these waters were the transportation trail for Chippewa and other Great Lakes Indian tribes. When lumber barons along the Saginaw River saw their supply of white pine dwindling, they found along the Au Sable high-quality red pine that floated like a fish bobber. Soon the Au Sable reverberated with sounds of falling timber, the vibrating ping of the blacksmith's anvil, and the clang of the camp dinner bell. By 1836, Oscoda was a sawmill town, with rows of taverns, Saturday night brawls after payday, and "shady ladies" along the back streets.

Its use as a log highway long vanished, the Au Sable has reverted to less intrusive business. Charter captains like Randy Hetzner in his *Mist E II* and Steve Paslaski in his *TMB II* join other boats heading for the waters of Lake Huron in pursuit of whitefish, perch, and, when they're running, salmon and steelhead.

◆ HURON NATIONAL FOREST    *map page 155, C-5*

The 22-mile-long **River Road National Scenic Byway** follows M-65 from Oscoda west along the south bank of the Au Sable through the Huron National Forest to Rollway, at Loud Pond. Outside Oscoda, a special area planted with jack pine

## THE LUMBERJACK CODE

*Mythic hero of Michigan's ancient forests, the lumberjack captured the American imagination in almost as grand a fashion as the cowboy. Paul Bunyan with his blue ox, Babe, were deliberately drawn larger than life, but beneath that legend lay a reality of derring-do and mind-boggling excess. The pioneering folk-life historian Richard Dorson sought to capture many of the tales and as much of the lore of that era as he could before it disappeared completely. This excerpt describes the inconsistent and highly contradictory code of that now-vanished way of life.*

The white pine lumberjack has grown into legend, the legend of a swashbuckling, ferocious, tenderhearted superman.... The life of the jacks followed an unwritten creed, and he who violated its articles suffered dishonor and dismissal from a proud fraternity.... More surely than any union contract, the lumberjack code extracted from the woodsmen unslacking, prodigious toil. "They worked all day from the first light until deep into the night; they'd work their heart out for you," Moonlight Schmidt said. To be the Number One jack in a camp was a coveted honor; to haul the most board feet of logs into camp was an incentive that spurred rival teamsters; to belong to the best camp was a proud assertion backed up with flying fists.

Skill and superstamina being taken for granted, the code next stressed the ability to brawl and the necessity to get insensibly drunk. The lumberjacks have been aptly styled "whiskey-fighting men." Every spring when camp would break, a jack must leave the woods where he has lived in monastic seclusion for six or seven months, hike to the nearest town and blow his entire stake of four or five hundred dollars on rotgut whiskey. During this spree he visited the brothels and mauled other jacks. When he was dead broke he made his way back to camp, to recoup his stake by working as a river-driver (or river-hog). Many jacks never escaped the woods because they blew every stake they made for liquor. Nat Kavanagh spent twenty years trying to see his mother but never got beyond St. Ignace. Just why the jack had to spend all his earnings thus futilely none of the old woodsmen can quite explain, all accepting the matter as fundamentalist doctrine quite beyond inquiry.

—Richard M. Dorson, *Blood-Stoppers and Bear-Walkers: Folk Tales of Immigrants, Lumberjacks and Indians,* 1952

ERECTED TO PERPETUATE THE MEMORY OF THE
PIONEER LUMBERMEN OF MICHIGAN THROUGH
WHOSE LABORS WAS MADE POSSIBLE THE
DEVELOPMENT OF THE PRAIRIE STATES

*The Lumberman's Monument.*

provides critical habitat for the tiny Kirtland's warbler. This forest and others developed within the Huron are the only nesting sites for the endangered gray and yellow songbird that winters in the Bahamas.

About 10 miles west of Wurtsmith Air Force Base at Oscoda is **Foote Site Village,** a mecca for steelhead and salmon anglers. Forgot your gear? All you'll need can be bought at Karen Usler's and Robert Lammi's **The Dam Store;** *1879 River Rd.; 517-739-9979.*

Eight miles farther west, on the shores of Foote Dam Pond, the white *Au Sable River Queen* paddlewheel riverboat is available for leisurely cruises along the seven- mile-long waterway. *1775 West River Rd.; 517-739-7351.*

On a bluff overlooking Cooke Dam Pond, another lake created by a power dam about 20 miles from Foote Dam Pond, the famous **Lumberman's Monument** is perched. It was erected to honor woodsmen: men who surveyed and harvested the trees, skidded logs to the rollways and into the streams; men who watered down the ice roads and drove the teams of horses. Displays include an interpretive visitors center, logging wagons, big wheels, and other equipment from the early years.

A few miles farther along the Au Sable, you reach a turnout. This is **Iargo Springs.** Some 294 steps descend a steep wooded hillside where a walkway spans a boggy glen under pines and spruce so tall one feels the urge to whisper. According to legend, Chippewas came to Iargo Springs to partake of its "mystical" waters which seep from springs at the bottom of the hillside. Here are low waterfalls and water plants greening in the seeps and the shallows of Cooke Dam Pond, where visitors toss coins to gleam among forgotten logs.

■ HARRISVILLE   *map page 155, D-4*

North of Oscoda, US-23 is lined with modest vacation cottages and year-round homes fronting on Lake Huron. A half-mile south of Harrisville at Harrisville State Park, campsites are set among groves of aromatic cedars and whispering pines.

Four miles north is the 1869 **Sturgeon Point Lighthouse and Museum.** Of Michigan's 117 lighthouse museums, this one is my favorite, still actively warning boaters of the deadly reef just offshore. Its fiery red window trim and doors contrast dramatically with the white of the keeper's quarters and connecting 70-foot conical tower. The tower is off-limits, but visitors are welcome in the plain kitchen with a cast iron stove (reached through the back door of the quarters). Furnishings in the first-floor rooms (kitchen, bedroom, and library) date from the early 1900s,

*Sturgeon Point Lighthouse was built in 1869.*

*Scenic US-23, shown here in autumn colors, follows the shoreline of Lake Huron.*

down to the pince-nez glasses resting on an open Bible. The walls are painted the same shade of green as they were when the keeper's family lived here in 1913. Outside displays include the rudder from the ship *Marine City,* a wooden steamer that caught fire in August 1880 and sank two miles north with 100 passengers and a crew of 41 on board—most of whom were rescued, you'll be glad to know. A room on the museum's second floor holds displays of the lifesaving station that once stood along the shore.

◆ HUBBARD LAKE    *map page 155, C/D-3/4*

Michigan's third largest inland lake, rated third cleanest, and second in clarity by Michigan's Department of Natural Resources, Hubbard Lake offers 30 miles of shoreline. The spring-fed lake has been a popular vacation destination for over a hundred years. It was also a favorite of Great Lakes Indians who considered a very large boulder at the head of the lake a holy place. In 1881, lumbering brought settlement to the area, and the tall, straight pines from around the lake were logged and shipped to the Atlantic seaboard as masts for oceangoing vessels.

Today the wooded shoreline is lined with 1950s–style resorts, small restaurants, ice cream and sandwich shops, marinas, and the occasional market. The community of South Shore is crowded with small private cottages and is as jam-packed as a third-grader's sleepover party. Boats and water toys are stacked along the shore, but because the lake is so large, it rarely seems over-populated.

"If I saw 12 boats at one time, I would say the lake was crowded," says Don Geib, owner of **Churchill Pointe Inn** on the East Shore. Hedged in greenery with banks of flowers circling the walkways, the 1927 inn and restaurant is a favorite with visitors and locals alike. From the long lakeside deck shaded by giant oaks boaters can order dockside dining served on board. *5700 Bennett Rd.; 517-727-2020.*

■ ALPENA    *map page 155, D-3*

Alpena, the largest city on the Sunrise Side, hugs the northern top of the 26-mile shoreline of Lake Huron's Thunder Bay. Approaching from the south on US-23 you pass through the marshlands of Squaw Bay, where waterbirds flit among the reeds, from mergansers in the shallows and plovers in the grasses to great blue herons circling overhead.

*The Brown Trout Festival in Alpena takes place in the fall.*

When surveyor Lewis Clason and his team arrived in 1839, they found little to their liking in what was then a pine and cedar swamp swarming with mosquitoes and stinging no-see-ums. They were so glad to finish the job that they demanded their pay in cash—three dollars a day—declining the offer of a deed to the township of their choice. They missed out: Alpena was to become the major shipping port in this part of Michigan. First for lumber, then concrete blocks made of area limestone, Alpena really reached its peak in fishing. Before 1835, when steamer captains Harvey Harwood and Walter Scott noted the large catches of a few fishermen living in scattered shacks, they set up a fishery. By the time they piloted the *Julius D. Morton* over the sand bars and into Thunder Bay River in 1852, other fisheries were also flourishing.

At that time, hand-made nets were used by lake fishermen; later, gill nets (illegal today) were used. About 15 miles south of Thunder Bay, fishermen developed pound nets which led fish through tunnels into a holding trap. These nets were soon used all along Lake Huron.

Commercial fishing on the Great Lakes was ill managed, with near depletion of some fishing grounds. In addition, lamprey eels, inadvertently introduced, had infested the waters, attacking larger fish such as lake trout and whitefish. The 1979 ruling by Federal District Judge Noel Fox in support of a Native American claim of exemption from all state commercial fishing regulations in the Great Lakes struck a final blow to the big commercial fisheries.

There are more lighthouses around Alpena than any other Michigan city: Alpena Light, Thunder Bay, and Middle Island, as well as the New Presque Isle and Old Presque Isle Lighthouse Museums. The waters of Thunder Bay have long been known as Shipwreck Alley due to the islands, rocks, shoals, and temperamental nature of Great Lakes storms.

Today, through sound management, Alpena is witnessing a strong recovery of lake trout, whitefish, perch, and other species. Recreational fishing is once again strong, especially in the Thunder Bay area, and the Native American fisheries have become the only commercial operations. Today, the city wears a charming Victorian air, its turreted mansions with wraparound porches interspersed with modern homes.

### Old Town

Electric streetlights first illuminated the town in 1883, two years after their invention, and telephones began ringing here one year after their invention. Old Town itself comprises three blocks of Second Avenue along which the brick streets and storefronts have been restored to their late-1800s appearance.

## John A. Lau Saloon

The 1893 **John A. Lau Saloon** stands on the site of the original, where lumberjacks came on payday—hell-bent on hell-raising. At that time, Lau kept three bartenders on hand—a German, a Frenchman, and a Pole—so that the language of most any lumberjack who bellied up to the bar could be understood. More sedate today, the saloon serves tasty barbecued ribs. *414 N. Second Ave.; 517-354-6898.*

## Thunder Bay Underwater Preserve

This preserve, one of 11 diving parks in Michigan, protects 88 shipwrecks within a 288-square-mile area, the heaviest concentration of shipwrecks per square mile in the Great Lakes. Within the preserve, the Michigan Nature Association manages 17 islands scattered in the bay, all key habitats for migrating waterfowl. *The Alpena Convention & Visitors Bureau, 235 W. Chisholm; 800-4-ALPENA.*

## Jesse Besser Museum

This museum features a re-created 19th-century **Avenue of Shops**, a general store, harness shop, post office, and clapboard houses with oil lamps and lace curtains at the windows, that allow a marvelous peek into bygone times. The museum's **Gallery of Early Man** displays 20,000 artifacts dating back 7,000 years, primarily from an area collection by the museum's historian and curator, Robert Haltiner, and his father, Gerald. *Closed Mondays; 491 Johnson St.; 517-356-2202.*

## Sportsmen's Island

On the west side of US-23 about three blocks from the museum, a gaggle of geese and ducks are sure to greet you at Sportsmen's Island, whether or not you invite them. Across the walkway to the nature area and wildlife sanctuary of islands with Thunder Bay River curling through, swans float on the river, warblers add background music, and an occasional barred or great horned owl sometimes make surprise visits.

◆ OLD PRESQUE ISLE LIGHTHOUSE AND MUSEUM    *map page 155, D-2*

The Old Presque Isle Lighthouse and Museum stands at Presque Isle Harbor off M-638, 19 miles north of Alpena. Somebody goofed in the 1840s when they built this one—the light could not be seen by down-bound ships! So another lighthouse was built a mile north. Recommissioned in 1870, they finally got it right. At 113 feet, it is the tallest on the Great Lakes and still a working light. *3550 E. Grand Lake Rd.; 517-595-3600.*

The Old Presque Isle Lighthouse features a spiral staircase with hand-chiseled stone steps that wind to the top. The English-style whitewashed brick light-keeper's cottage reflects the mid-1800s with displays of nautical instruments, foghorns, anchors, a windlass, a ship's wheel, and Fresnel lenses.

*Besser State Natural Area, on the shores of Lake Huron, lies across
False Presque Isle Harbor from Presque Isle.*

Along the road to the lighthouses lies the **Presque Isle Township Cemetery** and the graves of Bill Green, Fred Piepkorn, and Charlie Priest. During the Depression, when liquor was hard to come by, these three pals usually found more than their share. In a toast to their friendship, they pledged that as each pal passed on, the others would raise their bottles and pour a drink on their buddy's grave. In each cement slab is drilled a hole above the dearly departed buddy, waiting for his drink. Which buddy was the last to go? You'll have to check that out on your own. (Bring a flask!)

■ HILLMAN   *map page 155, C-3*

The tiny town of Hillman lies 22 miles due west of Alpena on M-32. In the summertime, breezes are warm and friendly, and the fields along the road are planted with sunflowers that raise their broad yellow faces eastward. In spring, delectable morel mushrooms grow in the forest, and in autumn, trees blaze red and gold.

Wintertime, after a good snowfall, is my favorite time to visit Hillman, because that is when I can view the elk at the **Thunder Bay Resort** from a horse-drawn sleigh on the way to a five course gourmet meal at **Elkhorn,** Jack and Jan Matthias's log cabin lodge. The wagon ride is offered throughout the year, but nothing beats a winter sleigh drawn by draft horses that puff clouds of breath into the icy air. Following the trail through the dense hardwood and evergreen forests along Anchor Creek, we leave the world behind; at the first bugling of a bull elk, we enter a magical world. I once counted more than 50 elk on the hour-long ride to the cabin.

Guests gather around an oversized fireplace against one of the pine-paneled walls. The aroma of crown roast of pork wafts from the ovens of the cabin's wood-fired stoves, and that is only the beginning of the feast. Rooms and chalets are available at the resort for overnights. Return in summer for golf and fishing. *27800 M-32; call for directions: 517-742-4875.*

*Waterfalls abound in Michigan's Lower Peninsula. Ocqueoc Falls,*
*is about 15 miles west of Rogers City,*

## ■ ROGERS CITY   *map page 155, C-2*

Twenty-nine miles north of Alpena lies Rogers City. The **Quarry View** platform reveals the workings in the three- by-two-mile-wide open limestone quarry, the largest such quarry in the world.

## ■ CHEBOYGAN   *map page 155, A-1*

Long ago, the combination of lakes and rivers along the Cheboygan was called the Inland Waterway, and it formed the dividing line between the Ottawa on the west side and the Chippewa to the east. Indian tribes planted summer gardens along the river banks. Today, quiet Cheboygan retains little of the rough and ready atmosphere that prevailed here 90 years ago when eight sawmills whined and screamed along the river day and night. They spit so much sawdust that it floated in the air, underfoot, and over the town, covering 12 acres and towering "higher than the tall masts of a schooner." In 1960, the mound still stretched a thousand feet long.

At the **1877 Opera House**, now restored to Victorian elegance, theatrical performances are staged throughout the season. The vaulted ceiling is supported by five ornate arches decorated with scrolls and garlands of pink and red roses highlighted in gold. *403 N. Huron St.*

Stop at the **Area Tourist Bureau** and ask about a theater tour. *124 North Main St.; 800-968-3302.*

At the mouth of the Cheboygan River, the **City Straits Park** walkway leads over the sand to the **Cheboygan Crib Light**. Here you'll find a beach, a playground, and picnic facilities. A raised boardwalk overlooks Michigan's largest cattail marsh, a nesting site for 54 bird species.

The river is home port for the U.S. Coast Guard cutter *Mackinaw,* the largest of the Great Lakes icebreakers. Visitors are welcome aboard when the cutter is in port. Car ferries make runs from the river to Pointe Aux Pins, a small village on the southern shore of Bois Blanc, a picturesque island and a mecca for sportsmen. *Cheboygan Area Tourist Bureau, 847 South Main St.; 800-968-3302.*

Just upriver from the mouth, the **1869 Cheboygan Lock** raises boats 15 feet onto the 30-mile-long waterway that the Great Lakes Indians called the "shortcut to nowhere," for after a relatively easy canoe trip, an eight-mile portage remained. Nevertheless, Indians and then fur trappers preferred it to the treacherous waters and long paddle through the Straits of Mackinac.

*A tugboat sits idly at an inland waterway lock in Cheboygan.*

# S O U T H W E S T
## & W E S T  C E N T R A L

■ HIGHLIGHTS

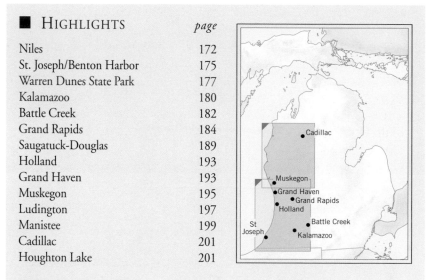

■ TRAVEL BASICS

**Area Overview:** Most of southwest and west-central Michigan is pretty flat and stays that way until you're north of Manistee. The major population and commercial centers are around Grand Rapids and Kalamazoo, but wide expanses of farmland, orchards, and vineyards beckon off the main highways, along with the small, intriguing towns and villages that make this part of Michigan so interesting.

**Travel:** The two main east-west arteries are I-94 (with commuters and semis between Battle Creek and Kalamazoo) and I-96 (the less heavily-traveled rocketway between Detroit and Muskegon).

**Weather:** Summer temperatures average around 85 and above, with balmy 60-degree nights. Fall and spring temps average in the low 70s with nights in the 50s. Rarely any snow before December, but the west side can receive heavy lake-effect snows.

**Food & Lodging:** Fine dining can be enjoyed in any of the major cities. The many B&Bs and small town lodgings often offer great food *and* great prices. *Please see listings beginning on page 274.*

# ■ HISTORY

Fort St. Joseph, on the St. Joseph River near the present city of Niles, was the center of the fur trade for the Illinois country and southwest Michigan. Strategically placed, the fort has flown the flags of France, Spain (for one day!), England, and finally the United States. After the War of 1812, the decline of the fur trade, and the displacement of the indigenous tribes, a strong military presence was no longer needed. Swampy and difficult to traverse, the area remained wilderness.

The region did not attract the interest of the ambitious settlers until the mid-1830s after the completion of the Erie Canal and the construction of the Chicago Road (US-12), a plank road road that connected Chicago with Fort Detroit. It followed the Old Sauk Trail that the Indians had used for centuries.

With the draining of "the Great Swamp," as the area was known, settlers uncovered the rich, black earth in which crops flourished. Today, the only reminders of Fort St. Joseph are the excellent artifact and history exhibits at the Fort St. Joseph Museum in Niles.

# ■ MICHIGAN'S FRUIT BASKET

Southwest Michigan abounds with small towns with colorful names such as Sodus, Cassopolis, Dowagiac, and Paw Paw. There are sleepy lakeside villages with street-side markets selling homegrown herbs, flowers, and vegetables. Out in the country, roadsides are dotted with fruit and vegetable stands, vineyards, and "U-pick" farms. In 1939, the authors of the WPA's guide to Michigan wrote: "Johnny Appleseed, the almost legendary eccentric who planted nurseries of apple trees in the Ohio River Valley and distributed the trees to the Indians, is generally credited with being the founder of southwestern Michigan's extensive fruit culture."

◆ **TREE-MENDUS FRUIT FARM** *map page 173, A-5*

*The* big event out here is **Teichman's International Cherry Pit Spitting Contest,** held every June at the Tree-Mendus Fruit Farm at Eau Claire. As Herb Teichman candidly states, "I started the contest 23 years ago when I was looking for something to do." The pit-spitting rules are strict *(see page 171).* When the contestant is ready, he or she carefully selects a freshly picked cherry, chews, and swallows. Keeping the pit rolling inside the cheek as the seconds tick away, the contestant arches back, gives a mighty forward thrust with the entire torso, and lets 'er fly.

"It's a wonder they don't get hernias," one spectator observed.

The record pit spit is 72 feet, 11 inches, set by Brian "Young Gun" Krause of Lansing in 1999, topping his father's record set in 1988. With three Krause family members former winners, and father Rick "Pellet Gun" Krause of Arizona an 11-time winner, Teichman calls them the "first family of spitting." For would-be contestants who feel they need a bit of practice, Teichman sells Cherry Pit Spit Training Kits. *tree-mendus.com; Seven miles west of Dowagiac of M-62; 9351 East Eureka Rd., Eau Claire; 616-782-7101.*

◆ WICK'S APPLE HOUSE   *map page 173, B-5*

Aromas of fresh fruit and vegetables mingle with the cinnamony fragrance of apple pies and other desserts as they pass from the see-through bakery window to the Orchard View dining room. There is always a representative member of the Wick family around willing to relate stories about this historic orchard. *52281 Indian Lake Rd., Dowagiac; 616-782-7306.*

◆ WINERIES

Southwestern Michigan is proud of its winemakers. **Tabor Hill Winery** at Buchanan, for example, gets high marks for its demi-sec sparkling white wine—it was served at the White House for the inauguration of Gerald Ford *(185 Mt. Tabor Rd.; 800-283-3363).* The **Lemon Creek Fruit Farm and Winery,** in operation for six generations, produces 15 blends from its 300-acres of varietals. Our favorites? The seyval blanc, the cabernet sauvignon, and the riesling. *533 E. Lemon Creek Rd., Berrien Springs; 616-471-1321.*

*Lake Michigan's moderating effect on the climate in Michigan allows cherries to grow as far north as Traverse City.*

# TEICHMAN'S INTERNATIONAL
# CHERRY PIT SPITTING RULES

1. The contest is open to everyone regardless of age or sex.

2. All contestants must register in qualifying court prior to spitting, unless spitter is awarded a special exemption by the official tournament judge. Registration deadline is 12:00 noon on day of Championship.

3. No foreign objects which may give an advantage in spitting the pit may be held in the mouth. Denture racks will be provided for those wishing to remove their teeth.

4. The contestant's foul line will be determined on a handicap basis according to height, in order to remove any advantage to taller contestants. The handicap will consist of a two-inch withdrawal from the base foul line for each one-inch of contestant height over four feet. Any contestant four feet tall or less will stand at the base foul line. The decision of the tournament line judge is final.

5. Contestants must select three cherries from the regulation variety (Montmorency) supplied by the tournament committee. Cherries must be washed and chilled to 55-60 degrees F pit temperature.

6. Each cherry must be inserted in the mouth whole, all solids eaten prior to spitting of the pit. No part of the cherry may be removed from the mouth after insertion.

7. Each contestant must spit his-her pit within 60 seconds of the time he-she is called to the line by the tournament judge. Three spits are allowed. The longest of the three is recorded. If the pit is swallowed, that spit is forfeited.

8. Contestants' hands must remain below the shoulders (to avoid popping one's cheeks).

9. Contestants' feet may not touch or cross the foul line.

10. Spitters must stand flat on the ground—or ground-level platform—to spit. Spitters are prohibited from using any kind of mechanical or other device to improve body thrust or spit length (including hydraulic hoists, wall support, etc.).

11. The pit-spitting range will be available for practice spitting from 10:00 A.M. until noon on the contest day. Practicing spitters will be allowed three spits.

12. Qualifying rounds for the Championship contest will be held Friday, the day *before* the Championship, at 11 A.M. and 3 P.M.; and on Saturday, day *of* the Championship, starting at 10 A.M. Deadline for reporting to qualifying court is noon on contest day. (All times listed are E.D.T.)

At Paw Paw, stop in at the **St. Julian Winery.** The guided winery tour ends in the tasting room where we found their merlot and chardonnay most drinkable. *(716 South Kalamazoo St.; 616-657-5568).* Nearby, choose a table in the wine garden restaurant at **Warner Vineyards** and watch the Paw Paw River flow past. *706 South Kalamazoo St.; 616-657-3165.*

■ NILES    *map page 173, B-6*

In 1691, the French built Fort St. Joseph at a point where the old Sauk Trail (now US-12) intersected the St. Joseph River just south of the present city of Niles. This was the second Fort St. Joseph, the first (at Port Huron) having been razed to the ground by its commandant prior to his return to Fort Michilimacinac. Fort St. Joseph made Niles the first settlement in western Michigan; the **Fort St. Joseph Museum** contains the best collection of 17th-century French and Indian artifacts in Michigan, including a fascinating set of pictographs made by the great Lakota chief, Sitting Bull. *508 East Main St.; 616-683-4702.*

*A commercial vineyard in the Paw Paw/Lawton area, Michigan's prime grape-growing region.*

SOUTHWEST &
WEST CENTRAL

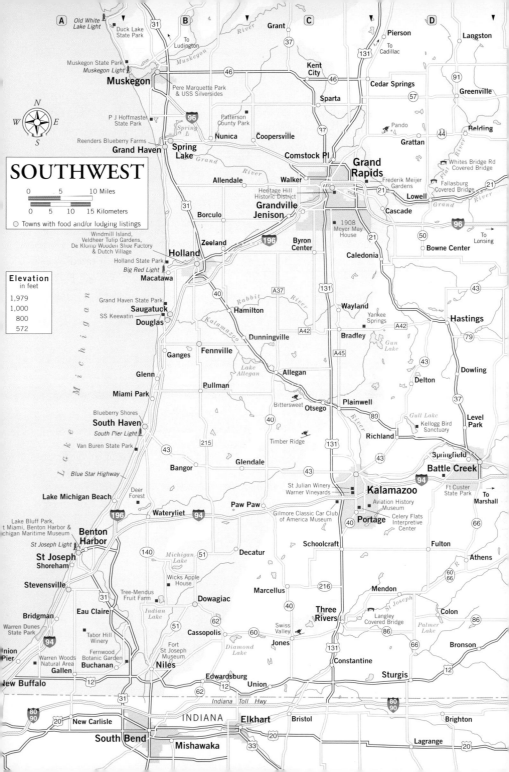

# SOUTHWEST

0   5   10 Miles
0   5   10   15 Kilometers

◯ Towns with food and/or lodging listings

**Elevation**
in feet
1,979
1,000
800
572

N
W   E
S

Old White Lake Light
Duck Lake State Park
31
To Ludington
Ⓐ
B
37
Grant
River
C
Pierson
To Cadillac
131
D
Langston

Muskegon State Park
Muskegon Light
Muskegon
46
Kent City
46
Cedar Springs
91
Greenville

Pere Marquette Park & USS Silversides
57
Sparta
Grattan
Belding
44

P J Hoffmaster State Park
96
Patterson County Park
37
Pando

Reenders Blueberry Farms
Grand Haven
Spring Lake
Nunica
Coopersville
Comstock Pl
Grand Rapids
Whites Bridge Rd Covered Bridge
21
Fallasburg Covered Bridge
21

Allendale
Walker
Frederik Meijer Gardens
Lowell
Grand River

Borculo
31
Heritage Hill Historic District
Grandville
Jenison
21
Cascade
96
To Lansing

Windmill Island, Veldheer Tulip Gardens, De Klomp Wooden Shoe Factory & Dutch Village
Zeeland
196
Byron Center
1908 Meyer May House
21
50
Bowne Center

Holland
Holland State Park
Big Red Light
Macatawa
40
A37
Rabbit
River
131
Caledonia
Wayland
43

Grand Haven State Park
Saugatuck
SS Keewatin
Douglas
Hamilton
A42
Bradley
Yankee Springs
A42
Hastings
79

Ganges
Fennville
Dunningville
A45
Gun Lake
Delton
Dowling
43

Glenn
Allegan
43
Richland
37
Level Park

Miami Park
Pullman
Lake Allegan
Otsego
Plainwell
89
Gull Lake
Kellogg Bird Sanctuary

Blueberry Shores
South Haven
South Pier Light
Van Buren State Park
Blue Star Highway
43
215
Glendale
Timber Ridge
Bittersweet
40
131
Richland
43
Springfield
Battle Creek
94

Bangor
43
St Julian Winery
Warner Vineyards
Kalamazoo
Ft Custer State Park
To Marshall

Lake Michigan Beach
Deer Forest
Watervliet
94
Paw Paw
Gilmore Classic Car Club of America Museum
Aviation History Museum
Portage
Celery Flats Interpretive Center
66

Lake Bluff Park, Ft Miami, Benton Harbor & Michigan Maritime Museum
196
Benton Harbor
St Joseph Light
St Joseph
Shoreham
140
Michigan Lake
51
Decatur
Schoolcraft
Fulton
Athens
60 66

Stevensville
31
Wicks Apple House
Marcellus
216
Mendon
60 66

Bridgman
Eau Claire
Tree-Mendus Fruit Farm
Dowagiac
40
Three Rivers
Langley Covered Bridge
86
Colon
86

Warren Dunes State Park
94
Tabor Hill Winery
Indian Lake
51
62
Cassopolis
60
Swiss Valley
Jones
86
Bronson

Union Pier
Warren Woods Natural Area
Gallen
Fernwood Botanic Garden
Buchanan
Fort St Joseph Museum
Niles
Diamond Lake
Palmer Lake
66
12

New Buffalo
12
Edwardsburg
Union
131
Constantine
Sturgis
12

31
62
Indiana Toll Hwy
Bristol
Brighton

80 90
20
New Carlisle
INDIANA
Elkhart
20
Lagrange
20

South Bend
Mishawaka
33

*This pictograph, drawn by the great Lakota Chief, Sitting Bull, is on exhibit at the Fort St. Joseph Museum. (courtesy Fort St. Joseph Museum, Niles)*

◆ THE FERNWOOD BOTANIC GARDEN
    AND NATURE CENTER

Fernwood is a 105-acre preserve that boasts more than 2,000 species of exotic plants and ferns. Kids enjoy plunging into the **Amazing Maize Maze.** Color keeps up with the seasons throughout the garden, building to an autumn peak in the arboretum with its wide variety of trees and shrubs. *Northwest from Niles off I-31, 13988 Range Line Rd.; 616-695-6491.*

■ RED ARROW HIGHWAY

From Paw Paw you can return to the Lake Michigan shore on truck-crowded I-94 or you can pick up the Red Arrow Highway at Warner vineyards. This is a leisurely drive through a bucolic countryside, past Paw Paw Lake and through Hartford to St. Joseph/Benton Harbor.

## ■ ST. JOSEPH/BENTON HARBOR   *map page 173, A-5*

Three blocks west of downtown St. Joseph, mile-long **Lake Bluff Park** stretches from **Maids of the Mist Fountain** to **Pioneer Watch**. This was the site of French explorer La Salle's Fort Miami, which he built in 1679 before heading south down the Mississippi River. Sculptures and monuments line the park's winding path, and steep steps descend to old town, where what were once fishermen's cottages are now tidy, trendy homes.

Sixty years ago, **Benton Harbor**, on the opposite shore of the St. Joseph River, was the rising star. In 1939, the Michigan WPA guide observed that the two cities were "so homogeneous that only residents can be perfectly sure of the boundary lines, and the existence of any marked difference, apart from size, is scarcely discernible even by them." In 1966, race riots changed that, but today Benton Harbor features a "New Territory," an art gallery district, and a revitalized downtown.

*Tower Dune, at Warren Dunes State Park, is a popular launching spot for hang gliders.*

SOUTHWEST &
WEST CENTRAL

The **Blossomtime Festival** is the state's oldest festival, with 25 communities participating in Southwestern Michigan parades and orchard tours. Apricot blossoms are the first to burst forth, followed by plum, pear, the wild pink of crab apples, cherries, peaches, and the wide sweep of apple blossoms as fresh and white as a bridal gown. The parade starts in St. Joseph and concludes in Benton Harbor. *Southwestern Michigan Tourist Council, 2300 Pipestone Rd., Benton Harbor; 616-925-6301.*

Once I'm ready to leave town, I have to make a choice: south to Warren Dunes State Park or north on the Blue Star Highway along the Michigan shore? It's not an easy decision! We're now smack in the middle of the longest continuous stretch of freshwater beach in the world and either direction offers unique pleasures. Today, I head south, still on the Red Arrow Highway as it continues to parallel I-94, meandering through shore villages and past elegant hotels and grand homes (many now B&Bs) that date from the coast's halcyon years in the early 1900s.

*From 1912 to 1953, the House of David baseball team, called the "Harlem Globetrotters" of baseball, represented Benton Harbor—when not touring the country. (Michigan State Archives)*

*This 1906 photo shows the cruise ship* City of South Haven *coming into port after crossing Lake Michigan from Chicago with more than 2,000 passengers. (Appleyards Studio, South Haven)*

Just south of St. Joseph/Benton Harbor, in Stevensville, there are two restaurants both highly rated by AAA: **Schuler's** *(5000 Red Arrow Hwy.; 616-429-3273)* and **Grande Mere Inn**. *Tue-Sat, dinner only, 5800 Red Arrow Hwy.; 616-429-3591.*

At Bridgman, just before you reach Warren Dunes State Park, the **Cook Energy Information Center** offers a three-theater exhibit on the science and history of electricity. Included are many fascinating, hands-on, interactive displays. *One Cook Pl.; 616-465-6101.*

◆ WARREN DUNES STATE PARK    *map page 173, A-5*

At Sawyer, the Red Arrow Highway passes through forest that gradually gives way to a succession of dunes and Warren Dunes State Park—two miles of light, granular sand piled into 240-foot dunes. When the wind is favorable, hang gliders take to the air from the summit of Tower Hill. Nearby, the 300-acre **Warren Woods State Natural Area** preserves a rare virgin remnant of the beech and maple forest that once covered this part of Michigan. *Exit 16 off I-94; 616-426-4013.*

## ■ BLUE STAR HIGHWAY

If you head north from St. Joseph/Benton Harbor, a lovely meandering Michigan road, the first stop is **South Haven** *(map page 173, B-4.)* The town is like a toy village, with shops stacked down the slope to the Black River. More shops and boutiques are tucked into **Old Harbor Village** on the riverbank.

Fresh lake fish is served aboard **The Idler,** a historic paddlewheel restaurant permanently docked in the Black River *(231-745-7541).* Across the river, the **Michigan Maritime Museum** recounts the area's water-travel history from Potawatomi Indians in birch-bark canoes to the era of hulking lake steamers. There is also a fine display describing Michigan lighthouses. *260 Dyckman Ave.; 616-637-8078.*

This is blueberry country. In August, the area stages a four-day National Blueberry Festival in Riverfront Park, with blueberry pizzas, blueberry sausages, blueberry shakes, blueberry popcorn, and a five-foot-wide community blueberry pie. After eating enough pie to "sink a ship," walk the 500-foot boardwalk along the river to the beach and the **South Haven South Pier Light.**

At the **Blueberry Store** (with the electric blue awnings) delicious aromas waft forth all year: blueberry candles, soaps, teas, and much more. Girls in blueberry-colored shirts help you select blueberry jams, jellies, books, and souvenirs. *525 Phoenix St.; 616-637-6322. South Haven–Van Buren County Lakeshore Convention & Visitors Bureau; 415 Phoenix St.; 800-764-2836.*

*(above and opposite) The rolling farmland in Cass County southwest of Kalamazoo.*

■ KALAMAZOO    *map page 173, D-4*

Titus Bronson is recognized as the first settler of "Kazoo," as it is called by those who know it best, and his original 1830 log cabin stands in downtown Bronson Park. But Kazoo's main claim to fame, besides being home to Western Michigan University, was the invention in 1885 of a dissolveable sugar coating used by Dr. William E. Upjohn to sweeten his pills. The rest, as they say, is pharmaceutical history.

Another claim to fame was celery, which flourished in the rich black muck of the marshlands along the Kalamazoo River and Portage Creek. Eventually, urban sprawl took over the celery farms, but a Michigan Historical Marker at the intersection of Crosstown Parkway, Balch, and Park Streets relates this early triumph: "A Scotsman named Taylor grew the first celery in Kalamazoo in 1856. Diners at the Burdick Hotel regarded it with curiosity. Cornelius De Bruyn, a gardener, who came here from The Netherlands in 1866, developed the modern type of celery from the earlier soup celery. J. S. Dunkley sold medicines and condiments made of celery. Soon Kalamazoo celery was known the nation over. Michigan has been a leading producer ever since."

*A replica of a 1930s Shell station is housed in the Gilmore Classic Car Club visitors center.*

The **Kalamazoo Aviation History Museum** houses legendary vintage aircraft such as Grumman Tigercat, Bearcat, and Hellcat, names that prompted museum supporters to dub it the "Air Zoo." *May–Oct., 3101 East Milham Rd.; 616 382 6555.*

At **Hickory Corners**, northeast of Kalamazoo, vintage automobiles are parked on the rolling lawns of the **Gilmore Classic Car Club of America Museum,** teasers for more than 140 antique and collector cars in the eight Michigan-red barns in the museum park. In a new interpretive center is housed the replica of a 1930s Shell filling station, with full-size service bay and grease pit. *6865 Hickory Rd.; 616-671-5089.*

**Langley Covered Bridge.** Did I say my car brakes for lighthouses? Well, it most definitely goes out of its way for covered bridges. And this is a great one. At 282 feet, the 1887 Langley Covered Bridge over the St. Joseph River is Michigan's longest covered bridge. *US-131 south to Three Rivers, then six miles east on M-86 to Centreville and north three miles on Covered Bridge Rd.*

*The Langley Covered Bridge, built in 1887, is Michigan's longest covered bridge.*

■ BATTLE CREEK   *map page 173, D-4*

Say "Battle Creek" to most Americans and breakfast-cereal commercials will likely come to mind. In 1894, while searching for a grain-based food to serve in their health sanatorium, brothers Dr. John Harvey and William Keith Kellogg started a morning dietary revolution when they created flaked cereal. Meanwhile, client and patient Charles W. Post conducted similar experiments in a nearby barn and came up with the hot cereal "Postum." Today Battle Creek is dubbed "Cereal Capital of the World." Visiting kids get to shake hands with Tony the Tiger at Kellogg's Cereal City USA, a large entertainment center along the downtown riverfront. It features a cereal assembly line and the Red Onion Grill, modeled after a 1930s diner. *171 W. Michigan Ave.; 616-962-6230.*

*Dr. John Harvey Kellogg.
(Michigan State Archives)*

Each June, **The World's Longest Breakfast Table** is set up downtown. Bowls of cereal are dished up to more than 60,000 people. In July, the city's skies come alive with brightly hued balloons during the **Team U.S. Nationals Hot Air Balloon Championship and Air Show.**

In the mid-19th century, Battle Creek was a major stop on the the the Underground Railroad, which helped slaves from the South to freedom in the North. In **Monument Park,** at the intersection of Division (M-66) and Main, a 12-foot bronze statue stands in tribute to the outspoken **Sojourner Truth**, who carried her rally for freedom all the way to President Lincoln. The six-foot-tall former slave called Battle Creek home for the last 27 years of her long, trailblazing life. Days before her death in 1883, she told her family, "I isn't goin' to die, honey, I'se goin' home like a shootin' star."

A TRIP THRO' Kellogg's

*Personally Conducted by
"The Sweetheart of the Corn"*

**Binder Park Zoo** is a 430-acre facility which is reknowned for its safari-style elevated boardwalk that winds through the "savannah" of its "African National Park." *Exit 100 off I-94, 7400 Division Dr.; 616-979-1351.*

## ■ MARSHALL

*map page 173, D-4*

With big plans to lure the state capital their way in the state's early years, the town of Marshall built a governor's mansion and enticed political leaders into building showy estates. When the new capital went to Lansing, Marshall was left with a legacy of well-preserved Greek, Gothic Revival, Queen Anne, Italianate, and other architec-

*Honolulu House in Marshall.*

tural delights. Downtown, ornate storefronts house cafés, specialty shops, boutiques, and antique stores. It's no wonder that this is designated a national historic landmark district.

Once a stagecoach stop along today's I-94, the 1835 **National House Inn** is a two-story redbrick inn with 16 guest rooms; rough planks cover the lobby floor and hand-hewn timbers frame the oversized hearth. *102 S. Parkview; 616-781-7374.*

After serving as U.S. Consul to the Sandwich Islands (later Hawaii), Michigan Supreme Court Judge Abner Pratt returned home to Marshall, but he couldn't leave the islands behind. In 1860 he built **Honolulu House** with liberal uses of teak and ebony, tall ceilings, wide doorways, and wall murals of tropical plants and animals. The judge even adopted the island style of tropical dress, a habit that contributed to his death. On a freezing-cold drive home from Lansing he caught pneumonia and died. *107 North Kalamazoo; 616-781-8544.*

■ GRAND RAPIDS    *map page 173, D-2*

Michigan's second largest city after Detroit, Grand Rapids straddles the Grand River at the junction of highways I-96, I-196, and US-131. Art and industry both flourish in this city. World-famous sculpture, scenic river walks, world-class manufacturing plants, elegant showrooms of style-setting furniture, the Heritage Hill historic district, the wild lupine along the highways, and friendly, down-to-earth residents all combine to make Grand Rapids a lovely city to visit.

The Grand Rapids of today is a far cry from the Indian fishing encampments along the rapids of the Grand River that Detroit fur trader Louis Campau found in 1826. Campau, called "The Fox" by the Indians, had already platted the new town of Saginaw and had assisted Gov. Lewis Cass in negotiating the Treaty of Saginaw with the Ottawa and Chippewa, purchased a 72-acre tract in what would later be the heart of the city. Slyly, he blocked access of the adjacent property to the river—property owned by surveyor and Michigan Territory delegate Lucius Lyon. The unfortunate legacy of this ploy is a frustrating jumble of dead-end streets in the heart of downtown.

*This 1856 panoramic by Grand Rapids artist Sarah Nelson shows her town. At far right is St. Mark's Episcopal Church, built in 1848 and still standing today. (Grand Rapids Public Library)*

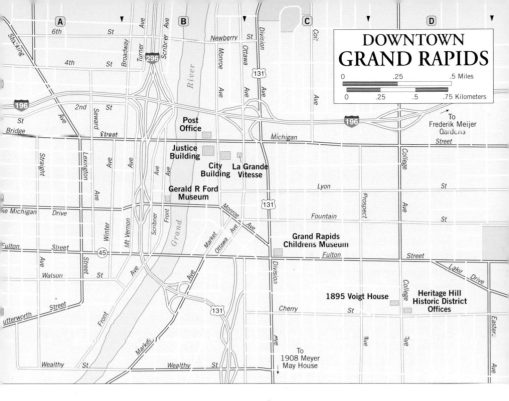

In 1838, Commissioner of Indian Affairs Henry Rowe Schoolcraft visited Grand Rapids and wrote:

> The fall of Grand River here creates an ample water power; the surrounding country is one of the most beautiful and fertile imaginable, and its rise to wealth and populousness must be a mere question of time, and that time hurried on by a speed that is astonishing. This generation will hardly be in their graves before it will have the growth and improvement which in other countries are the result of centuries.

It was an apt prediction. As the fur trade declined and the timber industry flourished, lumberjacks floated logs down the Grand River to the falls that had been harnessed to power sawmills. Attracted by the quality and low cost of the hardwoods here, cabinetmaker William Haldane moved to Grand Rapids and set up shop. By 1837, he had built a reputation for quality furniture that continues to this day.

The Grand River Trail from Chicago was surveyed in 1842, and a plank road (now I-96) was laid down to Kalamazoo. Mark Twain took this road once and commented that the ride would have been enjoyable had not "some unconscionable scoundrel now and then dropped a plank across the road."

## Gerald R. Ford Museum
*map page 185, B-2*
Across the steel-gray river from where Campau's trading post once stood is the museum honoring native son and 38th President of the United States Gerald R. Ford. Among the many interesting subjects on display are the burglary tools used to break into the offices of the Democratic National Committee at the Watergate Apartments during Richard Nixon's 1972 re-election campaign. *303 Pearl St., N.W.; 616-451-9263.*

## Sculpture
Grand Rapids is also home to one of the world's great sculptures, Alexander Calder's 40-foot red "La Grande Vitesse" *(map page 185, B-2).* This American classic is dramatically installed adjacent to the black Kent County Building on Ottawa Avenue between Michigan and Lyon. However, the huge **Frederik Meijer Gardens** *(map page 185, D-1)* now features a rival: Leonardo da Vinci's 24-foot bronze statue of a horse. In 1476, da Vinci was commissioned by Ludovico Sforza, the Duke of Milan, to create the world's largest equine sculpture, but the necessary bronze got used up making cannons during Milan's defense against France, leaving only a clay model and da Vinci's drawings to indicate its form and scale. Some 500 years later, Nina Akamu was tapped to cast the great horse. A duplicate casting resides in Milan.

Inside the five-story glass conservatory, paths meander across bridges and along pebbled streams that are surrounded by more than 300 tropical plants gathered from five continents. True, the orchids are extraordinary, but my favorite spot is a small brook that cascades down a 14-foot waterfall before burbling off through the garden. *Frederik Meijer Gardens; take East Beltline from I-96 West; 1000 E. Beltline N.E.; 616-957-1580.*

## Heritage Hill   *map page 185, D-3*
This 60-block historic district of vintage homes dates from the late 1800s to the 1920s. Here, turreted mansions share the same street with prim Victorian cottages. Most are private homes that are usually closed to the public, with two major exceptions: the 1895 **Voigt House** and the 1908 **Meyer May House** *(map page 185, D-3 and C-3 respectively).* The Voigt House features a wraparound porch and all the original furnishings of Carl G. A. Voigt and his family. A set of period china is set out upon the dining room table as if, at any minute, the whole family is about to arrive for dinner. *115 College Ave. S.E.; 616-456-4600.*

The Meyer May House has been completely restored and refurbished by its owner, the Steelcase Corporation, and now appears inside and out as it was originally designed. *Tuesdays, Thursdays, and Sundays; 450 Madison S.E.; 616-246-4821.*

Pick up free self-guided tour maps at Heritage Hill offices. *126 College Ave.; 616-459-8950.*

## Grand Rapids Children's Museum
*map page 185, C-2)*
An exciting venue for kids to play and learn at the same time. *11 Sheldon Ave. N.E.; 616-235-4726.*

*This replica of Leonardo da Vinci's 24-foot bronze horse stands in the Frederik Meijer Gardens.*

◆ Musketawa and White Pine Trail

The 26-mile-long Musketawa Trail is a 12-foot-wide asphalt "rails to trails" state park leading from Marne (off I-96 about 10 miles northwest of Grand Rapids) to Muskegon. In winter the bicyclists, joggers, and in-line skaters give way to snowmobilers and cross-country skiers.

The White Pine Trail State Park is another "rails to trails" park that traces a 92-mile path to Cadillac through forests, bucolic farmlands, and quaint rural towns. *For information: West Michigan Tourist Association; wmta.org; 800-442-2084.*

◆ Fallasburg and White's Bridge Road Covered Bridges

The 1871 white pine **Fallasburg Covered Bridge** spans the Flat River at the south end of Fallasburg Park. The 100-foot-long latticework truss bridge still bears a sign that reads, "$5 Fine for Riding or Driving on this Bridge Faster Than a Walk." *(M-21 to Lowell, then north on Fallasburg Park Dr. to the park.)* The weathered, narrow 1867 **White's Bridge Road Covered Bridge** over the Flat River is fastened with wooden pegs, handmade square iron nails, and is topped by a gabled roof. Jared N. Brasee of Ada, who built both bridges, used hand-hewn trusses sheeted over with rough pine boards. *Cross the Fallasburg Covered Bridge to McPherson Rd., turn north onto Potters Rd., then west onto White's Bridge Rd.*

■ Saugatuck-Douglas  *map page 173, B-3*

The natural beauty of the Kalamazoo River delights the eye as it flows between the towns of Saugatuck and Douglas, then widens into Kalamazoo Harbor before arcing into a wide oxbow and emptying into Lake Michigan.

The oxbow harbors an intriguing Michigan legend: the "lost city" of Singapore. Early in the 19th century, a sawmill town named Singapore thrived around the oxbow. It had sprung up in 1831 when Horace H. Comstock established a trading post for settlers moving inland. Over time, the outpost grew into a company mill town with a bank, three sawmills, boarding houses, two hotels, two general stores, and a lighthouse on the Lake Michigan shore. Its glory, however, was short-lived. By 1875, all the timber had been logged out and the last sawmill dismantled and loaded onto a ship bound for the tree country up the coast. Citizens moved on to areas with jobs, and the abandoned town was left to the drifting dunes.

Today, dunes are piled high above the site, but, alas, there is no city buried beneath them. Most of the buildings were salvaged for the new town of Saugatuck on Kalamazoo Harbor about four miles inland; the others, including the Singapore Bank Bookstore (now located at 317 Butler Street in Saugatuck), were slid out on logs and hauled down a frozen Kalamazoo River. "Sometimes I find handmade nails, old glass, or a dish or two," says local historian Kit Lane of Douglas. "It's the only evidence that the town was ever there."

The village of Saugatuck fared better. Soon after Singapore vanished, artists discovered Saugatuck, a delightful small town in the fork of the river behind the dunes. In 1910, the Chicago Institute of Art established a summer camp in the nearby oxbow with programs that drew artists from all over the world. The school

## SINGAPORE BANKING

My favorite story of Singapore is a reflection of the "wildcat" banking practices of the new state of Michigan. In 1837, the legislature passed a law that authorized any 12 landowners to form a banking association with capital stock of no less than $50,000, with 30 percent in specie (preferably gold) to support their paper currency. Banks sprang up all across southern Michigan. Since few of the banks actually had the gold, one bank would prop up the next when the inspectors came around every three months.

When the Allegan bank about 20 miles downstream on the Kalamazoo River from Singapore heard the inspector was on his way, it borrowed gold coins from two neighbors to pass the inspection. With Singapore the next stop, the Allegan banker handed off the bag of gold to a certain Maksaube, a friendly Ottawa Indian. He dashed out the back door, jumped into his canoe and paddled up the Kalamazoo well ahead of the banker who was making his way by horseback.

Four miles short of Singapore, Maksaube's canoe hit a snag, tipped, and the bag of gold splashed overboard into the deepest part of the river. While the banker summoned blacksmith James Harris to pound out a hook to drag the river, a runner was dispatched to the village of Richmond six miles downstream where the inspector was to cross the river. Obliging folks at Richmond's new tavern detained the inspector with a lively reception until word reached them that the Singapore team had indeed struck pay dirt. Oblivious of the to-do, the inspector continued on to Singapore to count the gold once again.

SOUTHWEST & WEST CENTRAL

at Oxbow (simply called "O") still conducts programs in painting, drawing, performing arts, and writing. It also offers permanent galleries and craft boutiques. *121 Butler St., 2nd Level; 616-857-1937.*

Saugatuck/Douglas, self-proclaimed as "The Art Coast of Michigan," may well have more galleries, studios, and B&Bs than any other location in Michigan. Adding to the fun is the 1838 **Saugatuck Chain Ferry**, a pedestrian-only connection between the two towns. Ring the bell and the operator hand-cranks the Victorian-style ferry along a 380-foot chain across the river. It's absolutely the best 50-cent ride in the state, and the only such chain-powered ferry remaining along the Great Lakes. Once across, climb up the 262-foot dune, Mount Baldhead, so named before it was planted with trees, to enjoy the view—especially at sunset.

Moored next to the Saugatuck-Douglas Bridge (Blue Star Highway and Union Street) is the 350-foot museum ship **SS *Keewatin,*** a 1907 coal-burning overnight steamer that operated along the Great Lakes until 1965, and the last of the Great Lakes passenger steamers. Wander through the many staterooms, the elegant ballroom with its chandeliers and finely carved mahogany bar, the captain's suite, the huge galley, and the ornate two-deck-high lounge with hand-painted skylights. Shades of *Titanic*-inspired luxury, but thankfully no Irish bagpipes to put it over the top. Good fun also can be had cruising the river and lake aboard either the 60-foot *City of Douglas* from Harbour Village *(616-857-2107)* or the 67-foot sternwheeler *Star of Saugatuck. 716 Water St.; 616-857-4261.*

*Saugatuck is known for its art galleries, craft boutiques, and shops.*

*A view of the Kalamazoo River and Saugatuck town as seen from Mount Baldhead.*

■ HOLLAND   *map page 173, B-2*

When Rev. Albertus C. Van Raalte led his 53 Dutch to the sandy shores of Lake Michigan in 1847, they brought along memories of windmills and wooden shoes. Choosing a site on Lake Macatawa, which connected to Lake Michigan via a shallow outlet, Van Raalte called his new town "Holland." The beginning years were hard: mosquitoes, no-see-ums, and smallpox plagued these pioneers who were ill-equipped for the rigors of the new land.

When the government refused to dredge the outlet to Lake Michigan less than a half-mile away, townsfolk picked up their shovels and dug it themselves, thus opening Holland to trade; the town soon became famous for its fine woodwork.

### Holland Tulip Time Festival

No matter what your ancestry, anybody can pretend to be Dutch during this May festival. A clanging brass bell signals the beginning: "Hear ye! Hear ye! The streets are dirty and they must be scrubbed," the town crier calls in Dutch, then English. With splashes from wooden water buckets, swishes of brooms, and clacks of the klompen (wooden clogs that were popular here long before they became a fad on the dance floor) echoing along the streets, 10 days of

parades and festival begin. Young men in baggy pants dance past with lovely girls in billowy skirts. Children march in tulip-shaped hats. Bands play.

**Windmill Island**

At Seventh Street and Lincoln Avenue, a drawbridge leads to a 30-acre miniature Dutch town that features DeZwann—a 1780s windmill given to the city by Amsterdam. Lazily turning in the wind, it powers a flour mill. *616-355-1030.*

**Veldheer Tulip Gardens**

A maze of windmills, canals, drawbridges, these gardens feature more than a hundred varieties of tulips. On the grounds is the **De Klomp Wooden Shoe Factory** which makes wooden shoes, along with **Delft-**

**ware**, the only factory in the nation producing this particular hand-painted porcelain. *12755 Quincy St.; 616-399-1900*

**Dutch Village**

A theme park off US-31 North, this replicates an old world village, with shops selling Dutch chocolates, cheeses, and other imported specialties *(616-396-1475).* Across the canal, the **Queen's Inn**, an authentic Dutch restaurant with a beamed ceiling, serves such fare as *saucizenbroodjes,* (spicy sausage pigs) wrapped in flaky crusts, and *hutsput* ("housepot" stew).

**Big Red**

This Holland lighthouse at the end of South Shore Dr. is not open to the public, but it's a great place for a stroll or a picnic.

■ GRAND HAVEN  *map page 173, B-2*

As you approach Grand Haven driving north on US-31 at Tawas Street, watch for **Reenders Blueberry Farms.** Pick your own or select a ready-to-go basket filled with delicious marble-sized berries. *14079 168th Ave.; 616-842-5238.*

The mouth of the Grand River was the site for several pre-settlement dramas, none more fascinating than that observed by the American Fur Company's fur trader Gordon Hubbard. In his autobiography, Hubbard relates how in 1819 he and his men were invited to observe a "Feast of the Dead." Assembled on a high dune overlooking Lake Michigan, a chief and his family awaited the return of a man condemned for killing the chief's son. On that day he was to pay the ransom for his crime with furs or with his life. After trapping all through the hard winter with poor results, the condemned man returned with his family to the dune and stood empty-handed before the chief. With his family watching, the proud Indian stood without flinching while the chief's remaining son thrust a knife into his chest and killed him.

*The Veldheer Tulip Gardens in Holland.*

Like most other port cities, Grand Haven began as a sawmill town. It got a boost in 1855 when the railroad from Detroit was completed. Later, the line was called the "Emigrant Route," as pioneers rode the trains to Grand Haven and then boarded steamers to cross Lake Michigan to settle in Wisconsin.

Grand Haven's nightly spectacle is **The Musical Fountain**, largest fountain in the world, with waterspouts and colored lights synchronized to perform "duets" to the music. *View from Waterfont Stadium; 616-842-2550.*

❖

Ten miles northwest along US-31, turn west on Pontaluna Road and follow the signs to the thousand-acre **P. J. Hoffmaster State Park** in the heart of towering sand dunes and long stretches of white sand beaches. The glass-fronted **Gillette Nature Center and Michigan Sand Dune Interpretive Center** is one of the best, with hands-on classroom dunes exhibits. *6585 Lake Harbor Rd.; 231-798-3711.*

*Grand Haven Beach and State Park is a favorite weekend spot on hot summer days.*

*Grand Haven Lighthouse.*

## ■ MUSKEGON   *map page 198, A-6*

In the 1880s, when it became known as Lumber Queen of the World, Muskegon boasted 40 lumber millionaires, with 47 sawmills buzzing along the Muskegon River. The Victorian mansions of Thomas Hume and of philanthropist Charles H. Hackley stand side-by-side as house museums of the same era; both are listed on the National Register of Historic Places. *West Webster at Sixth St.; 888-843-5661.*

During summer, a bright red double-decker trolley makes rounds downtown past Victorian storefronts alongside modern department stores, office buildings, city parks, and beaches. The schedule is casual. A sign reads "So don't be upset if we are a little late—or a little early. Just flag us down." *(231-724-6420)* If you drive here, bring a map: it's easy to get lost in the maze of downtown streets.

From **Rafferty's Dockside Restaurant** you can enjoy a view of Muskegon Lake while you're eating dinner (they serve pretzel-crumbed walleye). Or pull your boat up to the dock and dine on board. *601 Terrace Point Rd.; 231-722-4461.*

SOUTHWEST &
WEST CENTRAL

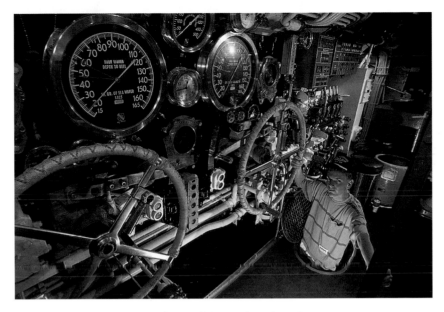

*The control room of the* USS Silversides *submarine.*

At **Pere Marquette Park,** the beach comes alive with volleyball tournaments in summer while pleasure boats parade up and down the river and out past the cherry-red lighthouse and into Lake Michigan. The submarine USS *Silversides* is permanently docked here. Commissioned on December 15, 1941, only eight days after the Japanese attacked Pearl Harbor, this 312-foot submarine sank 23 ships in World War II, ranking third highest in total tonnage sunk. During the tourist season, visitors squeeze their way along the cramped passageways and listen for the resounding klaxon that sounded the "Dive!" command during its many attacks. *1346 Bluff; 231-755-1230.*

■ LUDINGTON   *map page 198, A-3*

On the Lake Michigan shore, behind a strip of barrier dunes, lies the safe deep-water harbor of Pere Marquette Lake—long an important shipping center, and today the docking point for the only car ferry to regularly cross Lake Michigan.

*(opposite) The mansions built by Hackley (foreground) and by Hume (background) in Muskegon are fine examples of Victorian fantasy homes.*

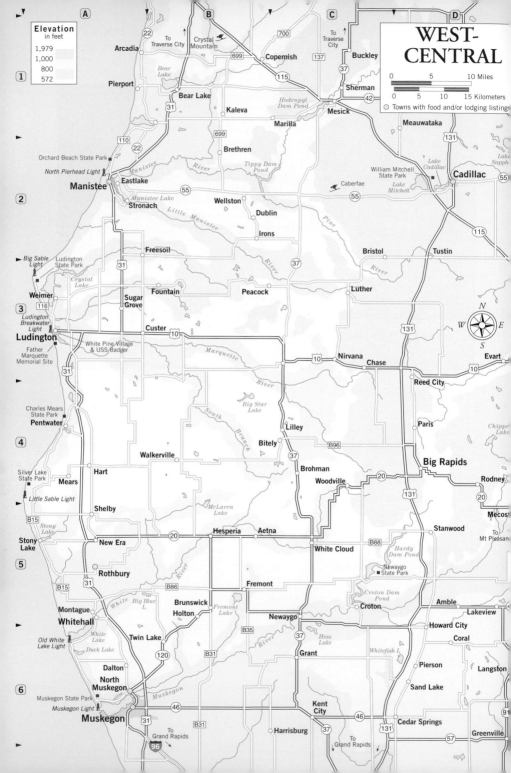

# WEST-CENTRAL

**Elevation**
in feet

1,979
1,000
800
572

0    5    10 Miles

0    5    10    15 Kilometers

○ Towns with food and/or lodging listing

M-10 terminates its east-west crossing of the mitten here, becoming wide Ludington Avenue which runs through the town all the way to Lake Michigan.

The story of Ludington could easily be the story of any other lumber town, but it's not. Originally named Marquette in honor of Father Jacques Marquette, the missionary-explorer who presumably died here in 1675, the name was pre-empted by a well-heeled Chicago businessman named James Ludington, who bought up lumber mills and property—basically the whole town—and had the town named after him. Nothing untoward here, given the scope of 19th-century egotism, except that he required that all the property deeds stipulate that no liquor would be sold on the premises, stating: "So long as I can control the matter I will not allow a liquor saloon to live in the village that bears my name." Ludington, unique among lumber towns, was dry.

Historic **White Pine Village,** on the southern outskirts of Ludington, is a cluster of 20 restored buildings, including the trappers cabin built by French trapper William Quevillon about 1850. The village stages festivals and special events throughout the year. *1687 South Lakeshore Dr.; 616-843-4808.*

In summer, take the 4,200-ton **SS** *Badger* car ferry on one of its daily 60-mile round-trips across Lake Michigan to Manitowoc, Wisconsin. During the four-hour crossing, the renovated Great Lakes steamer offers its 620 passengers two restaurants, movies, games, shopping in the Badger Boutique, an interesting maritime historical exhibit, and even an overnight stay in a *Badger* stateroom. Or just loll about on deck enjoying the cooling breeze and gazing out at the lake. Reservations recommended. *701 Maritime Dr.; 800-841-4243.*

A few miles north on M-116, beautiful **Ludington State Park** arcs around Lake Hamlin, popular with canoeists and fishermen. It offers excellent hiking, swimming, and all the requisites for generally goofing off. A trail follows a two-mile route to the **Big Sable Point Lighthouse;** *231-843-8671.*

■ MANISTEE *map page 198, A-2*

If Ludington was dry, not so Manistee. "At Manistee," writes Milo M. Quaife of the little town 20 miles north, "open barrels of whiskey were placed in the streets, into which passersby who were reluctant to imbibe were sometimes thrust headfirst by the merry loggers." *Merry,* of course, being a euphemism for rip-roaring hammered.

SOUTHWEST & WEST CENTRAL

*The Manistee Kitchen Band plays at Orchard Beach State Park's annual Open House.*

Now, Manistee primly wears the title of the "Victorian Port City." Restored Victorian "painted ladies" boasting gingerbread trim and fanciful gables are found around most every corner, and downtown is listed on the National Register of Historic Places. They take their Victoriana seriously; the Manistee Victorian Christmas features a Sleighbell Parade with horse-drawn floats and a Victorian Santa waving from his sleigh. Even the conductors in the bright-red tour trolley wear period costumes. The 1889 fire engine–red brick firehouse, a Romanesque Revival-style hall with a copper dome, remains today Michigan's oldest continuously operating fire station. *Manistee County Convention & Visitors Bureau; 50 Filer St.; 800-288-2286.*

◆ MANISTEE NATIONAL FOREST

Inland from Manistee are five National Wild and Scenic Rivers: Pere Marquette (emptying into Pere Marquette Lake at Ludington), Pine, and Manistee, Little Manistee, Big Sable, and their tributaries. For generations, people have come to these exquisite rivers to fish, canoe, and camp.

SOUTHWEST &
WEST CENTRAL

After decades of replanting, a lot of it by the CCC during the 1930s, a mixed forest of pine and hardwood now stands thick and tall across northwestern Michigan, especially in the **Manistee National Forest**. In the springtime people come for mushrooming and fishing, in winter snowmobiling and cross–country skiing.

■ CADILLAC   *map page 198, D-2*

Forty-eight miles east of Manistee on M-55 lies Cadillac, surrounding Lake Cadillac, which is itself connected by a narrow inlet to larger Lake Mitchell. Little wonder that water sports are the main summer attraction. When winter covers the hills with snow, recreation turns to skiing and snowmobiling. We Michiganians love our snow, being out in it bundled up against the cold, and we relish the adrenaline rush of a downhill ski plunge or cross-country trail.

Five cross-country ski trails wind through dense forests here; some even lit for night skiing. A network of 200 miles of groomed snowmobile trails connects with other marked trails throughout northern Michigan. The big event of the year is the **North American Snowmobile Festival** in early February that brings up to 10,000 snowmobilers to ice-capped Lake Cadillac, with races, outdoor picnics, sleigh rides, and fireworks. *Cadillac Area Visitors Bureau; 222 Lake St.; 800-225-2537.*

■ HOUGHTON LAKE   *map page 155, A-5*

Thirty miles east of Cadillac, M-55 connects with US-27 and then with I-75 some 18 miles north. Inside the triangle formed by these converging highways are Houghton and Higgins Lakes. Houghton Lake, ten miles long, eight miles wide, with a 72-mile shoreline, is Michigan's largest inland lake. Although camping and fishing are popular year-round, nothing on any of Michigan's lakes creates more excitement than the annual **Tip-Up Town U.S.A.** held on the third and fourth weekends of January. While fishermen gather to drill holes in the ice on Houghton Lake and set their fishing gear for "tip-ups" that signal that a fish is on the line, the carnival on ice goes into full swing. One highlight is the polar bear dive through a hole in the ice. After you!

*For information about the area contact the Houghton Lake Chamber of Commerce; 1625 West Houghton Lake Dr.; 800-248-5253.*

SOUTHWEST & WEST CENTRAL

# N O R T H W E S T
## & M A C K I N A C   I S L A N D

■ HIGHLIGHTS    *page*

■ TRAVEL BASICS

**Area Overview:** This area—from Grand Traverse Bay to Mackinac Island—is the heart of Michigan's most scenic, and most visited, vacationland. Included are Mackinac Island, the nation's sixth-most visited national park, and Gaylord, one of America's golf meccas.

**Travel:** Main travel arteries are south to north US-31 and US-131; I-75 the mid-state corridor, borders the region on the east. Interconnecting highways form a network of good road systems. Air travel is from Traverse City and Pellston.

**Weather:** Generally mild with prevailing westerly winds. As with the rest of Michigan, summertime highs can reach the 90s with low humidity and gentle breezes. Fall can bring temperatures in the upper 70s. Winters, with the westerly lake effect, average an annual snowfall of 130 inches, with freezing temperatures that can reach zero.

**Food & Lodging:** Some of Michigan's best places to dine and to stay are found here. From the vineyard B&Bs on the Leelanau Peninsula to the ultra-luxurious Grand Hotel on Mackinac Island, the choices are many. *Please refer to the listings, which begin on page 274 .*

# ■ HISTORY

The Straits of Mackinac mark the transition between Lake Huron to the east and Lake Michigan to the west—a kind of Great Lakes Cape Horn. Fearsome gales and treacherous waves can make it exceedingly dangerous to cross, and because it straddles two great bodies of water, Indian tribes and European nations sought to control the area and keep others out.

The French were the first Europeans to establish a fort (Fort Du Buade) across the Straits at what is now St. Ignace. The Algonquin name for the site, *Michili-mackinac,* proved more enduring, a name which followed the fort across the Straits and then to Mackinac Island. The first transition came after the French under Cadillac abandoned the fort in order to take command of the new, and more strategic, fort at Detroit. The French burned Fort Du Buade to the ground and then rebuilt it on the other side of the Straits in what is now Mackinaw City.

*This 1842 lithograph depicts Fort Michilimackinac when it stood on Mackinac Island; Round Island is in the background. (Bentley Historical Society)*

During the period of French supremacy in the Northwest, the entire upper Great Lakes region was known as the Province of Michilimackinac, or "Mackinac country." After the British defeated the French in the French and Indian War (1756–63) they occupied Fort Michilimackinac. In 1781, however, fearing an American invasion after the Revolutionary War, they moved the fort yet again, this time to Mackinac Island. In spite of the paper ownership of the territory by the Americans, the British dominated trade and travel through the Straits until 1813, when they were finally given the boot by the Americans during the War of 1812.

Until 1813 and the death of the legendary Shawnee chief Tecumseh, the entirety of Michigan, as well as most of Indiana, Ohio, and Kentucky, was figuratively and literally dominated by his Confederation of Algonquin-speaking tribes: Ojibwa, Ottawa, Wyandot, Potawatomi, Miami, Shawnee, Kickapoo, Fox, Iowa, Winnebago, Seneca, and Osage. Even the Seminoles in Florida were involved. Tecumseh's death all but ended indigenous resistance to the inundating flood of settlement sweeping westward through the Ohio Valley and onto the Great Plains. Andrew Jackson's "Indian Removal Act" (famous for the Cherokee "Trail of Tears") was the final step of "ethnically cleansing" the Ohio Valley.

In Michigan, settlement in the early 1800s revolved around the fur trade. John Jacob Astor established his American Fur Company on Mackinac Island, followed by a consortium of railroads that built the Grand Hotel, and launched an extravaganza of Victorian construction among the enclaves of the rich. After the trees were logged out, farmers tilled the opened land at the north end of the peninsula. The soil was not as rich as in the southwest, and they began planting orchards, finding cherries especially suited to the climate. These days it's tourism that powers the economies of Traverse City, Bay Harbor, Petoskey, Mackinaw City, and Mackinac Island. So, what's to see?

## ■ FRANKFORT  *map page 205, A-6*

Heading to the Lake Michigan shoreline, we follow M-115 to the charming small town of Frankfort, on the south shore of Crystal Lake. Aptly named, the 10-mile-long lake sends sun sparkles fairly dancing across its surface. Tucked between a hill and Lake Michigan, Frankfort boasts a deep-water recreational harbor on Betsie Lake with an outlet to Lake Michigan.

NORTHWEST & MACKINAC ISLAND

NORTH MANITO ISLAND

North Man Visitors Cen

South Man Visitors Cen

SOUTH MANITOU ISLAND

P

Manitou

Sleeping Bear Dunes National Seashore   Glen Arl

Dune Climb

Empire
Visitors Center &
Park Headquarters

Platte B

Point Betsie Light

Crystal Lake

Ferry to Wisconsin

North Breakwater Light

Frankfort   115   Beulah

Elberty   Benzonia

22

Upper Herring Lake

31   Mc

C

22   Michigan Art Park

A

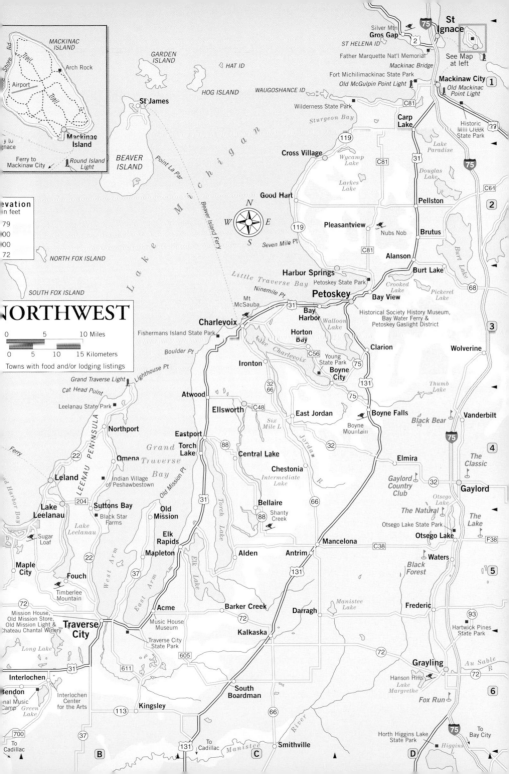

# NORTHWEST

## Mackinac Island inset
MACKINAC ISLAND
Arch Rock
Airport
Trail
Trail
Mackinac Island
Round Island Light
Ferry to Mackinaw City
North Shore Rd

## Elevation (in feet)
79
00
00
72

0    5    10 Miles
0    5    10    15 Kilometers
Towns with food and/or lodging listings

St Ignace
See Map at left
Silver Mtn
Gros Gap
ST HELENA ID
Father Marquette Nat'l Memorial
Mackinac Bridge
Fort Michilimackinac State Park
Old McGulpin Point Light
Mackinaw City
Old Mackinaw Point Light
Historic Mill Creek State Park

GARDEN ISLAND
HAT ID
HOG ISLAND
WAUGOSHANCE ID
Wilderness State Park
Sturgeon Bay
Carp Lake
Lake Paradise

St James
BEAVER ISLAND
Point La Par
Beaver Island Ferry

119
Cross Village
Wycamp Lake
C81
31
Douglas Lake
Larkes Lake

Lake Michigan

Good Hart
N W E S
119
Pleasantview
Nubs Nob
Brutus
Pellston
2
C61
75

Seven Mile Pt
C81
Alanson
Burt Lake
Burt Lake

Harbor Springs
Petoskey State Park
Little Traverse Bay
Ninemile Pt
Mt McSauba
31
Bay Harbor
Petoskey
Bay View
Crooked Lake
Pickerel Lake
68

NORTH FOX ISLAND
SOUTH FOX ISLAND

Charlevoix
Fishermans Island State Park
Boulder Pt
Lighthouse Pt
Grand Traverse Light
Cat Head Point
Leelanau State Park

Historical Society History Museum, Bay Water Ferry & Petoskey Gaslight District

Horton Bay
Walloon Lake
Lake Charlevoix
C56
Young State Park
75
Clarion
Wolverine
3

Ironton
Boyne City
131
Thumb Lake

Atwood
32 66
East Jordan
Boyne Falls
Black Bear
Vanderbilt
4

Ellsworth
C48
Six Mile L.
Boyne Mountain
32
The Classic

Northport
22
LEELANAU PENINSULA
Omena
Indian Village of Peshawbestown
Old Mission Pt
Grand Traverse Bay

Eastport
Torch Lake
88
Central Lake
Jordan R
Elmira
Gaylord Country Club
32
Gaylord

Leland
204
Suttons Bay
Black Star Farms
Old Mission
Chestonia
Intermediate Lake
Otsego Lake
The Natural
The Lake

Lake Leelanau
Sugar Loaf
Elk Rapids
Bellaire
88
Shanty Creek
66
Otsego Lake State Park
F38

Maple City
22
Fouch
37
Mapleton
Torch Lake
Elk Lake
Alden
Antrim
Mancelona
C38
Waters
5
Black Forest

Timberlee Mountain
West Arm
East Arm
131

Mission House, Old Mission Store, Old Mission Light & Chateau Chantal Winery
Acme
Music House Museum
Barker Creek
72
Darragh
Manistee Lake
Frederic
93
Hartwick Pines State Park

72
Traverse City
Traverse City State Park
605
Kalkaska
72
Grayling
Au Sable River

Long Lake
31
611
Hanson Hills
Lake Margrethe
Fox Run
6

Interlochen
Bendon
onal Music Camp
Green Lake
Interlochen Center for the Arts
South Boardman
113
Kingsley
131
66
Smithville
Horth Higgins Lake State Park
75
To Bay City
Higgins L

700
To Cadillac
37
131
To Cadillac
Manistee River
C
D

B

*Point Betsie Lighthouse in summer.*

Some believe that the Jesuit missionary and explorer Father Jacques Marquette died here in 1675. A wooden cross marks the supposed spot, although conventional wisdom has it that the priest died further south in Ludington. Whether Frankfort or Ludington, the intrepid priest's faithful Indian friends returned the following year and carried his remains north to St. Ignace for final burial.

A favorite lighthouse of mine lies just off M-22 about five miles north of Frankfort—the **1858 Point Betsie Lighthouse**. Thanks at least in part to its backdrop—rolling dunes, sandy beach, driftwood, green lawn—the white brick tower is one of the most photographed lighthouses in Michigan.

### ■ SLEEPING BEAR DUNES NATIONAL LAKESHORE
*map page 205, A-5*

The hilly dunes of the 71,000-acre Sleeping Bear Dunes National Lakeshore stretch for 35 miles along Lake Michigan. Maple and beech forests encircle the inland lakes and climb the hills nearby. Beautifully juxtaposed are pale and powdery dunes, which roll from forested inland valleys all the way to the blue waters of

NORTHWEST &
MACKINAC ISLAND

Lake Michigan, in some places reaching 460 feet high—making them the highest sand dunes outside the Sahara Desert.

Pick up a map at the **Visitors Center** and follow the route to Pierce Stocking Scenic Drive, a steep 7.4-mile route for cars and bicycles, to a high bluff overlooking the dunes. It also offers an impressive view of North and South Manitou Islands, about 17 miles offshore. The legend of the Sleeping Bear:

Long ago, along the Wisconsin shoreline, a mother bear and her two cubs were driven into Lake Michigan by a raging forest fire. The bears swam for many hours, but eventually the cubs tired and lagged behind. Mother bear reached the shore and climbed to the top of a high bluff to watch and wait for her cubs. Too tired to continue, the cubs drowned within sight of the shore. The Great Spirit Manitou created two islands to mark the spot where the cubs disappeared and then created a solitary dune to represent the faithful mother bear.

*Leland, a historic fishing town along the Leelenau Peninsula, is today the jumping-off point for ferries to the Manitou Islands.*

◆ MANITOU ISLANDS    *map page 205, A-4*

During the summer months, ferries run from Leland on the west shore of the Lee-lanau Peninsula to North and South Manitou Islands, part of Sleeping Bear Dunes National Lakeshore. At South Manitou, there are guided walking tours from the ferry docks. They're great outings. Late one evening I tried hiking along the beach toward the 104-foot South Manitou Island Light, intrigued by the little map I carried that showed an abandoned farm and a "Valley of the Giants," with a stand of virgin white cedar trees. However, I missed them—I was chased back to the boat by ferocious sand flies that stung like little devils.

◆ DUNE CLIMB

Near the northwest arm of Glen Lake on the Lakeshore mainland is the Dune Climb. Climbers labor to reach the crest of this 400-foot dune and start out eager enough, but it doesn't take long for them to shuffle into a sand dance that lasts all the way to the top—if they make it that far. It's two steps forward and one step back. Kids know how to do it best. They climb for a while, then fall down and roll back to the bottom. *Sleeping Bear Dunes National Lakeshore; 9922 Front St., Empire; 616-326-5134.*

(above) Sleeping Bear Dunes in winter.

(opposite) A view of Sleeping Bear Dunes from Empire Bluff.

NORTHWEST &
MACKINAC ISLAND

■ LEELANAU PENINSULA   *map page 205, B-4*

The 35-mile-long peninsula between Lake Michigan and Grand Traverse Bay, with Lake Leelanau extending up the middle, is circled by sand beaches and cliffs. Lake breezes blow gently across the vineyards and herb farms. A drive around the Leelanau is an autumn right of passage for those familiar with the burst of colors in the forest and the crispness in the air. Fruit and vegetable stands are set up along the roadsides staffed by folks who find time to chat. It seems every small town has a winery, shop, gallery, restaurant, or bed-and-breakfast inn, and each different from those of its neighbors. The most interesting and certainly the most ambitious is **Black Star Farms**. This B&B is home to a winery, a distillery, and an equestrian training center. *blackstarfarms.com; 231-271-4886.*

Leland, built along the west side of the Leelanau, began in 1853 as a cluster of shacks hastily built by lumbermen and seasonal fishermen. The main attraction is still **Fishtown**—gray weathered shacks along the Carp River that have been converted to gift shops and boutiques. Some of the other original buildings are still ice- and smokehouses for local fishermen. **The Manitou Islands Ferry** leaves from here each morning at 10 A.M. and returns at 6 P.M.; *231-256-9061.*

*For general information contact the Leelanau Peninsula Chamber of Commerce; 105 Phillips, Lake Leelanau; 231-256-9895.*

■ TRAVERSE CITY   *map page 205, B-5*

It wasn't until 1839 that the Grand Traverse region, so named by the French *voyageurs*, was settled. First to come was the short, hardworking Rev. Peter Dougherty who established a Presbyterian mission at the tip of what is now called the Old Mission Peninsula, a narrow strip of land that divides Grand Traverse Bay into its East and West Arms. The mission has been reconstructed as **Mission House** and sits in the midst of a kind of living museum consisting of the **Old Mission Store** which began serving settlers—out of a wigwam—shortly after Peter Dougherty arrived. It has remained in continuous operation ever since, essentially unchanged for a century or so. To enter the store is to take a remarkable step into the past. *18250 Mission Rd.; 231-223-4310.*

The **Old Mission Light**, a working lighthouse that is also the official marker for the 45th parallel, perches on the peninsula. Mid-century brought settlers to the head of the bay, with Horace Boardman's sawmill on Kid's Creek buzzing out lumber for new housing. Then came more people, more mills, and nearby settlements. As pine was cut for lumber, homesteaders planted cherries, which flourished in the bay breezes. The first Blessing of the Blossoms in 1924 became in 1926 the **National Cherry Festival**, still celebrated annually the first part of July, with parades, cherry treats, orchard tours, fireworks, and much more. *National Cherry Festival; cherryfestival.org; 800-872-8377.*

**Clinch Park**, in Traverse City at the bottom of the West Arm of Grand Traverse Bay, is so green I want to instantly plop down on a park bench and gaze north along the bay at the sailboats and other watercraft cutting patterns in the waves. Kids head for the park's zoo, aquarium, or beach. Or stroll along the Broadman River to the downtown district with its nautical shops and sidewalk cafes.

Vineyards have replaced many of the apple orchards, spreading an old-world atmosphere across the rolling hills. Tours and tastings are offered at **Chateau Chantal Winery**—also a fine B&B; *www.chateauchantal.com; 15900 Rue de Vin; 800-969-4009.*

◆ TALL SHIP *MANITOU*

Few things are more romantic than boarding the windjammer **Tall Ship** *Manitou,* for a sunset sail across Grand Traverse Bay. In July and August, the 114-foot, two-masted, gaff-rigged replica of an 1800s schooner also operates as a floating bed and breakfast. As the huge sails billow in the breeze and with the smells of freshwater all about, passengers dive hungrily into their picnic lunches. The 12 cabins are equipped with comfortable double bunks, wash basins, and electric bedside reading lights. Red geraniums, petunias, and trailing vines brighten the skylights and the companionways.

When morning light streaks across the bay, a hearty breakfast is served in the galley. Afterward, with sea legs steady, passengers reluctantly head for land. In spring and fall, the *Manitou* reverts to three- and five-day cruises out of Northport to nearby islands and through the Straits of Mackinac. The *Manitou* is one of two Tall Ships that sail the bays. *Traverse Tall Ship Co.; 13390 S. West Bay Shore Dr.; 800-678-0383.*

*A crow's nest view of the deck of the Tall Ship Manitou.*

◆ INTERLOCHEN  *map page 205, B-6*

Interlochen is home to one of the premier art centers in the nation. The 1,200-acre campus of the **Interlochen Center for the Arts** includes an academy for gifted students in grades nine through 12. The **National Music Camp** attracts students from around the world. The **Interlochen Arts Festival and International Concert Series** brings the best artists to the north woods *(interlochen.org; 231-276-9221).* If you strolls along the wooded paths in summer, you may hear young musicians practicing under the trees, oblivious to everything except their music. *For information contact: Traverse City Convention & Visitors Bureau; mytraversecity.com; 101 W. Grandview Pkwy.; 800-TRAVERS.*

◆ MUSIC HOUSE MUSEUM  *map page 205, B-5*

Back along Grand Traverse Bay, follow US-31 along the curve of East Arm for six miles to the Music House Museum at Acme. It's on the edge of hokey, but music makes it fun with sound everywhere, from small music boxes to player pianos to a 97-key pipe organ. Linger to sip a soda in the **Hurry Back Saloon** while nickelodeons spin old-fashioned tunes. *7377 US-31; 231-938-9300.*

*(opposite) Students practice in the woods at Interlochen.*

Watch for roadside fruit stands. At **Amon Orchards,** climb aboard a wagon for orchard tours or pick your own. The gift shop offers samples from its vast array of cherry and apple jams, spreads, butters, and relishes, all lined up on the counter. The fruit pies? To *die* for. *8066 US-31; 231-938-9160.*

## ■ FISHERMAN'S ISLAND STATE PARK    *map page 205, C-3*

Six miles from Charlevoix, watch for the sign directing you to Fisherman's Island State Park. The island can't even be seen from the main campground and beach, but it is absolutely the best place in the state to find Petoskey stones, Michigan's official state stone. A stroll along the pebble beach is like walking barefoot on jellybeans. The various shapes and colors of the stones show up best where the sand is damp. The brown and tan stones patterned in hexagonal polyps are pieces of the 350-million-year-old Devonian fossilized coral reef offshore, polished and deposited along the beach by waves.

Keep an eye out for fulgurites—pieces of cigar-shaped glassy tubes formed when lightning strikes high-silica sand. They can be several inches long.

*Several homes in Charlevoix were designed by architect Earl Young, known for his unique use of boulders and Lake Michigan stones.*

*Charlevoix's Venetian Festival in full swing.*

## ■ CHARLEVOIX  *map page 205, C-3*

It's no wonder that the city at the top of Lake Charlevoix is known as "Charlevoix the Beautiful." The cobalt-blue water of Lake Michigan stretches to the north, and to the south is Round Lake, with a channel to Lake Charlevoix. A boardwalk runs along the navigable half-mile-long Pine River from Round Lake and the town to Lake Michigan's Charlevoix South Pier Light.

Summer residents, boaters, and visitors stroll the waterfront streets through the lingering twilight hours. Stop by **Koucky Gallery;** its silly and funky art offerings can run as high as $55,000. *325 Bridge St.; 231-547-2228.*

Late one mid-July evening, some friends and I sailed down the Pine River Channel into Round Lake only to discover it packed with boats of every description, and all decorated with lights, banners, flags, and streamers. It was the annual July **Venetian Festival.** Before we knew it, the bridge closed behind us, forcing us to quickly seek a mooring. The only spot we could find was hard against the bridge. When the fireworks started, they came from atop the bridge directly behind us! Soon hot ashes began falling on deck, and we hastily formed a water

NORTHWEST & MACKINAC ISLAND

bucket brigade, dousing every spark and ember, praying that none landed in the sails. Finally it was over and the bridge lifted for our departure. *Charlevoix Area Convention & Visitors Bureau; 408 Bridge St.; 800-367-8557.*

## ■ BEAVER ISLAND   *map page 205, B-2*

Beaver Island owns the dubious distinction of being the site of one of the more bizarre occurences in American history: the Kingdom of James Strang. *(See essay on page 217).* Today, a hundred miles of road left by the island's Mormon colonists wind through green forests to pristine beaches. Old-model cars and bicycles are for rent in St. James, the island's only village, which overlooks the bowl-shaped natural harbor. As I wend my way along the roads, it takes a great stretch of the imagination to picture Beaver Island as a kingdom of anything but natural beauty.

Catch the **Beaver Island Ferry** at Round Lake in downtown Charlevoix. It's an enjoyable 32-mile jaunt out to the 13- by six-mile island. *Beaver Island Boat Co., bibco.com; 103 Bridge Park Dr.; 231-547-2311.*

For accommodations on the island contact: *Beaver Island Chamber of Commerce; 231-448-2505.*

## ■ HORTON BAY   *map page 205, C-3*

The biggest happening in Horton Bay is the Fourth of July parade. On every even year at 1 P.M., the one-store village of 49 residents closes its only street (County 56) for an hour-long slapstick parade that sometimes draws up to 10,000 spectators. They perform a humorous parody of other hometown parades, beginning with an auction for a spectator's choice seat on the limb of a roadside tree—it's left to the winner to climb the tree. Parade drill teams are popular, such as the Precision Lawn Mower Team with maneuvers choreographed to music, while an accompanying team performs with lawn chairs. Bands march backward, and family floats in rusted pickup trucks toss water balloons until a portly gentleman in a gaudy woman's dress brings up the rear—and the fat lady sings. *Horton Bay General Store; 231-582-7827.*

This is Hemingway country; he spent a few summers of his youth here and on Walloon Lake. *(See page 252.)*

NORTHWEST & MACKINAC ISLAND

## STRANG'S KINGDOM

The only kingdom ever to exist in the United States belonged to James Jesse Strang, King of Beaver Island. Born March 21, 1813 in western New York state, Strang early on harbored visions of grandeur, comparing himself to Caesar and Napoleon. He became a lawyer noted for his hypnotic oratorical skill, but left the profession to join the Mormon Church where he was baptized by its founder, Joseph Smith. The murders of Joseph and Hyrum Smith (in 1844 in Carthage, Ill. by a mob inflamed, in part, by Smith's presidential ambitions) created a vacuum of leadership to which Strang leapt to fill, producing an apocryphal letter from Joseph Smith endorsing him as the true heir. Excommunicated for his efforts, Strang established a rival church at Voree, in southeastern Wisconsin. He sanctified his community with the miraculous discovery of a set of ancient tablets—much as Smith did. The tablets could only be read by using magic "peep stones," by the use of which Strang generated *The Book of the Law of the Lord*—a direct challenge to *The Book of Mormon*.

Persecuted and harassed in Wisconsin, Strang found refuge for his church on remote Beaver Island, inhabited by a few Irish fishermen. The industrious Strangite Mormons built roads, acquired more land, appropriated the better fishing grounds, renamed the harbor St. James, and generously bestowed biblical names to geographic features. The resident Irish were not amused. When President Millard Fillmore refused Strang's petition for title to all the uninhabited islands in Lake Michigan, Strang pronounced them his by God's decree. This wonderment was announced during Strang's coronation on July 8, 1850, a costume pageant in which Strang wore a crimson robe and an actor-turned-saint crowned him.

Hostilities with the Irish persisted, and the conflict came to a head when President Fillmore learned of Strang's kingdom and ordered his arrest. Acting as his own lawyer, Strang won an acquittal, then rigged a local election to gain a seat in the Michigan legislature. The end came when two disgruntled followers, Thomas Bedford—who had been whipped for allegedly supporting his wife's refusal to wear bloomers—and Alexander Wentworth, shot the King one June evening in 1856. The resulting chaos invited invasion, and on July 5, 1856, a mob of drunken rowdies descended upon the kingdom, burning the tabernacle and ferrying 2,600 men, women, and children off the island. A turn-of-the-century historian, Byron M. Cutcheon, called it "the most disgraceful day in Michigan history." Today, all that remains of Strang's kingdom are the **Mormon Print Shop Museum** and a few names such as King's Highway, Lake Geneserath, and Mount Pisgah.

*The interior of the Horton Bay General Store.*

■ BAY HARBOR    *map page 205, C-3*

Until 1994, the shoreline along Little Traverse Bay was lined with industrial smokestacks, silos, buildings, and gravel pits left behind by a cement factory that was operated here from 1910 to 1981. In 1995, the site became the largest land reclamation project in the nation. Today, the vista takes one's breath away.

Surrounded by green lawns and golf courses, the upscale development of Bay Harbor has its own lake, marinas, shops, restaurants, and condominiums. The sprawling white **Inn at Bay Harbor,** with its staggered raspberry-red roofline outlined against the blue waters of the bay, offers elegant seclusion. From the dining room of **Sagamore's,** the beauty of the bay pulls me outside where patios and walkways afford more expansive views. Settling into one of the Adirondack chairs on the beach, I am lulled into daydreams, feeling as lazy as the waves that gently lap the shore. *3600 Village Harbor Dr.; 231-439-4000.*

*(previous pages) The town of St. James awaits visitors to Beaver Island.*

NORTHWEST &
MACKINAC ISLAND

# ■ PETOSKEY    *map page 205, C-3*

From Bay Front Park, you can see the elegant Victorian homes of Petoskey dotting the hills across the bay. The marina stretches into the bay, where fishermen cast off for deep water, pleasure boaters reach for the breeze, and the **Bay Water Ferry** waits to board passengers for a bay cruise or a shuttle to Bay Harbor. *1549 Glendale, Bay View; 231-347-5550.*

The flower-banked **Little Traverse Historical Society History Museum,** housed in the 1892 railroad station, traces the area's history through lumbering, transportation, and the tourism of today. Hemingway spent a few summers of his youth here, and his aficionados gravitate toward displays of his books and memorabilia, including a childhood chair. *100 Depot Ct.; 231-347-2620.*

Petoskey earned its reputation as a resort town early, but it started out in the usual manner of other Michigan river-port settlements. Lumbermen came to harvest timber, establish mills, and eventually move on once the forest was levelled—typical of the boom-and-bust pattern all along the Lake Michigan shore.

*Downtown Petoskey, dressed up for Christmas.*

On the evening of November 25, 1873, the Pennsylvania Central Railroad chugged into Petoskey with officials on board to celebrate the completion of the 193-mile line from Grand Rapids. George Gage, newspaper reporter for the *Grand Rapids Times,* rode along. Later he wrote stories describing the village at the end of the line and the million-dollar sunsets over Little Traverse Bay. Soon three trains a week were bringing tourists from "down below." By the turn of the century, 13 hotels were accommodating tourists in downtown Petoskey, with more in Charlevoix, Harbor Springs, and Mackinac Island. *For additional information contact: Petoskey–Harbor Springs–Boyne Country Visitors Bureau; 401 E. Mitchell St.; 800-845-2828.*

◆ BAY VIEW    *map page 205, D-3*

Around the same period that Petoskey was developing into a tourist town, the Methodists of Michigan were searching for a summer campground site. In 1875, they purchased land for it and founded the Bay View Association on Little Traverse Bay, which still exists today. From tents, they moved on to build over 400 Victorian summer homes in the hills above the bay, with a summer university and Chautauqua programs. It's easy to identify where Petoskey ends and Bay View begins by Bay View's salmon-colored street curbing.

◆ GASLIGHT DISTRICT

In Petoskey's Gaslight District you'll find Victorian buildings, modern-art galleries, brick sidewalks, softly glowing streetlights, park benches, flower boxes, canopied doorways, and—my favorite—the redbrick 1879 **Symon's General Store**. Inside, pots, pans, baskets, and other goods hang from the high tin ceiling, and the aisles offer a plethora of cheeses, wines, and ethnic foods, all begging to hop into your picnic basket. *401 East Lake St.; 231-347-2438.*

■ HARBOR SPRINGS    *map page 205, D-3*

North of Bay View, US-31 is intersected by M-119, which leads to Harbor Springs and continues along the lakeshore to Cross Village. In winter, Harbor Springs is almost deserted with virtually all the summertime "cottage" mansions shuttered. Indeed, Harbor Springs is so deserted in winter that those remaining hold a bowling tournament down Main Street on the first of April and shoot off a cannon to end the celebration.

NORTHWEST & MACKINAC ISLAND

When the French explorers and fur traders arrived, Harbor Springs was one of dozens of Ottawa villages that stretched for 30 miles up the coast from Little Traverse Bay to what is now Cross Village. L'Arbre Croche, or Crooked Tree, near the present village of Good Hart, was the seat of the Ottawa nation. A tall white pine with a twisted crown once stood along the cliff above Lake Michigan marking the council place of Great Lakes Indian chiefs and serving as a landmark for paddlers on the lake.

Ottawa Indian Andrew J. Blackbird grew up in L'Arbre Croche, went away to what is now Eastern Michigan University, and returned to serve as postmaster while writing two books on Michigan Indians. In one, *History of the Ottawa and Chippewa Indians of Michigan,* Blackbird describes the area in the early 1800s:

*In* my first recollection of the country of Arbor Croche, which is sixty years ago, there was nothing but small shrubbery here and there in small patches, such as wild cherry trees, but the most of it was grassy plain; and such an abundance of wild strawberries, raspberries and blackberries that they fairly perfumed the air of the whole coast with fragrant scent of ripe fruit. The wild pigeons and every variety of feathered songsters filled all the groves, warbling their songs joyfully and feasting upon these wild fruits of nature; and in these waters the fishes were so plentiful that as you lifted up the anchor stone of your net in the morning, your net would be so loaded with delicious whitefish as to fairly float with all its weight on the sinkers. As you look towards the course of your net, you see the fins of the fishes sticking out of the water in every way. Then I never knew my people to want for anything to eat or to wear, as we always had plenty of wild meat and plenty of fish, corn, vegetables, and wild fruits. I thought (and yet I may be mistaken) that my people were very happy in those days.

◆ TUNNEL OF TREES SCENIC DRIVE

Today there are few reminders of those years. The narrow road from Harbor Springs north is one of the most scenic in Michigan. The twisting, turning road dips and climbs through the thick forest of birch, maple, and evergreens that form a tunnel over it. There are only occasional glimpses of Lake Michigan to the west. Spring brings out the fresh mint greens of the forest with splashes of flowering sugarplum and pin cherries; autumn cocoons the road in radiant shades of red, gold, and orange. *Chamber of Commerce, 368 E. Main St.; 231-526-7999.*

*Tunnel of Trees Scenic Drive (on M-119 north of Harbor Springs).*

# ■ INLAND DIVERSION

◆ **GRAYLING**   *map page 205, D-6*

We'll begin our inland journey along the I-75 corridor at Grayling, which was named for the beautiful trout-like fish that vanished in the face of overfishing, logging, and fire. The Au Sable River flows fast through the city and gets top billing as a catch-and-release trout stream. Some fishermen still use the flat-bottom Au Sable riverboat, guided with a long pole, made popular during logging drives of the late 1800s. *Grayling Area Visitors Council; 213 N. James St.; 800-937-8837.*

◆ **HARTWICK PINES STATE PARK**   *map page 205, D-5*

Seven miles northeast on M-93 lies Hartwick Pines State Park, the fifth largest in Michigan. What makes this park unique is an 86-acre remnant of Michigan's original white pine forest. Standing tall, cool, and dark, these trees are all that remain of the glorious forest that once covered Michigan. Why this tract wasn't logged is something of a mystery. In 1893 the Salling Hanson Company of Graying purchased the land and logged all of it except for this small area. Was the market weak, the trees too small back then? No one is really sure. *517-348-7068.*

◆ GAYLORD    *map page 205, D-4*

Designed after its sister city of Pontresina, Switzerland, downtown Gaylord offers ornate clock towers, flower boxes, sidewalk canopies, and shake-shingled rooftops. The popular **Alpenfest** fair is held the third week of July.

Gaylord prides itself on being a "swinging" region—that is, swinging golf clubs. With over 22 major courses, Gaylord offers more world-class golf per square mile than any other place in the United States. Among the sterling attractions are two of the courses at **Treetops:** one, the **Masterpiece,** was designed by Robert Trent Jones, Sr.; the **Premier** was designed by Tom Fazio. In addition, **The Natural,** near **Beaver Creek Resort,** has been declared a wildlife sanctuary by the National Audubon Society. *For more information contact: Gaylord Golf Mecca; gaylord-mich.com/golf or the Gaylord Area Convention & Tourism Bureau; 101 West Main St.; 800-345-8621.*

There is also great fishing here, on the Sturgeon, Pigeon, Black, Manistee, and North Branch of the Au Sable Rivers.

*The Treetops Signature golf course was designed Rick Smith.*

## GOLFING IN GAYLORD

One of America's premier golfing destinations is the area in and around the Otsego County town of Gaylord, which lies off I-75, 57 miles south of Mackinaw City and 35 miles southeast of Petoskey. Clustered here are no less than 15 separate golf resorts and a total of 22 courses—some of which are rated among the best in the country. Following is a brief list of what we consider the top courses, along with their basic amenities. For a virtual tour of all 22 courses, go to: *www.gaylord-mich.com/golf*

### BEAVER CREEK RESORT & GOLF CLUB    *map page 226, A-1*
*Open year-round,*
*5004 W. Otsego Lake Dr.,*
*five miles south of Gaylord;*
*517-732-1785.*

This Jerry Mathews-designed course, on the west side of Otsego Lake, is called "The Natural" and features a beautiful clubhouse which overlooks all 18 holes and a wetlands wildlife preserve.

### WILDERNESS VALLEY & BLACK FOREST GOLF RESORT
*map page 226, A-1*
*Open Apr.-Oct., 7519 Mancelona Rd.*
*15 miles southwest of Gaylord;*
*231-585-7090.*

The Black Forest Course is one of the highest ranked courses in Michigan featuring difficult bunkers and sculptured greens.

*The boardwalk on the back nine at Elk Ridge Golf Course.*

## ELK RIDGE GOLF CLUB
*map page 226, B-1*
*Open May-Oct., 9400 Rouse Rd., Atlanta; 517-785-2275.*
Some 35 miles east of Gaylord on M-32 and then north six miles on M-33. *Golf Digest* magazine honored the Elk Ridge course as runner-up for Best New Public Golf Course in America, 1991. Relatively expensive, but in lovely surroundings. Watch for bull elk in the fall. Designed by Jerry Mathews.

## FOX RUN COUNTRY CLUB
*map page 226, A-2*
*Open Apr.-Oct.,*
*5825 W. Four Mile Rd.,*
*517-348-4343.*

Three miles south of Grayling, 31 miles south of Gaylord, at I-75 exit 251. This course has a reputation for having a knowledgeable staff with lessons available from a PGA pro. Nice course out in the middle of nowhere.

## GARLAND GOLF RESORT
*map page 226, B-2*
*Open Apr-Oct., in Lewiston;*
*517-786-2211.*
Thirty miles southeast of Gaylord, east on M-32 about 20 miles to CR-491, then south for 10 miles.

*Four courses:*

### The Fountains
This course, opened in 1999, offers six par fives, and the "longest single-span, log bridge in the world" (it crosses CR-489 to connect two holes).

### The Monarch
A *Golf Digest* reader avows that this is the "Augusta of northern Michigan" (he also says this resort has the "most luxurious lodge rooms in Michigan." Water hazards come into play on 14 of the 18 holes.

### The Swampfire
This course winds its way through, well, swamps. A challenging course with lots of wildlife to view.

### Reflections
This is considered the easiest of the four courses and perhaps the most scenic.

*The Robert Trent Jones Sr. Masterpiece course pictured above at hole 15.*

### TREETOPS SYLVAN RESORT
*map page 226, A-1*
*Open Apr.-Oct.,*
*3962 Wilkinson Rd.; 517-732-6711.*
Perhaps the premier Gaylord area golf resort, Treetops features five courses; two are considered world-class links. The resort offers include indoor/outdoor pools with spas and two restaurants.

*Five Courses:*

**Robert Trent Jones** *Masterpiece Course*
Ranked among the top 30 courses in America by *Golf Digest.* In October the extraordinary fall foliage may divert you from your bogeys.

**Tom Fazio** *Premier Course*
Rated as the best at Treetops and also the most difficult. Some consider it the best course in Michigan with its wide fairways and imaginative holes.

**Rick Smith** *Signature, Tradition,* **and** *Threetops Courses*
Smith's award-winning *Signature* course is another challenging set of links with fabulous views. The *Tradition* course is described as having a "classic look," perhaps because Smith designed the course for golfers who *walk* between holes: there's less hilly terrain, and shorter distances between holes. The par-3, nine-hole *Threetops* course is geared toward the beginning golfer.

### OTSEGO CLUB
*map page 226, A-1*
*(Various locations)*
*M-32 one mile east of Gaylord*
*www.otsegoclub.com*
*517-732-5181.*
Features three world-class courses—all designed by William H. Diddel.

OTSEGO CLUB *(cont'd)*

*Three Courses:*

**The Loon**
*Open Apr.-Oct.,*
*4400 Championship Dr., Gaylord*
Opened in 1994, this has proved to be one of northern Michigan's most popular courses. Listed as one of the top fairwaysby *Golf for Women* magazine for its "user-friendly" landscaping.

**The Classic**
*Open Apr.-Oct.,*
*696 M-32 East, Gaylord*
The founding course in the "Gaylord Golf Mecca," it is considered to have some of the finest greens in Michigan.

**The Lake**
*Open Apr.-Oct.,*
*5750 Opal Lake Rd., Gaylord*
Combines three distinct terrains: six alpine holes around ski hills, six Scottish holes (tall and plentiful roughs), and six holes over and around water hazards. Voted third best of new resort courses by *Golf Digest* when it opened in 1988.

GAYLORD COUNTRY CLUB
*map page 226, A-1*
*Open Apr-Oct.,*
*M-32 W in Gaylord; 231-546-3376.*
Following the rolling hills five miles west of Gaylord are 18 holes of scenic golf. A spacious practice range and budget-friendly greens fees.

*Many consider the lodgings at Garland to be the finest in the state.*

■ MACKINAW CITY    *map page 205, D-1*

From Cross Village, drive east on County 66, then north on US-31 and I-75 to Mackinaw City at the top of Michigan's mitten. This village of 875 full-time residents swells to thousands of visitors in the summer months. Of interest are the historic sites, the five-mile-long Mackinac Bridge to the Upper Peninsula, and the waters of the Straits of Mackinac where Lake Huron meets Lake Michigan. Mackinaw Crossing, a Disneyesque web of shops is replete with fountains, park benches, and entertainers every hour on the hour.

◆ MACKINAC BRIDGE    *map page 205, D-1*

Twin towers rise 552 feet above the Straits of Mackinac, supporting a web of cables for "Big Mac," the only ground transportation link between the two peninsulas. With a length of 8,614 feet, it ranks among the world's longest suspension bridges. Every Labor Day, the two southbound lanes are closed to vehicular traffic for the Mackinac Bridge Walk from St. Ignace to Mackinaw City, with over

*An ore freighter passes under the Mackinac Bridge as some 70,000 souls cross the bridge during the Labor Day walk.*

NORTHWEST &
MACKINAC ISLAND

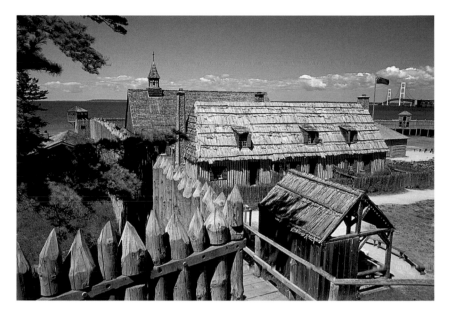

*A view of colonial Michilimackinac with the Mackinaw Bridge in the background.*

70,000 walkers participating. Folk dancers and a ballerina dance their way across, people pull tired kids in red wagons, and politicians walk across shaking hands. At 7:30 A.M., when the walk begins, sunlight streaks across Lake Huron, casting long shadows of the bridge toward Lake Michigan.

Until construction of the bridge, people either paddled or sailed across the Straits. In winter, the Straits froze into icy slabs like jagged concrete, cutting off transportation. In 1888, the *St. Ignace* ferry was carrying both rail and passengers between the two peninsulas. In 1923, the first ferry transported a dozen or so cars across the Straits. During hunting season, travelers sometimes lined up for 23 miles, with drivers napping at the wheel. The first driver to pay the toll and drive across the Big Mac did so on November 1, 1957.

◆ HISTORIC MILL CREEK STATE PARK    *map page 205, D-1*

The present site of Mackinaw City across the Straits from St. Ignace—the site of the original French Fort Du Buade—was originally a low sand beach of swamp grasses. It remained so until Sieur Antoine de la Mothe Cadillac abandoned Du Buade, razed it, and marched off to build Fort Pontchartrain at Detroit. In 1715,

NORTHWEST &
MACKINAC ISLAND

the French returned to rebuild Fort Du Buade, but this time on the southern banks of the Straits (where the reconstructed Colonial Michilimackinac now stands). Michilimackinac fell to the English in 1761. In 1779, fearing attacks from the Americans after the Revolutionary War, British Major Patrick Sinclair dismantled the fort and re-built it on Mackinac Island. He also "borrowed" timbers from a sawmill four miles southeast. The mill has been reconstructed and is the central feature of Historic Mill Creek State Park. *US-23; 231-436-7301.*

❖

**Fort Michilimackinac** was the scene perhaps the most dramatic episode of the French and Indian War. The great Ottawa chief Pontiac had assembled a large confederation with the aim of ousting the British and returning the French to control of the fur trade. "Pontiac's War" involved simultaneous assaults at forts all along the Great Lakes and the Ohio Valley, what was then the western frontier.

On June 2, 1763, two bands of Chippewa and Sauk, part of Pontiac's "secret" Indian confederation gathered in front of Fort Michilimackinac to stage a game of baggatiway (similar to lacrosse). Although he had been warned of possible trouble, Fort Commander George Etherington took it lightly. On that June morning, soldiers leaned idly at their posts along the stockade and watched as the game heated up. Soldiers cheered as the wooden ball went back and forth in a near frenzy of plays. Suddenly the ball sailed over the stockaded walls. The teams swarmed through the open gate, grabbed tomahawks and knives hidden under the blankets worn by their women waiting inside the walls, and started hacking, stabbing, shooting, and scalping every English soldier to be found.

Civilians watched or cowered in their houses. British fur trader Alexander Henry was sitting in his room writing a letter when the massacre began. Although a servant girl hid him, he was nevertheless captured. Henry, Etherington, his lieutenant, and 12 privates were loaded in canoes bound for Beaver Island *(map page 205, B-1)* where supposedly they were to be killed, boiled, and eaten.

Meanwhile, the Ottawa at L'Arbre Croche heard about the massacre and were furious, in part because they had not been consulted. They gathered a band of a hundred warriors and set out for Michilimackinac. The two parties met halfway. The Ottawa prevailed and rescued Henry and nine of the soldiers. Henry lived to tell the story in graphic detail. *(See literary extract page 234.)*

The drama is reenacted every Memorial Day weekend. *Mackinac State Historic Parks; 231-436-5563.*

*A sawyer in early Federal-period costume works the mill at Historic Mill Creek State Park.*

NORTHWEST &
MACKINAC ISLAND

■ MACKINAC ISLAND   *map page 205, D-1 and map page 239*

Arriving by ferry from St. Ignace or Mackinaw City, the predominant sight is the island's long white **Grand Hotel** crowning West Bluff. This world-famous hotel-

## A GAME OF BAGGATIWAY

*In this passage, Alexander Henry describes the game of baggatiway—a lacrosse-like game played by Indian tribes in the Northeast. Pontiac used a baggatiway match as a ploy to catch the British soldiers unprepared to defend their fort.*

*T*he game of baggatiway...is necessarily attended with much violence and noise. In the ardor of contest the ball, as has been suggested, if it cannot be thrown to the goal desired, is struck in any direction by which it can be diverted from that designed by the adversary. At such a moment, therefore, nothing could be less liable to excite premature alarm than that the ball should be tossed over the pickets of the fort, nor that having fallen there, it should be followed on the instant by all engaged in the game, as well the one party as the other, all eager, all struggling, all shouting, all in the unrestrained pursuit of a rude athletic exercise. Nothing could be less fitted to excite premature alarm—nothing, therefore, could be more happily devised, under the circumstances, than a stratagem like this; and this was in fact the stratagem which the Indians had employed...

—Alexander Henry, *Travels and Adventures in Canada and the Indian Territories Between the Years 1760 and 1776*

*Chippewas in period garb play a game of baggatiway at Fort Michilimackinac.*

*Arch Rock on Mackinac Island.*

mansion, built in 1887 by a consortium of railroads during the heyday of timbering, is flanked on either side by a line of Victorian summer mansions replete with gingerbread trim, turrets, and wraparound porches. To the north and east, the 14 original buildings of Fort Mackinac rise above thick stone walls, with a sloping ramp reaching down the limestone cliff to the village on the shore.

Cars have been banned here since the 1890s, and the effect of stepping onto the island, with its horse-drawn buggies, bicycles, false storefronts and Victorian extravagance, is like walking through a portal into the past.

Some visitors come to experience the history, others to indulge in the luxuries offered by many of the island hotels, while others rent a carriage or bicycle and set out to explore the miles of trails that crisscross the island. **Mackinac Island Carriage Tours** offers an insider's view of the island, including Arch Rock, cemeteries, and woodland glades full of wildflowers. *Across from Arnold Ferry dock on Main St.; 906-847-3573.*

## MACKINAC ISLAND

*F*or a while, Mackinac Island was the biggest trading post in the New World—John Jacob Astor's fur trading company was based here—but its real glory dates from the late nineteenth century when wealthy people from Chicago and Detroit came to escape the city heat and enjoy the pollen-free air. The Grand Hotel, the biggest and oldest resort hotel in America, was built and the country's wealthiest industrialists constructed ornate summer houses on the bluffs overlooking Mackinac village and Lake Huron. I walked up there now. The views across the lake were fantastic, but the houses were simply breathtaking. They are some of the grandest, most elaborate houses ever built of wood, twenty-bedroomed places with every embellishment known to the Victorian mind—cupolas, towers, domes, dormers, gables, turrets, and front porches you could ride a bike around. Some of the cupolas had cupolas. They are just incredibly splendid and there are scores of them, standing side by side on the bluffs flanking Fort Mackinac. What it must be to be a child and play hide-and-seek in those houses, to have a bedroom in a tower and be able to lie in bed and gaze out on such a lake, and to go bicycling on carless roads to little beaches and hidden coves, and above all to explore the woodlands of beech and birch that cover the back three-quarters of the island.

—Bill Bryson, *The Lost Continent, Travels in Small-Town America,* 1990

*Mrs. Potter Palmer, queen of Chicago society, here enjoys a carriage ride on Mackinac Island, circa 1890. (Michigan State Archives)*

*A costumed reenactor plays his flute at Fort Mackinac.*

The Chippewa Indians called it Michilimackinac (Great Spirit or Great Turtle) and considered the island a holy place for all tribes. Their belief holds that the great God Manitou ascended from his home in the depths through the great limestone sweep of Arch Rock overlooking Lake Huron. The French may have honored that tradition, but the British had a more practical view of the island: as a strategic point of defense against the Americans. In 1781, they transported Ft. Michilimackinac from Mackinaw City to the island. The Americans nevertheless gained possession in 1813 at the close of the War of 1812.

Perhaps the island's greatest days occurred during the era of John Jacob Astor's American Fur Company, which headquartered itself there in the early 1800s. Abandoned in 1894, the restored 18th- and 19th-century British and American military outpost became part of Michigan's first state park in 1895. Reenactments of historic episodes are performed on the Parade Grounds by interpreters in 1880s military dress. *Mackinac State Historic Parks; 213-436-5563.*

The north side of the island is much less crowded than the popular south side. In winter, the entire north side is snowmobile free and is reserved for cross-country skiing and other "quiet" sports.

NORTHWEST & MACKINAC ISLAND

### ◆ Mackinac Island Highlights

Fudge! Purchase it at several shops downtown. Granted, fudge is no substitute for lunch or dinner, but you're not a visitor to Mackinac Island until you've succumbed to your instincts and sampled the island's most famous export from its shops on Main Street.

**Beaumont Memorial**
At the corner of Market and Fort Streets, this monument recounts the story of fort physician Dr. William Beaumont who made significant discoveries about the human digestive system. Beaumont was called upon to attend 19-year-old Alexis St. Martin, a French *voyageur* who had been accidentally shot in the stomach, leaving a

hole in his abdomen "large enough to insert a fist." Beaumont was able to save young St. Martin, but the stomach adhered to the wound, leaving a "window" into St. Martin's digestive system. Beaumont conducted extensive experiments with St. Martin, eventually becoming heralded as the "leader and pioneer of experimental physiology in America."

**Stuart House Museum**
This magnificent two-story white mansion-museum on Market Street *(906-847-8181)* was one of the four warehouses built by fur trader John Jacob Astor in the early 1800s. Only two of Astor's warehouses remain: the Stuart House and a second warehouse that is now the **Mackinac Island City Hall.**

**Grand Hotel**
The front porch of this stunning, world-famous 1887 Victorian Hotel is longer than two football fields and is lined with classic columns, white wicker rockers, and flower boxes that hold 2,000 red geraniums. Throughout the salons, hallways, dining area, and private rooms, the hotel takes on the quality of a living museum. Guests lounge on antique sofas, enjoy viewing fine art, and often sleep on antique beds. *One Grand Dr.; 906-847-3331.*

*The Grand Hotel's front porch stretches more than 600 feet along the lakefront.*

## GETTING TO MACKINAC ISLAND

Mackinac Island is serviced by three ferry lines. All of them depart from the docks at St. Ignace and at Mackinaw City. All charge about the same ($15) per round trip. Parking is free. Schedules change with the seasons, so be sure to check to confirm departure times. You can also get there by air. For information on accomodations, contact: *Mackinac Chamber of Commerce; Mackinac Island; 800-4-LILACS.*

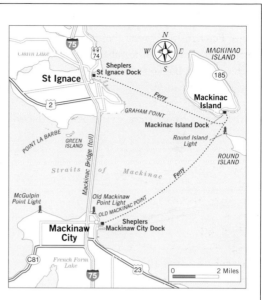

**Arnold Line.** *arnoldline.com; 800-542-8528.* Traditional ferries.
**Shepler's Ferries.** *sheplerswww.com; 800-828-6157.* Hydroplane ferries.
**Star Line.** *mackinacferry.com; 800 638-9892.* Hydro-Jet ferries.

### Directions to St. Ignace Dock

When traveling north on I-75 across the Mackinac Bridge, take Exit 344 and follow US-2 to the north end of town. From the west, follow US-2 east to the north end of town. If you're heading south on I-75 take Exit 348 (Business Loop 75) to dock.

### Directions to Mackinaw City Dock

When traveling north on I-75 (or US-31, which merges into I-75) take exit 337 or 338 and follow the signs. If you take Exit 339, turn right, and continue to stoplight (Central Avenue). Turn left and continue to the docks. When traveling south across the Mackinac Bridge, take Exit 339 off I-75. Turn left at the stop sign. Continue to Central Avenue. Turn left and into the Gateway.

**Great Lakes Air.** *906-643-7165.* Departs from the St. Ignace airport at the north end of town off N. State St.; $40 round trip.

# UPPER PENINSULA

## ■ HIGHLIGHTS *page*

## ■ TRAVEL BASICS

**Area Overview:** Surrounded on three sides by Lakes Superior, Huron, and Michigan, the U.P. begins with low rolling hills to the east that rise to form "Midwest mountains" inland. It is a land of waterfalls, inland lakes, long stretches of sandy beaches and sandstone cliffs along the lakes.

**Travel:** Main travel routes are east to west, by way of US-2 and M-28, bisected by US-41 running north and south. Commuter air service is offered at Sault Ste. Marie, Marquette, Escanaba, Houghton, and Ironwood.

**Weather:** Visitors have traditionally come to the U.P. to escape the summer heat. Nights are refreshingly cool, and humidity is generally low. The drawback? Summers are black fly and mosquito season. September and October, however, can be idyllic, with cool northern air bringing autumn's palette to the hardwoods. The first snow is expected in November. Annual snowfall averages 200 inches.

**Food & Lodging:** Chains dominate the landscape, but as in so many places in Michigan, small town diners and B&Bs can often prove surprisingly good. Please refer to the listings that begin on page 274.

# ■ MICHIGAN'S UPPER PENINSULA

Three of the largest freshwater lakes in the world—Superior, Huron, and Michigan—draw the 1,100-mile boundary of Michigan's Upper Peninsula, reaching 384 miles from Drummond Island on the east to Ironwood on the west, and 233 miles from Menominee on the south to Copper Harbor at the tip of the Keweenaw Peninsula far out in Lake Superior. Yet in all this vastness only three cities claim a population of more than 13,000: Marquette, Sault Ste. Marie, and Escanaba.

The Upper Peninsula, locally called the U.P. (residents call themselves "yoopers") is greater in size than all of southern New England combined. Its western border is as far west as St. Louis, Missouri, and its northern shore extends farther north than Montreal. In fact, the distance between Detroit and Isle Royale is about the same as that between Detroit and New York City.

It claims Michigan's largest wilderness and largest state park, and of Michigan's 152 significant waterfalls, all but two are on the peninsula. There are 200-foot cliffs, beaches, dunes, 4,300 inland lakes, and 12,000 miles of trout streams. It's no wonder the peninsula appeals so strongly to nature lovers and sportsmen alike.

*A family strolls along windswept Twelve Mile Beach in Pictured Rocks National Lakeshore.*

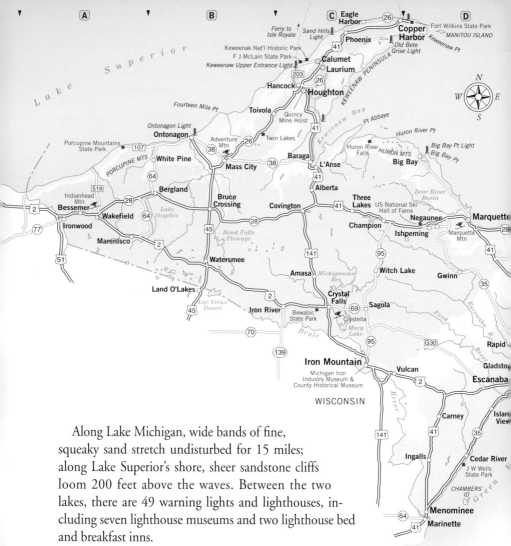

Along Lake Michigan, wide bands of fine, squeaky sand stretch undisturbed for 15 miles; along Lake Superior's shore, sheer sandstone cliffs loom 200 feet above the waves. Between the two lakes, there are 49 warning lights and lighthouses, including seven lighthouse museums and two lighthouse bed and breakfast inns.

The U.P. is the Michigan frontier, where most residents are aggressively provincial; diners wearing jackets and ties sit comfortably alongside others wearing swamper boots and Mackinaw jackets. As self-described Yoopers, U.P. denizens teazingly refer to those living below the Mackinac Bridge as "Trolls." Yoopers are known for their dedicated work ethic as well as a high tolerance for eccentricity. The U.P. economy is based on iron mining, forestry, and tourism. Temperatures in the summer season (from May through October) are especially pleasant, but Yoopers joke about having "10 months of winter and two months of poor sledding."

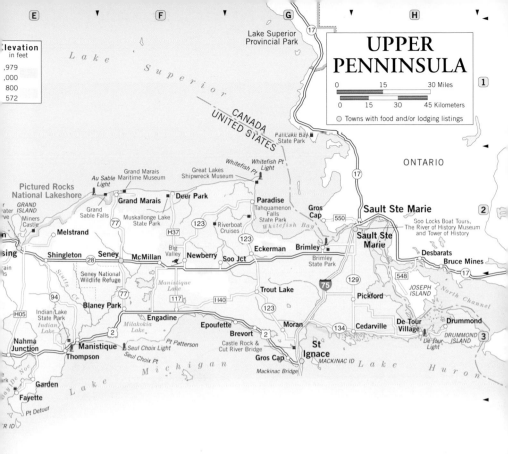

The first day of whitetail deer hunting season is considered a Yooper holiday. They will root equally for either the Green Bay Packers or the Detroit Lions, depending on their mood. Yoopers favor pasties—the meat pie in a crust introduced by miners who emigrated from Cornwall, England—and bratwurst. Most winter events include mushers and sled-dog races.

## ■ HISTORY

In the early 1600s, while the English were dropping anchor from the *Mayflower* at Plymouth Harbor, the Dutch were building New Amsterdam (New York), and the Spanish were claiming lands on the Gulf of Mexico, French explorers and missionaries were paddling up the St. Lawrence River, headed for what is now Michigan's Upper Peninsula. Chippewa (Ojibwa) Indians inhabited the eastern end of the peninsula, with Menominee Indians in the west.

*In this painting by Paul Kane circa 1845, two canoes of Menominee Indians spear fish at night by the light of pine-knot fires. (Royal Ontario Museum)*

Young Étienne Brûlé may have been the first European to see the Upper Peninsula. Sent by Samuel de Champlain to explore the possible water routes to China, which he believed lay just to the west of the Lakes, Brûlé found neither China nor the fabled Northwest Passage, but he did find Native Americans, in this case Hurons. A talented linguist, Brûlé was soon speaking their language, and, as was often the case in those years, was accepted into the Huron world as part of an extended family. The warm feelings soured. Following a fierce argument, the Hurons killed and ate him. (Ritual cannibalism was an act of great respect, by the way).

Following in Brûlé's footsteps came explorers, traders, and zealous black-robed priests. Among this group were Jean Nicolet, Father René Menard, Father Claude Allouez, Louis Jolliet, and Robert Cavelier de la Salle. In 1668, Jesuit missionaries Jacques Marquette and Claude Dablon built a mission at St. Marys Rapids, naming Michigan's first settlement Sault Ste. Marie for the Virgin Mary.

Two years later, when Marquette moved south to the Straits of Mackinac, his mission, settlement, and New France's nearby Fort Du Buade became the second Michigan settlement. Marquette named it St. Ignace for St. Ignatius of Loyola, founder of the Jesuit order, but it was better known by its Algonquin name, Michilimackinac.

The compulsion to claim more souls for God, and incidentally more lands for France, soon drove Marquette and Jolliet westward into the wilderness. Willis F. Dunbar and George S. May state in the book *Michigan:*

> *O*n May 17, 1673, Jolliet and Marquette, together with five other Frenchmen, departed from St. Ignace. Following the Lake Michigan shore of the Upper Peninsula into Green Bay, they ascended the Fox River, portaged to the Wisconsin, and on June 17, a month after the start of the trip, they entered the Mississippi, "with a joy which I am unable to make known," Marquette later declared.

After Cadillac abandoned Fort Du Buade (in order to construct the more strategically placed Fort Ponchartrain at Detroit) little was heard of the U.P., until Michigan sought entry into the Union, when the U.P. regained prominence, even notoriety. In 1835–36, as politicians and business leaders clamored for statehood—all the while engaged in a heated argument with Ohio over a strip of land around Toledo—Congress offered Michigan the Upper Peninsula in return for granting Ohio the disputed Toledo Strip. It was a shotgun marriage, and Michigan's politicos, unaware of the rich mineral resources it contained, grudgingly accepted the 16,538-square-mile "barren waste of the Upper Peninsula."

Then, in 1841, state geologist Douglass Houghton presented the legislature with a report on the copper along the Keweenaw Trap Range fueling a "copper rush" to the north. Three years later, state surveyor William Austin Burt discovered iron on Teal Lake in what is now Negaunee, and soon the stampede for iron was on. The mineral wealth of the U.P. turned out to be enormous, generating more wealth than did the gold fields of California and Alaska combined.

*The Étienne Brûlé exhibit at the Great Lakes Shipwreck Museum in Whitefish Point.*

## THE DISCOVERY OF IRON

*In order to become a state, Michigan was forced to cede a slice of itself called the "Toledo Strip" to Ohio. In return, Michigan was granted the "godforsaken willderness" of the Upper Peninsula. It turned out to be a wilderness that contained some of the richest mineral deposits in the world.*

Late in the afternoon of September 19, 1844, the region just south of Lake Superior ceased to be a howling wilderness. At that hour the needle of a magnetic compass held by William A. Burt dipped and jittered furiously. Then it quivered with uncertainty a moment and, like a man lost in the woods and gone wholly mad, it darted west and east and south, describing wild arcs, pointing nowhere for long.

Burt was amazed ... "Boys," he said, "look around and see what you can find." The boys looked around, and without any trouble they found a score of outcroppings of ore that appeared to be almost pure iron. There it was, hard, black ore in abundance, seemingly an entire hill, almost a mountain of it.

M. Everett of Jackson, in lower Michigan, who thought he wanted to own a copper mine and had gone looking for one, heard of Burt's findings. Everett also came in contact with an Indian chief who claimed to know where there was an entire mountain of strange rock.

This Indian labored under the name of Madjigijig, or sometimes Marji Gesick, in paleface spelling. He told Everett that the queer mountain was of black and blue and red and many colors. Everett asked to see it. The chief replied that the mountain was strictly Bad Medicine, filled with countless devils and spirits of one kind and another.

Whether or not Marji Gesick, the Chippewa, had any inkling of the value of this mountain to the palefaces isn't known. In any case, he grunted and muttered—which was hemming and hawing—until Everett offered to give the chief a part of the value of the find, if find it were.

Old Marji Gesick led Everett and his party to a spot on high land near the present city of Negaunee. It was rough, broken ground, with outcroppings of rock all over its surface. The chief, doubtless sweating from fear of Bad Medicine, directed Everett to a huge pine tree lying flat on the ground. He wouldn't approach the windfall himself.

"Catch um there," said Marji Gesick, pointing.

Everett went over to look. Exposed under the big roots was a broad expanse of black ore—heavy magnetic stuff that caused Everett's pocket compass to dip and flutter. It was a June day in 1845, six months after Burt had surveyed along this very hill.

—Stewart H. Holbrook, *Iron Brew*, 1939

# ■ ST. IGNACE *map page 243, G–3*

As you drive across the Mackinac Bridge toward St. Ignace, you are presented with vast expanses of water on either side. To the east is Lake Huron, with Mackinac Island floating on its blue-green waters. To the west is Lake Michigan, with three small islands in the distance. On clear summer days, the lakes turn azure blue with low, whitecapped waves when the wind is up. The impressive "big salties" (sea-faring freighters) dwarf the lake freighters as they pass under the bridge through the Straits of Mackinac.

St. Ignace itself is not visible from the bridge, but, on the west side after the toll booth, is the Michigan State Police post, and to the east are the bridge headquarters and a welcome center. US-2 becomes State Street as it goes through town, which can be slow going during the peak summer months, when tourists come to enjoy Mackinac Island, and St. Ignace becomes a virtual bedroom community for budget-minded vacationers seeking cheaper quarters than those on the island. Low key and friendly, St. Ignace offers convenient dining and lodging; many establishments have been operating since the 1920s. *For lodging information contact: Ignace Area Tourist Assn.; 560 North State St.; 800-338-6660 or the St. Ignace Welcome Center; I-75 North; 906-643-2361.*

State Street continues on and swings down the bluff to East Moran Bay where the ferries dock. *map inset, page 239.*

## ◆ CASTLE ROCK AND CUT RIVER BRIDGE

Four miles north of St. Ignace on I-75 is 195-foot Castle Rock. Once a lookout for Great Lakes Indians, the climb to the top rewards you with a dramatic panoramic view of Lake Michigan and the Straits of Mackinac. US-2, heading west out of St. Ignace, wanders past numerous low dunes and miles of Lake Michigan beaches. East of Brevort the shallow Cut River—meandering through a deep forested gorge—is spanned by the 641-foot-long cantilevered Cut River Bridge. Known as "the million-dollar bridge over a ten-cent river," it is, at 147 feet, the second highest bridge in Michigan. (Big Mac, at 199 feet, is highest.)

# ■ SAULT STE. MARIE *map page 243, H–2*

For eons, Indian tribes fished the half-mile-long rapids where Lake Superior's Whitefish Bay takes a 21-foot drop into St. Marys River and Lake Huron. In

1668, noting the large encampments of Chippewa there, Fathers Marquette and Dablon built a mission on the east side of St. Marys Rapids in the hopes of netting converts. The founding of the mission makes this city of 14,700 the Midwest's oldest settlement and the third oldest in the nation. The mission was abandoned in 1670, but in the late 1760s it was resurrected as a fort to protect the fur traders.

When the British lost their Great Lakes naval dominance during the War of 1812—at the hands of Comm. Oliver Hazard Perry in 1813 at the Battle of Lake Erie—they abandoned "their" fort to the Americans. In 1855, in response to expanding industries, particularly in terms of the ores being extracted in the north, the first of four U.S. navigational locks was dug, connecting Lake Superior to the St. Lawrence Seaway.

Today, the Soo Locks rank as one of the world's busiest waterways. The U.S. Army Corps of Engineers Visitors Center displays a working model of the locks and offers a history of the locks system. From any of the three observation platforms outside, one can view the huge freighters easing their way through the locks. As Soo native Bud Mansfield states, "We all rush dockside when the 'big salties' lock through." *From I-75 take Exit 394, the last before the International Bridge. Go left over I-75 to next stop sign, then right to Portage. Visitors Center; 906-632-2394.*

*This Paul Kane painting, circa 1845, shows Ojibway at Sault Ste. Marie, always a strategic site for both the Indians and the Europeans. (Royal Ontario Museum)*

*An ore freighter passes through the Soo Locks of Sault Ste. Marie.*

**Soo Locks Boat Tours**
To observe this close-up, take a two-hour "sunset dinner cruise" along the river and through the locks. **Soo Locks Boat Tours,** *515 and 1157 East Portage Ave.; 800-432-6301.*

**Soo Locks Tour Train**
Cross the 2.8-mile International Bridge to Soo, Ontario for an interesting perspective on Locks history. *315 West Portage Ave.; 800-387-6200.*

*Valley Camp*
This is a 550-foot Great Lakes freighter transformed into a museum. Included among the exhibits are lifeboats recovered from the *Edmund Fitzgerald,* which sank in Lake Superior in 1975. *501 East Water St.; 888-744-7867 or 906-632-3658.*

**River of History Museum**
Displays capture river history from early Chippewa Indian days to modern times; *209 East Portage Ave.; 906-632-1999.*

**Tower of History**
For a panoramic view of the locks, rapids, river, and the view into Ontario, ride the elevator up the 210-foot-tall **Tower of History.** *326 East Portage Ave.; 888-744-7867 or 906-632-3658.*

**Great Lakes Shipwreck Museum**

For a truly haunting experience of Great Lakes history, head west from Sault Ste. Marie on M-28 about 20 miles to M-123, then head north to Paradise. Just north of Paradise, on Whitefish Point Road, is the Great Lakes Shipwreck Museum. It stands on the lake at a point where more than 300 ships met their violent ends. The artifacts from the *Edmund Fitzgerald* are quite sobering, especially with the glow from the Fresnel lens at the entrance reflecting off the ship's recovered bell. Each time I visit, I recall lines from Gordon Lightfoot's song "Wreck of the *Edmund Fitzgerald*":

*The legend lives on from the*
                    *Chippewa on down,*
*Of the big lake they called Gitchigumi.*
*"Superior," they said, "never*
                    *gives up her dead*
*"When the gales of November come early."*

A quiet walk through the keeper's quarters, past the iron-pile lighthouse, then along the lonely beach scattered with driftwood and banded agates continues the mood of reflection. *110 Whitefish Point Rd.; 906-635-1742.*

■ TAHQUAMENON FALLS    *map page 243, G–2*

South of Paradise on M-123 at Tahquamenon Falls State Park, the tea-colored Tahquamenon (Ta-kwah'me-non) River meanders through the tamarack and

*One of many victims of Lake Superior's unpredictable storms and hazardous shoals, the* George M. Cox *ran aground on Isle Royale in May of 1933. (U.S. Army Corps of Engineers)*

*The tannin-dyed waters of Lower Tahquamenon Falls.*

northern forests, draining Michigan's largest swamp, and then sheets over a 200-foot-wide sandstone ledge into a fury of foam and bubbles 40 feet below. In his famous poem *Hiawatha,* Henry Wadsworth Longfellow described Hiawatha voyaging on the Tahquamenon: "And thus sailed by Hiawatha / Down the rushing Tahquamenaw / Sailed through all its bends and windings, / Sailed through all its deeps and shallows."

At Lower Falls, the river drops in cascades to circle an island accessible by paddleboats. The 40,000-acre Tahquamenon Falls State Park has campgrounds, hiking trails, fishing, cross-country skiing, and snowmobile trails *(906-492-3219).* The **Toonerville Trolley and Riverboat Tour** runs from Soo Junction to Upper Falls. *888-77-TRAIN.*

■ SENEY    *map page 243, F–2*

In the heyday of tall timber, Seney, at the junction of M-28 and M-77, was as wild as any Western cow town, with brawls in crowded saloons when lumberjacks came to their "Hell Town in the Pines." In *Call it North Country,* John Bartlow Martin

## BIG TWO-HEARTED RIVER

*T*he train went on up the track out of sight, around one of the hills of burnt timber. Nick sat down on the bundle of canvas and bedding the baggage man had pitched out of the door of the baggage car. There was no town, nothing but the rails and the burned-over country. The thirteen saloons that had lined the one street of Seney had not left a trace. The foundations of the Mansion House hotel stuck up above the ground. The stone was chipped and split by the fire. It was all that was left of the town of Seney. Even the surface had been burned off the ground.

Nick looked at the burned-over stretch of hillside, where he had expected to find the scattered houses of the town and then walked down the railroad track to the bridge over the river. The river was there. It swirled against the log spiles of the bridge. Nick looked down into the clear, brown water, colored from the pebbly bottom, and watched the trout keeping themselves steady in the current with wavering fins. As he watched them they changed their positions by quick angles, only to hold steady in the fast water again. Nick watched them a long time.

—Ernest Hemingway, *The Short Stories of Ernest Hemingway*, 1960

described the town's legendary ladies of pleasure. "Many of them chewed 'Peerless' [tobacco]. One was called Razorback; her peculiar forte, perfected at bagnio dances, was to waltz her partner near the door so the pimps could seize him and drag him outside and beat and rob him."

Seney is now a peaceful village, with the only evidence of its wild past the wooden 'Died fightin' markers in a half-forgotten cemetery on the north side of town. Hemingway aficionados alert: you can easily imagine what it must have been like here when, in the short story "Big Two-Hearted River," Nick Carter stepped off the train in a deserted, burned-out Seney and stood on the little bridge looking down at the trout swimming in the Fox before hiking on to the Big Two-Hearted River. *(See literary extract above.)*

Five miles south on M-77, in the Great Manistique Swamp, is the **Seney National Wildlife Refuge**, the largest contiguous national refuge in the United States. Within its maze of marshes, swamps, and forests can be found a treasure trove of rare and endangered bird and animal species, including bald eagles and timber wolves. There are hiking trails, canoeing, 80 miles of biking trails, and the seven-mile self-guided Marshland Wildlife Drive. In the evening, if you're lucky, you may hear wolves howling in the distance—unforgettable. *906-586-9851.*

For 25 miles across the Seney Stretch, Highway M-28, voted Michigan's dullest highway by readers of the *Detroit Free Press,* shoots straight and monotonous as a west Texas two-lane, but as it approaches Munising, M-28 enters another gorgeous portion of the U.P.

■ MUNISING    *map page 243, E–2*

Grand Island is the largest island on Lake Superior's south shore, standing guard at Munising's front door, protecting the town from the wrath of storms. Nowhere is Lake Superior more spectacular, but if you choose to venture forth, make certain that you understand her moods. It takes a brave soul to enter the water more than big-toe deep—the lake seldom comes within 40 degrees of body temperature, even on an August day. Despite clear waters that can lie as smooth as glass, and cool breezes that caress, at least 30 known shipwrecks are known to lie in the **Alger Underwater Preserve,** a favorite site for scuba divers, attesting to Superior's temperamental nature. The glass-bottomed **Shipwreck Tours** runs two-hour narrated cruises out to the shipwrecks, including the 150-foot wooden schooner *Bermuda,* which sank in 1870. *906-387-4477.*

◆ PICTURED ROCKS NATIONAL LAKESHORE    *map page 243, E–2*

The same Paul Bunyan–sized, frenzied ice-age sculptor who carved the shores of Michigan's peninsulas was particularly inspired when he created Pictured Rocks. Rising over 200 feet above Lake Superior, the Lakeshore extends about 15 miles, with the four-square-mile **Grand Sable Dunes** on the east end.

Among the picturesque formations and sites are "Miners Castle" and the 1874 **Au Sable Light Station.** The 300-foot-long Log Slide was used by lumbermen in the late 1800s to slide their logs down to Superior for rafting to market. Visitors enjoy running down the dunes, but remember: It's a joyous three minutes down and a grueling 30-minute climb back up. *Pictured Rocks National Lakeshore and Hiawatha National Forest Visitors Center, 400 E. Munising Ave.; 906-387-3700.*

**Pictured Rocks Cruises** makes two-hour boat trips along the painted cliffs, past more than a dozen weather-sculpted formations. In the fall, bluffs are topped with blazing autumn colors. *Off M-28; 906-387-2379.*

*Lake Superior Lighthouse in Marquette.*

■ MARQUETTE    *map page 242, D–2*

Marquette, the peninsula's largest city (pop. 22,000), makes a wide sweep along Lake Superior, with a fiery-red lighthouse announcing safe passage to the lower harbor. Some people see comparisons here to the Oregon coast, with its beaches, rocky cliffs, and blue waters that can brew ocean-type storms. Fine old brownstone buildings line Marquette's Washington Street and the historic East Ridge Street residential district, called "Big Bug Hill" in early days for the wealthier mining and lumbering barons, the "big bugs," who built the district's Victorian homes.

The campus of Northern Michigan University here includes a U.S. Olympic Education Center. Athletes from around the world attend the year-round training programs in 23 sports. In summer, it's not unusual to see cross-country skiers training on the backroads on roller-blade skis.

*(previous pages) The spectacular sweep of the Grand Sable Banks at Pictured Rocks National Lakeshore.*

UPPER PENINSULA

# ■ IRON MINING

State surveyor William Austin Burt found the first iron mountain in 1844 when his magnetic compass danced erratically near what is now Negaunee. He developed a solar compass to get around the problem, reported the iron discovery, and continued his work. Douglass Houghton, who headed the survey team that had set off the copper rush in the Keweenaw Peninsula three years earlier, did the same thing again, only this time the rush was for iron.

Once metals were discovered, miners arrived. They dug into the earth, shored up tunnels with heavy timbers, and followed the veins for miles with picks and blasting powder, toiling by the light of candles clamped to their tin hats. They came from all across Europe, first from the tin and copper mines of England's Cornwall district. Then came Norwegians, Swedes, Finns, Slovenians, Irish, Germans, and others, contributing to the ethnic mix of today. They were clannish, with their own churches, customs, baseball teams, holidays, and communities. Mines worked around the clock. Beds in crowded boardinghouses were never empty; as one miner rolled out, another rolled in.

From Cornwall, miners brought the tradition of the pasty (rhymes with "nasty," not "hasty," like another sort of pasty), the meat pie in a crust they carried underground in tin buckets. Pasties remain the area's "national dish," available at many shops, restaurants, and church suppers.

Information: *Marquette County Convention & Visitors Bureau, 2552 US-41 West, Suite 300, Marquette; 800-544-4321. Marquette Welcome Center, 2201 US-41 South, Marquette; 906-249-9066.*

At Negaunee, on the Carp River, stands the site of the Jackson Mining Company's forge, where iron was first wrought in Michigan. Now the **Michigan Iron**

*Cargo trains deliver iron ore to Marquette's docks in this 1860s photo. (Michigan State Archives)*

**Industry Museum,** it features hands-on, interactive displays that guide us through the history of iron mining in the U.P. *73 Forge Rd., Negaunee; 906-475-7857.*

At the **Marquette County Historical Museum,** Burt's solar compass is displayed, invented after his magnetic compass failed in the presence of iron. *213 N. Front St., Marquette; 906-226-3571.*

■ SKIING

In the snowy, hilly U.P., ski resorts abound: Marquette Mountain at Marquette, Indianhead at Wakefield, Powderhorn at Bessemer, Porcupine Mountains at Ontonagon, Mont Ripley at Hancock, Norway Mountain at Norway, and ski jumps at Suicide Hill in Negaunee and Pine Mountain at Iron Mountain.

At Ishpeming, the **U.S. National Ski Hall of Fame and Museum** follows skiing history from its birth on the iron ore tailings of Ishpeming and Negaunee, where European immigrants made skis from barrel staves, to the early developed ski runs down the taller hills, and eventually to the peninsula's ski resorts. *skihall.com; US-41 West at Second St. in Ishpeming; 906-485-6323.*

*(above) A team of competitors in Marquette's Up Zoo Sled Dog Race greet their fans.*
*(opposite) Cross-country skiing at Al Quaal Recreation Area in Ishpeming.*

*In 1956, fire destroyed the weatherbeaten shaft house of the Quincy Mine, one of the region's premier copper mines in the late-19th and early-20th centuries. (Michigan State Archives)*

■ KEWEENAW PENINSULA    *map page 242, C–1*

Call it Copper Country: The 100-mile-long crook of land that curves into Lake Superior at Michigan's northernmost point is a land apart for more reasons than geography. Bony ridges give way to lakes, streams, waterfalls, hills that burn with autumn colors, and in winter the dancing rays of the aurora borealis. The mining towns have all but disappeared, with garden flowers gone wild and mine shaft houses crumbling around heaps of rusting machinery near piles of leftover copper ore. The abandoned mine shafts have become winter homes for hundreds of thousands of hibernating bats, and the many shafts are being fitted to protect their winter habitats.

◆ COPPER'S HISTORY

Shallow mining pits at Isle Royale, the Keweenaw Peninsula, and Ontonagon River date back at least 3,000 years to the Old Copper Indians, credited as the first people to work with metals in the Western Hemisphere. Pits were less than six feet deep and about twice that wide. The copper, some of the purest in the world, lay close to the surface. Prehistoric Michigan copper has been found as far east as New York and as far south as Kentucky, demonstrating that a widespread trading network connected these early Indian groups.

Although French explorers of the 1600s knew about the copper, it was ignored until state geologist Douglass Houghton submitted his report of its presence to the legislature in 1841. Ransom Shelden, one of the first promoters, advertised the Keweenaw in words not found in any dictionary, describing it as a "veritable Ophir of delitescent, metalliferous treasure."

How one of the world's richest mines was discovered is a matter of some debate. Old timers say that a man named Billy Royal was standing in a dusty road in front of his bar near Calumet when along came a man named Ed Hulbert. Billy's pigs had escaped their pens, and Hulbert offered to join the search. Following a faint squealing sound, they found the pigs trying to scramble out of a 12-foot-deep ancient mining pit. In their scrambling and snorting around the bottom of the pit,

*Copper bars are rolled out of the smelter of the Calumet & Hecla mine. (Underwood Photo Archives, San Francisco)*

## CORNISH PASTIES

*Miners' wives made these portable savory pastries for their husbands to take into the mines,*

| Crust: | Filling: |
|---|---|
| 1⅓ c. flour | ⅓ c. each, diced; potatoes, turnips, carrots |
| ½ tablespoon salt | 1 medium onion, diced |
| ⅓ c. lard or shortening | 2 T minced parsley |
| ⅓ c. cold water | 1 lb. boneless beef, cubed |
| | salt and pepper to season |

*where eating quarters were cramped at best.*
Sift together the flour and salt. Cut in the shortening, and add water a little at a time, just enough to moisten. Mix and knead lightly (do not overwork); then divide the dough into two parts. Roll each into a 9-inch circle.

Mix the filling ingredients and season with salt and pepper. Put half of filling on each pastry circle. *A pat of butter set on top of the filling adds richness and flavor (optional).* Moisten edges of dough with water and fold in half to enclose filling. Crimp edges to seal. Bake at 375° for 45–60 minutes. Serve with chutney. *Makes two pasties.*

the pigs had uncovered a 20-ton nugget of conglomerate copper ore, thus launching the Calumet & Hecla mine at Calumet.

In copper's heyday, men sank vertical shafts two miles deep and bored two thousand miles of horizontal tunnels to produce 95 percent of the nation's copper. The last copper mine closed in the 1980s.

***Information:** Keweenaw Tourism Council, 56638 Calumet Ave.; 800-338-7982.*

■ HOUGHTON    *map page 242, C–1*

The twin cities of Houghton (named for Michigan's first state geologist Douglass Houghton) and Hancock (named for John Hancock) perch on 500-foot hills above the Portage Canal. Houghton is home to **Michigan Technological University,** while Hancock is home to **Suomi College.** The **Quincy Mine Hoist,** in Hancock, offers underground tours of a fascinating old copper mine. *US-41 at top of Quincy Hill; 906-482-3101.*

Headquarters for the 45-mile-long Isle Royale National Park are located in Houghton as is one of the ferries that commutes to the island. *(See following page.)*

*Stunning fall colors on Highway 41 north of Hancock.*

■ ISLE ROYALE NATIONAL PARK   *map opposite*

Isle Royale is a roadless wilderness island and is the best place I know to read the bones of the earth. Isle Royale's stone spine is 1.2 billion years old; the whole park and its 200 attendant islands lie in the same direction, with parallel striations and upheavals.

Isle Royale boasts the largest island in a lake on an island in a lake—that's Ryan Island in Siskiwit Lake on Isle Royale in Lake Superior. Around Rock Harbor, like other parts of the island, the terrain is rocky with low shrubs, spruce, fir, cedar, and mixed northern hardwood. Wave-stained boulders covered with orange lichen line coves and bays. There is evidence here and there of failed mining operations in the late 1800s, such as the small cemetery all but hidden under the trees where a few crosses encrusted with an inch of moss mark the graves of forgotten residents.

In summer, Isle Royale is a mass of wildflowers and you may very well encounter a moose as you take an afternoon stroll. In fact, with the island's large moose population, it's hard *not* to see a few. The famous Isle Royale wolves are a different story. Given their wild nature and their fear of humans, they can sometimes be heard, but rarely seen. *(See essay, page 266-267)*

Rock Harbor Lodge runs daily tours. My favorites include the **Edisen Fishery** for a visit with the interpreter-fisherman and a short walk through the woods to tour the **Rock Harbor Lighthouse.**

◆ HISTORY AND LEGENDS OF ISLE ROYALE

Approaching Rock Harbor on the ferry from Copper Harbor, the first visible sign of the island is long, spiny Greenstone Ridge, which runs its length and towers over the hundreds of timbered islands, boulders, and ledges scattered offshore. After swinging through the channel at Rock Harbor Lighthouse, the ferry enters the still waters of the seven-mile-long Rock Harbor. To the right is Mott Island, park headquarters and docking point for the ferry from Hougton, the island where former *voyageur* Charlie Mott and his tall Chippewa bride, Angelique, were dropped off by copper speculators in the summer of 1845. Promising that they would return before winter, the prospectors hired the Motts to protect their find on the deserted island until they could make a run back to Sault Ste. Marie for supplies. The supplies of a few beans, rancid butter that turned white like lard,

# GETTING AROUND ISLE ROYALE

## ◆ ACCESS

**Ferry, seaplane, or private boat:** *Reservations and permits are required.*

MV *Ranger III.* 165 feet, 125 passengers, six hours. Leaves from Houghton; *906-482-0984.*

MV *Isle Royale Queen III.* 81 feet, 100 passengers, four hours. Leaves from Copper Harbor; *906-289-4437.*

Isle Royale Seaplanes. *906 482-8850.*

**Marina for transient boaters** is at Rock Harbor's north end, where ferries dock.

## ◆ ACCOMMODATIONS

**Rock Harbor Lodge.** Offers cabins and motel-type lodging tucked into the forest and along the lakeshore. *Rock Harbor Lodge: in summer, 906-337-4993; in winter, 270-773-2191.*

**Camping.** Isle Royale has 36 official campgrounds, one of which is next to Rock Harbor, connecting with 165 miles of trails. Reservations and permits are mandatory. Camping is "leave no trace:" No trash left behind, no fires, no pets. Most park facilities are open from mid-May to mid-September, including Rock Harbor Lodge.

**Things to remember:** Temperatures seldom top 80 degrees F. Bring jackets and gloves, even in August.

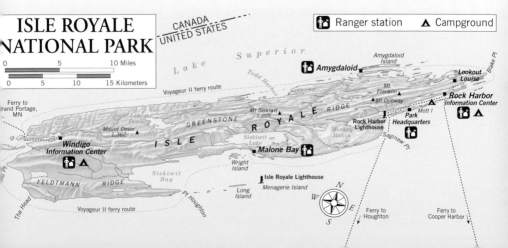

# THE WOLVES OF ISLE ROYALE

*A small slice of the Pleistocene—the interplay of wolf and moose—endures on Isle Royale. On this stage an ancient drama re-enacts itself every year, and though much the same from one eon to the next, the script itself is filled with subtlety, each character finding his or her place in an ecological morality play—the endless cycling of life and death. Dr. Rolf Peterson has spent a lifetime studying this drama.*

The most famous inhabitants of Isle Royale are of the four-legged variety, especially the gangly moose, largest member of the deer family, and its predator, the gray wolf. The population swings of these animals spawn an annual scientific trek to the island in the dead of winter, when this national park is closed and its wildlife can be truly wild, outside any limits set by humans. As a member of that winter study crew for the past 30 years, I am always excited to learn "How many wolves? How many moose?"—a question of interest to the general public and scientists alike. Initially, as a graduate student in wildlife ecology and now, as project director, I have been grateful for the privilege of studying these fascinating creatures. The goal of wolf-moose research on Isle Royale was, in the beginning, to understand the effect of wolves on an isolated moose population but has now expanded to study the importance of wolves to the entire island ecosystem, including beaver and the tree species eaten by moose and beaver. Also, DNA fingerprinting has shown us that the island's wolves are highly inbred, so I am eager to learn how long the wolves can survive, isolated from other wolves.

Wolves and moose are both relatively recent arrivals to Isle Royale, the moose arriving in the early 1900s (they are strong swimmers) and the wolves following in the late 1940s. Before wolves came to the island, the moose population fluctuated in a boom-and-bust pattern that jeopardized the trees and other plants that moose need to survive. When they arrived, wolves not only killed the sick, very old and young moose but also eliminated coyotes (and thereby made life easier for red foxes), trimmed the beaver population, and safeguarded the island's forests. The landscape of the island is largely determined by, on average, just a couple dozen wolves. While the wolf population is small and indeed heavily inbred, the number of wolves per square mile is among the highest in the world. Likewise, moose density is some five times higher than on the Ontario shore, some 20 miles distant, where moose must deal with bears and human hunters as well as wolves.

The balance between predator and prey, however, is far from constant. Both fluctuate at an interval of about 20 years, with peaks and crashes in moose followed about a decade later by similar trends in wolves. It is the characteristic pattern of wolves killing primarily calves and old moose that sets up these patterns. It goes something like this—when wolves are scarce, more moose calves survive, fueling a moose population increase that leads to abundant old-age moose, the bread and butter in a wolf's diet, a decade later. With more food available, wolves then increase and make inroads on moose calf survival, ultimately reducing the moose population. And so it goes—when moose are increasing wolves are down, and vice versa. In the past 40 years, moose have ranged between 500 and 2,000 animals, while wolf numbers have been as low as 12 and as high as 50.

It is easy to understand the high vulnerability of young moose, relatively small and inexperienced. But old moose usually fall victim to wolves only after they begin to suffer a variety of ailments familiar to humans—bad teeth, osteoporosis, and arthritis. There is even a wolf tapeworm that has as part of its life cycle a cyst that gradually accumulates in the lungs of each moose on Isle Royale, eventually reducing its lung capacity and increasing the likelihood that the moose will fall victim to wolves, thereby completing a critical stage of the tapeworm life cycle. While wolves limit the moose population, the wolves themselves are controlled by food abundance. When lean times prevail, fewer pups are born, their survival may be poor, and real estate among the packs is rearranged. In the late 1990s, for example, one of the three wolf packs on Isle Royale faced dwindling moose numbers and expanded into the territory of a neighboring pack. It was a case of 12 wolves against the home pack of only two wolves, so the takeover seemed uncontested. In other cases, wolves are killed by other wolves in skirmishes that can ultimately be traced to inadequate food. In this way, the numbers of this top carnivore are effectively adjusted to the food resources that support it.

For much of the late 20th century the only wolves in Michigan were those on Isle Royale. Now, wolf populations are recovering in northern Wisconsin and Upper Michigan and can be found throughout the northern part of Minnesota. Finding success on Isle Royale, and greater public acceptance, the wolf promises to add new excitement to wildlands throughout the Upper Great Lakes.

—Rolf O. Peterson, Michigan Technological University, 12 July 2000

(following pages) A view from Lookout Louise: the Canadian shoreline is visible in the distance

and a bit of salt and flour were soon spent, snow was falling, and still the prospectors did not return. Charlie starved to death, and Angelique pulled hairs from her head to weave a snare to catch a rabbit now and then. Eventually, she built a lean-to with fallen limbs nearby, moved her fire, and left Charlie in the cabin so she would no longer be tempted to eat him. The prospectors returned on the spring wind, but Angelique never forgave them. Her story is well documented in newspapers of that time. For the rest of her years, nightmares often wakened her at night as she screamed, "I did not eat Charlie!"

Scandinavian fishermen discovered the island's bountiful fishery in the late 1800s. The island reminded them of their homeland, and they brought their families here. It was a rough yet idyllic life where men fished and women gathered greenstones from the beaches to sell each spring when the agent from Tiffany's in New York circled the island on the Booth Fisheries boat. Everybody moved back to the mainland in winter, either to Wisconsin or Minnesota, both of which are closer than Michigan.

The big cruise boats of the early 1900s found the island a tour destination. They sailed up and down the long finger peninsulas to enjoy the rugged beauty of boulder-strewn cliffs and moss-covered ridges, and anchored offshore near one of the small resorts.

Then, in 1931, the National Park Service claimed Isle Royale. All the fisheries were claimed and homeowners were allowed to retain their homes until that generation died or moved away. Most are gone now, and I find it a sad thing to visit the few remaining homesteads, with their sagging roofs and vanished memories. But in the yard beside the door there is almost always a clump of roses or lilacs that bloom in spring. Congress established the park in 1940 and it was dedicated in 1946. Presently the park service is proposing the removal of all support services, for a wilderness island to be left to nature.

■ CALUMET    *map page 242, C–1*

The village of Calumet is a study in sandstone—its 1900 **Opera House and Calumet Theater** (the only place where John Philip Sousa played twice) are particularly excellent examples of its use. In fact, the entire five-block downtown area is part of the **Keweenaw National Historic Park**. The park consists of 12 "cooperating" sites strung along the peninsula from Ontonagon to Copper Harbor that tell the story of copper mining in the Upper Peninsula.

*Calumet is Michigan's snowiest town. In the days before snowplows, the snow had to be hauled off the streets and out of town in sleighs. (Michigan State Archives).*

"The park is more than technology," explained a ranger, referring to the mining equipment. "It is miners who lived and sometimes died here, women who made and kept their families going, children who played in the streets, slapping mosquitoes, dodging the wagons and sometimes going underground to work beside the men."

# ■ SNOWMOBILE COUNTRY

North of Mohawk, Keweenaw County's snow gauge annually records huge snow-falls, with a record 390.4 inches (over 32 feet) for the winter of 1978–79. In Michigan, lots of snow means lots of snowmobiles, and networks of groomed trails are spread like highways, complete with trail signs throughout northern Michigan. In fact, these trails connect with other trails across the snow country all the way to Alaska.

Back when vehicles moved slower and groomed trails were a thing of the future, the ability to ride above three and four feet of powder was as heady as champagne, opening up hills and valleys previously sealed off with snow from all except snow-shoers and cross-country skiers with their limits of distance. Sure, the engine was loud but with the rush of wind past my ears, the cold nipping at my cheeks, and the friends riding alongside me, I hardly noticed. I loved crossing frozen lakes in the moonlight, packing a picnic lunch to spread below a frozen waterfall, going on safari where we drove all day and gathered around a roaring fire at night in some remote lodge.

Snowmobiling can be dangerous. Nearly 40 snowmobilers died in Michigan last season, with most deaths attributed to alcohol and recklessness.

# ■ COPPER HARBOR    *map page 242, D–1*

The drive along M-41 up the Keweenaw Peninsula wends its way through almost forgotten mining communities, crosses sparkling streams and cuts through deep forests. The peninsula is glorious in September, when autumn colors erupt in red, orange, and gold. There is a wonderful view from atop 700-foot Brockway Mountain of the vast stretch of Superior and the village of Copper Harbor, with the white barracks of Fort Wilkins toy-like in the distance. *(Take Brockway Mountain Drive from Copper Harbor for the 9.5-mile drive to the top of the mountain.)*

In 1844, after copper mining began, the U.S. Army built Fort Wilkins and sent in soldiers, ostensibly to protect the miners from the Indians. But the only people from whom the miners needed protection were themselves. On payday, they flocked to the bars to let off steam, became rowdy, and inevitably found reason to take great umbrage with one another. Now **Fort Wilkins State Park,** the stockade with its 18 buildings (12 are original) was restored in the 1930s by the Work Projects Administration. *906-289-4215.*

◆ PORCUPINE MOUNTAINS WILDERNESS STATE PARK    *map page 242, A–1*

From the rocky escarpment 600 feet above it, the long finger of Lake of the Clouds stretches teal-blue against the multi green forest that carpets the mountains. There are many jewels in this 70,000-acre park. For instance, follow the park trail to the Carp River mouth where a short walk leads to a low, rocky ledge that stretches into Superior. If you rise early enough, you are treated to a special show: sunrise over the Queen of the Great Lakes. *412 South Boundary Rd., Ontonagon; 906-885-5275.*

◆ FAYETTE STATE HISTORICAL PARK    *map page 243, E-3*

A sandstone bluff rises above Lake Michigan's Snail Shell Harbor, with overlooks of a green hillside dotted with 19 weathered structures—the ghost town of Fayette. From 1867 to 1891, charcoal pig iron was manufactured here. The townsite, including a company store, hotel, and kilns, is part of Fayette State Historical Park. *Turn off US-2 at Garden Corners; continue south for 17 miles; 906-644-2603.*

*The kilns at Fayette State Park.*

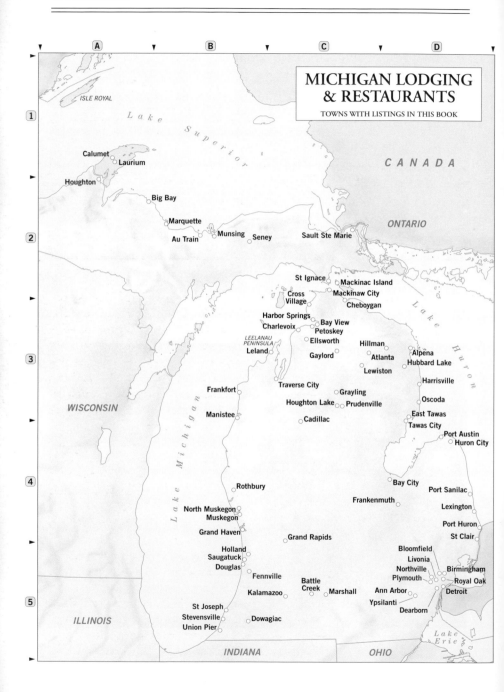

A  B  C  D

1

# MICHIGAN LODGING & RESTAURANTS

TOWNS WITH LISTINGS IN THIS BOOK

ISLE ROYAL

Lake Superior

CANADA

Calumet
Laurium

Houghton

Big Bay

Marquette

Au Train
Munsing  Seney

Sault Ste Marie

ONTARIO

2

St Ignace  Mackinac Island
Cross Village  Mackinaw City
Cheboygan

Harbor Springs
Charlevoix  Bay View
Petoskey

LEELANAU PENINSULA  Ellsworth  Hillman
Leland  Gaylord  Atlanta  Alpena
Hubbard Lake

Lewiston

Harrisville

Frankfort  Traverse City  Grayling
Houghton Lake  Prudenville  Oscoda

Manistee  Cadillac  East Tawas
Tawas City

Port Austin
Huron City

WISCONSIN

Lake Michigan

Lake Huron

3

Rothbury  Bay City  Port Sanilac

Frankenmuth  Lexington

North Muskegon
Muskegon

Grand Haven  Grand Rapids  Port Huron
St Clair

Holland  Bloomfield
Saugatuck  Livonia
Douglas  Fennville  Northville  Birmingham
Plymouth  Royal Oak
Battle Creek  Marshall  Ann Arbor  Detroit
Kalamazoo  Ypsilanti

St Joseph  Dearborn
Stevensville  Dowagiac
Union Pier

ILLINOIS

4

5

INDIANA  OHIO

Lake Erie

# L O D G I N G &
# R E S T A U R A N T S

⊟ *Lodging Rates:*
*per night, one room, double occupancy*
$ = under $80; $$ = $80–130; $$$ = $130–200; $$$$ = over $200

✕ *Restaurant Prices:*
*average dinner entrée*
$ = under $10; $$ = $10–17; $$$ = $17–25; $$$$ = over $25

### Alpena    *map page 274, D-3*

⊟ **Waters Edge.** 1000 State Ave. (US-23); 517-354-5495 $
This small motel is one of the few in the city directly on Thunder Bay. There are 11 rooms, five with kitchenettes and all with coffeemakers, cable TV, phone, small refrigerator, and air conditioning. Each has two double beds. Outside, there's a wide beach on Lake Huron's Thunder Bay.

*WATERS EDGE*

✕ **John A. Lau Saloon & Steakhouse.** 414 N. Second Ave.; 517-354-6898 $$–$$$
Want steak? This is the place to come in Alpena. Named for the original 19th-century owner of the watering hole that survived two devastating fires, this historic saloon is famed for serving slab-sided cuts of American beef at its finest. There's a decidedly masculine atmosphere, with dark wood paneling and tables to hold up its huge, eclectic menu while guests peruse wall photos of Alpena's beginnings. Choices range from a basic like soup in a bread bowl with the eatery's signature fruit and nut salad featuring dried Michigan cherries atop crumbled blue cheese and nuts.

For your main course, try the 20-ounce porterhouse. Other cuts available include sirloin and Kansas City steak, plus prime rib on Fridays and Saturdays. Fresh-fish lovers are soothed, too, with baked whitefish, pan-fried perch, and even farm-raised bluegill. Pizzas and burgers are offered, and its location (next to the Thunder Bay Theater, Alpena's professional playhouse) makes it perfect for a pre- or post-show bite.

LODGING & RESTAURANTS

## Ann Arbor  *map page 274, D-5*

▣ **The Artful Lodger.** *artlodger.com;* 1547 Washtenaw Ave.; 734-769-0653 $–$$
Just four guest rooms and a house full of cool theater memorabilia. Breakfast and private baths, of course.

*THE ARTFUL LODGER*

▣ **Bed & Breakfast on Campus.** 921 E. Huron; 734-994-9100 $–$$
On the edge of campus, right off State Street, the Bed & Breakfast on Campus nestles four rooms into a unique chalet-style building.

▣ **Bell Tower Hotel.** *belltowerhotel.com;* 300 S. Thayer St.; 734-769-3010 or 800-562-3559 $$$
A seeming world of its own in the midst of the U-M campus, the Bell Tower is elegantly restored and appointed.

▣ **Campus Inn.** 615 E. Huron;
✕ 734-769-2200 or 800-666-8693 $$–$$$
One of Ann Arbor's finest, the 200+ guest rooms in this inn and conference center uniformly guarantee a good night's sleep—and excellent access to both downtown and

campus. **Victors** *(734-769-2282)* does fine renditions of classic beef, seafood, and chicken dishes, with an occasional surprise. Open for breakfast, lunch, and dinner.

▣ **Embassy Hotel.** 200 E. Huron; 734-662-7100 $
Downtown. Inexpensive. Most rooms with a microwave and mini-fridge. It's the Embassy, and it'll outlive us all.

▣ **First Street Garden Inn.** *firststreetgardeninn.com;* 549 S. First St.; 734-741-9786 $–$$
A nifty little—and we do mean little—B&B just southwest of the Main Street area. Homey, comfortable, and low-key. Highly recommended, so call early.

▣ **Vitosha Guest Haus.** 1917 Washtenaw Ave.; 734-741-4969 $–$$
Ten rooms with private baths in an 80-year-old Swiss-chalet home, including continental breakfast and afternoon tea.

*VITOSHA GUEST HAUS*

✕ **Amadeus Café & Patisserie.** 122 E. Washington St.; 734-665-8767 $
Amadeus features authentic central European–style dinners. Highly recommended.

✕ **Amer's.** 300 S. Main St.; 734-668-1500 $

This "Mediterranean deli" will set you up with New York kosher-style sandwiches, Italian coffees, and other international flavors, not to mention pastries. If you're lucky, you might even grab a sidewalk table.

✕ **Bagel Factory & Deli.** 1306 S. University Ave.; 734-663-3345 $

Forget that this is the home office of Shaky Jake. For breakfast, lunch, and dinner, good fast food makes this place a favorite of nearby students.

✕ **BD's Mongolian Barbeque.** *bdsmongolianbarbeque.com;* 200 S. Main St.; 734-913-0999 $

Pick your own polyglot of meats, seafoods, cut vegetables, and spices, then have it stir-fried to your specifications. It's a tricky idea and can be fun. Long waits for a table can be a minus.

✕ **Bird Feeder.** *thebirdofparadise.com;* 207 S. Ashley St.; 734-662-8310 $

The clear attraction here is the location— inside the top-line Bird of Paradise jazz club. But don't let that stop you. The food is better than most bar food, much of it quite good.

✕ **Blimpie's Subs and Salads.** *blimpie.com;* 115 E. Liberty St.; 734-741-2567 $

Good, quick subs and salads. Open until midnight. Any other questions?

✕ **The Brown Jug.** 1204 S. University Ave.; 734-761-3355 $

A South U. hangout for over 60 years, The Brown Jug gives students, profs, and locals homemade cooking at hard-to-beat prices. From sandwiches to specials, this place is all right.

✕ **Café Felix.** 204 S. Main St.; 734-662-8650 $

Coffee and cappuccino, accompanied by light sandwiches, soups, and pastries. Watch for the tapas specials.

✕ **Café Zola Crepe and Coffee Bar.** 112 W. Washington St.; 734-769-2020 $

Plenty of room here to nurse a caffe latte. And if you're dining, Café Zola offers unique veggie omelets, crepes with a multitude of fillings, and generous sandwiches.

✕ **Dominick's.** 812 S. Monroe St.; 734-662-5414 $

Relaxing outdoor seating mixes with sublime sangria for a fine experience.

✕ **The Earle.** *theearle.com;* 121 W. Washington St.; 734-994-0211 $–$$

Considered by many to be Ann Arbor's most romantic restaurant, the award-winning Earle is dark and cozy—with an inventive rotating French and Italian menu.

✕ **Escoffier.** 300 S. Thayer St.; 734-995-3800 $$

Honored year after year, the Escoffier blends classic and contemporary French with continental cuisine—and some of the area's best wines. Serving dinner in the elegant Bell Tower Hotel, it remains one of Ann Arbor's finest restaurants.

✕ **Fleetwood Diner.** 300 S. Ashley St.; 734-995-5502 $

An A² institution, the Fleetwood is always open. At this classic diner, you're never quite sure who you'll see or what short-order specialty they'll be having. The wall-to-wall conversation is free and itself worth the price of admission.

✕ **Gypsy Café.** 214 N. Fourth Ave.; 734-994-3940 $

Gypsy Café is more than just a coffeehouse with some good sandwiches. Live music on weekends and some week nights, along with poetry, performance art, original art on the walls, AA meetings, and writers' forums, make Gypsy Café atypical—and engaging—every time you enter.

✕ **Le Dog.** 410 E. Liberty St.; 734-665-2114 $

These are some damn good hot dogs, even when they compete with the surprising roast duck. An unusual and fun place for lunch—and, since they open late and close early, only for lunch. $

✕ **The Original Cottage Inn.** *cottageinn.com;* 512 E. William St.; 734-663-3379 $

Ann Arborites take this pizza joint to heart. The deep-dish is measured in fathoms, the thin-crust in micrometers. Expect good pizza and a boisterous atmosphere.

✕ **Park Avenue Café.** 211 S. State; 734-665-9535 $

Heart-healthy. Good for what ails you.

✕ **Red Hawk Bar & Grill.** 316 S. State St.; 734-994-4004 $

The locals love the sandwiches here. A better-than-average selection of microbrews doesn't hurt.

✕ **Thano's Lamplighter.** 421 E. Liberty; 734-996-0555 $

The world is blasting past Thano's, and that's all right. This Italian/Greek place will put an excellent pizza or moussaka in front of you, minus the lights, noise, and fanfare of newer, more happening places. Thanks, Thano.

✕ **Sweet Lorraine's Café and Bar.** *sweetlorraines.com;* 303 Detroit St.; 734-665-0700 $

Friendly and relaxed, Sweet Lorraine's is a good spot to relax on the outdoor patio and enjoy a warm day. From signature pecan chicken to sandwiches and salads, the food's excellent; order a merlot to go with dinner.

✕ **Zanzibar.** *ameritech.net/users/zanzibar;* 216 S. State St., 734-994-7777 $

The chefs take culinary risks at this place, and some are bound to work better than others. But if you love new and different dining, there may be no better place in Ann Arbor to find it.

✕ **Zingerman's Delicatessen & Zingerman's Next Door.** *zingermans.com;* 303 Detroit St.; 734-665-0700 $

One-of-a-kind in these parts, legendary Zingerman's brings New York City to the shores of the Huron River. The sandwiches are stacked high and the place is never empty. This is not fast food.

## Battle Creek
*map page 274, C-5*

▦ **Greencrest Manor.** *greencrestmanor.com;*
6174 Halbert Rd.; 616-962-8633
$$–$$$$
This romantic French Normandy 1935 mansion on the highest elevation of St. Marys Lake, about five miles north of downtown, is constructed of sandstone, slate, and copper. Eight rooms are decorated in French style by innkeepers Kathy and Tom VanDaff, with double, king, and queen beds. Explore the 20-acre grounds with formal gardens that include fountains and stone urns. Breakfast includes fresh fruit, cereal (this is Battle Creek, remember) breads and coffee, and juice.

*GREENCREST MANOR*

▦ **McCamly Plaza Hotel.**
50 Capital Ave. SW; 616-963-7050 or 888-622-2659 $$$
There are 242 rooms in 16 stories, with an indoor pool and exercise room. All rooms have irons and ironing boards and free cable TV.

✕ **Clara's on the River.** *claras.com;*
44 N. McCamly; 616-963-0966 $
In a former train station along the Kalamazoo River, the menu has a wide variety of offerings. My favorite is the chicken Caesar salad.

## Bay City   *map page 274, D-4*

✕ **Krzysiak's House Restaurant.**
1605 Michigan Ave., southeast side of town; 517-894-5531 $
This restaurant has been feeding Bay City's Polish roots proudly for 20 years. Before that, it was a Polish neighborhood bar. Polka up the entrance ramp to Polish music emanating from outside speakers. Then turn right through the small store that sells Polish beer, breads, and other items. Dining room is decorated with murals depicting the old country. Prices are cheaper than cheap. The all-you-can-eat buffet includes sausage in kraut, chicken, vegetables, ham, salad, and dessert. Menu items are just as inexpensive. Polish platters feature *pierogi* (stuffed dumplings), *golabki* (cabbage rolls), and homemade kraut and sausage. Steaks also are on the menu, including Delmonico and strip.

✕ **Terry & Jerry's O Sole Mio Restaurant.**
1005 Saginaw St. (downtown); 517-893-3496 $$
Arguably one of the state's best Italian restaurants. On offer are calamari pasta, cannelloni, and, for meat lovers, steaks. Fun, homey atmosphere.

## Birmingham/Bloomfield
*map page 274, D-5*

▦ **Hamilton Hotel.**
35270 Woodward Ave., Birmingham;
800-334-8086 $$$
This well-kept hotel on the northern outskirts of downtown Birmingham has 64 rooms and a fitness center. Stays include an extensive breakfast buffet including fruit, eggs, juice, and cereals.

▦ **Townsend Hotel.** 100 Townsend St.,
Birmingham; 248-646-7300 $$$$
Birmingham's premier hotel with a distinct European atmosphere. There are 87 rooms in four stories, and afternoon tea is served in the lobby.

*TOWNSEND HOTEL*

✕ **Big Rock Chop & Brew House.**
245 S. Eton St., Birmingham;
248-647-7774 $$$
Located in the former Birmingham passenger train station, the restaurant brews its own beers and offers steak, lamb chops, and fish, plus gourmet pizzas.

✕ **Forte.** 201 S. Old Woodward Ave.,
Birmingham; 248-594-7300 $$$
In the heart of downtown Birmingham, this restaurant specializes in northern Italian food, including pasta with seafood.

## Cadillac  *map page 274, C-3*

▦ **Herman's European Café & Inn.**
✕ 214 N. Mitchell; 231-775-9563 $$–$$$
Austrian-born owner-chef Hermann Suhs has brought a touch of Europe to this quiet, romantic restaurant that's a mixture of a French bistro and Austrian gasthof. It's very continental, with exposed brick walls, pressed tin ceiling, and mauve tones. There are both booths and tables. Suhs's eclectic menu reflects his travels and his homeland, including apple wood-smoked pork loin with potato dumplings. Traditionally in Europe, wild game such as pheasant, venison, or reindeer is served in the fall, and Suhs does so here, too. Suhs also runs the deli and bakery next door, which serves breakfast, and next to that, the wine and butcher shop. Upstairs there's a seven-room hotel furnished in country style with lots of natural wood, high ceilings, and private baths. There is a handicapped-accessible room. Continental breakfast is served in all rooms.

▦ **McGuire's Resort & Conference Center.**
7880 Mackinaw Trail; 231-775-9947
$$$
Perched atop one of the highest hills overlooking the Manistee National Forest and Lakes Cadillac and Mitchell, McGuire's has been a fixture in many families' vacation plans for both summer and winter for more

than 30 years. Several buildings spread out from the lobby contain 12 rooms with whirlpools. Visitors may reach the sauna, whirlpool, and indoor pool through an enclosed walkway. In winter, there is snowmobiling and lighted cross-country skiing, while golfers take over in summer to play 27 holes.

*MC GUIRE'S RESORT*

## Calumet/Laurium   *map page 274, A-1*

*LAURIUM MANOR INN*

⊞ **Laurium Manor Inn.** 320 Tamarack St.,
✕ 906-337-2549 $–$$$
Neoclassical 1908 mansion with pillared

wraparound porch and balcony, 10 guest rooms, 1,300-square-foot ballroom, library, and gilded elephant hide and leather wall coverings. Furnished in period antiques. Two dining rooms with full breakfast. On the National Register of Historic Places.

## Charlevoix   *map page 274, C-3*

⊞ **Weathervane Terrace Inn & Suites.**
*weathervane-chx.com;*
111 Pine River Lane, just off US-31 at the bridge; 231-547-9955 $$
From a distance, it looks like a castle. Stone turrets pop up like mushroom caps at this 68-room city landmark on a hill on the north side of the Pine River channel. Oversized rooms come in three versions, including ones with a patio. All include a small refrigerator, microwave, VCR, hair dryer, irons, and cable TV. There are two rooms with whirlpool tubs and one-bedroom suites with a fireplace and kitchenette. Relax in the hot tub or the outdoor pool surrounded by stonework. Breakfast is included with the room.

✕ **Rowe Inn.** *roweinn.com;* 231-588-7351 $$$
With a dining room captained by Wes Westhoven and chef Todd Veenstra, the Rowe is located in former a 1940s fast-food restaurant. The menu changes weekly, with prices a bit more earthly. Entrées may include such delights as rainbow trout with shrimp stuffing, or chicken and portobello crepes with mushroom crème. Morel mushroom dishes are a specialty. Desserts might include delicate white chocolate brownies.

LODGING & RESTAURANTS

✕ **Stafford's Weathervane Restaurant.** 106 Pine River Lane at the US-31 bridge; 231-547-4311 $$$

Sharing the name but not the ownership with the inn up the hill, the restaurant is under the tutelage of Stafford Smith, who also operates Stafford's Bay View Inn *(see Petoskey)*. Sailboats headed to and from Lake Charlevoix and ships like the *Beaver Islander,* which ferries goods and tourists to that Lake Michigan island, bring a constantly changing panorama for dining. Be here for the Venetian Night parade in mid-July when colorfully lit boats fill the Pine River channel. There's a decidedly nautical theme in the decor, and the menu reflects that and the waterfront location. The planked whitefish is baked on an oak plank and served with plank-baked duchess mashed potatoes. Weathervane bay scallops sautéed in garlic and sherry are presented over tricolor pasta.

✕ **Tapawingo.** 9502 Lake St., Ellsworth; 231-588-7971 $$$

Just south of Charlevoix and at the northern tip of Ellsworth Lake, the tiny town of Ellsworth holds one of the best restaurants in the Midwest. Chef-owner Harlan "Pete" Peterson's spot is generally booked months in advance. The food, the ambiance of the rambling country home, and the bright, simple dining room with windows nearly floor to ceiling are all worth checking out. Summer lunch is served on the patio.

Recent dishes on the daily-changing menu have included roasted parsnip and apple soup, and sautéed lemon sole with seared sea scallops, Israeli saffron couscous, and sautéed spinach in a red pepper coulis.

Desserts include wonders like molten chocolate, a warm chocolate mousse cake with a molten bittersweet chocolate center, served with vanilla ice cream and blood orange sauce. Wonderful.

✕ **Whitneys of Charlevoix.** 305 Bridge St.; 231-547-0818 $$

One of the region's best places to enjoy a summery evening. All three floors offer views of Round Lake (part of Lake Charlevoix). On top is an open-air deck with an awning to protect diners from the weather. The nautical decor—sailboat cloths on the tables, and old boats built in below the high tin ceiling in both bar areas. The restaurant is famed for its seafood, including oysters; Maryland crab cakes made with blue back-fin crab; and shrimp and scallops in a spicy marinara served over spinach fettuccini.

## Cheboygan  *map page 274, C-2*

▣ **The Gables.** *mich-web.com/gablesbb;* ✕ 314 S. Main St.; 231-627-5079 $$$

Kenneth and Annetta Coates run this restored, comfortable multi-peaked Victorian inn. Complimentary desserts—cakes, pies, and various berry treats—are served each evening on the wraparound porch, in the fireplace room, or in the parlor. There's also an eight-person hot tub in the Queen Anne gazebo. Kenneth, who has run several fine kichens, prepares the food and will even make dinner by arrangement. The six guest rooms at this 5,600-square-foot, 1890s former lumber-baron home include one with a private bath, two with half-baths, and the rest with shared facilities. Guest robes in each room. Parking in the back.

☖ **Hack-Ma-Tack Inn.** 8131 Beebe Rd.;
✗ 231-625-2919 $$$
Moored beside the Cheboygan River and the east end of Mullett Lake, this century-old log lodge was built as a fishing and hunting retreat by Watson Beebe. *Hack-Ma-Tack* is Native American for tamarack, and lots of tamarack went into the lodge's construction, says Mike Redding, whose family has owned the inn for the last two decades. Stroll through the dining room and read the local Native American legends inscribed on ceiling beams; check out the various display cases as well as two canoes and two rowing skulls which hang from the ceiling. House specialties include the Lake Huron whitefish almondine, and prime rib that's been roasted then lightly char-grilled, imparting a unique, smoky flavor. Six spartan rooms are also available for rent.

✗ **The Boathouse.** 106 Pine St.;
231-627-4316 $$
Watch the water and boats go by on the inland waterway downtown and enjoy the summery evenings Michigan's north country is famous for. Originally built as a vacation house with an attached boat garage, local old-timers like to tell about the 1920s and '30s, when it housed one of northern Michigan's principal whiskey distributors and was controlled by Detroit's infamous Purple Gang. In the 1980s, it became a restaurant. Look up at the windows overlooking the Cheboygan River/waterway, and you'll notice the original boat hoists and the foundations for the boathouse doors. Instead of watching rum-runners with a fresh shipment from Canada, these days diners can watch as pleasure boaters tie

up outside. The restaurant is known for Lake Huron walleye sautéed in honey and sprinkled with pecans, and breast of duck drizzled with cherries Jubilee sauce.

## Cross Village *map page 274, C-2*

✗ **Leg's Inn.** *Mid-May to mid-October.*
6425 Lake Shore Dr.; 231-526-2281
$–$$
The family-owned inn on a bluff overlooking Lake Michigan has been a traditional stop for tourists on the Tunnel of Trees Highway (M-119) since 1921. The stone house was named for the row of inverted white cast-iron stove legs along the roof ledges. Inside are log walls and an eccentric mix of tables and chairs handmade from tree trunks and twisted limbs. Indoor and outdoor dining in summer. The full-service menu features Polish dishes such as a plate of golabki, pierogi, kielbasa, and sauerkraut.

## Dearborn *map page 274, D-5*

☖ **Dearborn Bed & Breakfast.**
*laketolake.com/dearborn/index.htm;*
22331 Morley, West Dearborn;
313-563-2200 $$$
Four guest rooms in this 1927 brick house built in 1927, which is listed on the Michigan Register of Historic Places and located in west Dearborn, close to shops, museums, and fine dining. Nancy Siwik and Rick Harder have furnished the one suite and all four rooms (three with private baths) in Victorian Renaissance antiques. Guests enjoy down comforters, fine lace and linens in a romantic, relaxing atmosphere.

⊡ **Dearborn Inn.** 20301 Oakwood Blvd.;
✗ 313-271-2700 $$$$
Built in the 1930s by Henry Ford to house visitors and to serve his airport across Oakwood Blvd. (now part of a Ford vehicle test area), the hotel has 222 rooms, with some rooms within five replicas of homes owned by famous Americans. Two restaurants, heated pool, and tennis courts.

⊡ **Hyatt Regency Dearborn.**
✗ Michigan Ave. and M-39;
  313-593-1234 $$$$
This all-glass-sided, 13-story hotel is opposite Ford World Headquarters. Its 772 recently renovated well-appointed rooms bend around an open atrium. Pool, sauna, whirlpool, and two restaurants.

✗ **Big Fish.** 700 Town Center Dr., on the
  south edge of Fairlane Town Center
  mall; 313-336-6350 $$
One of the region's best seafood restaurants. Entrees include whole fish, and pasta with shrimp, scallops, and chunks of salmon surrounded by mussels in a light garlic sauce over homemade linguine. Can be noisy.

✗ **La Pita.** 22435 Michigan Ave. in West
  Dearborn; 313-565-5115 $$
Dearborn's Middle Eastern influence is apparent in the crop of good, inexpensive restaurants that have been opened in recent years. Combination plates of lamb, dolmas, shish kebab, and hummus with flat bread prevail. Good fresh fruit puree drinks also.

✗ **Mati's On Monroe.** 1842 Monroe;
  313-277-3253 $
Housed in a former service station, this deli stacks some of the best sandwiches on the

planet. Try the Ellen's—corned beef, cole slaw, and Swiss on rye. Finish off with carrot cake or a cream cheese brownie.

**Detroit** *map page 274, D-5*

*Here are just a few of the restaurants in a city described as having some of the best choices of dining styles in the nation.*

⊡ **Atheneum Suite Hotel.** 1000 Brush St.;
✗ 313-962-2323 $$$$
The anchor of Greektown, this 10-story hotel has 174 rooms, including some suites and 160 two-bedroom units. Restaurants on premises include the highly regarded **Fishbone's Rhythm Kitchen Café,** *313-965-4600.*

⊡ **Courtyard by Marriott.**
  333 E. Jefferson Ave. (opposite the
  Renaissance Center); 313-222-7700 $$
Comfortable 21-story downtown hotel: 250 rooms, heated pool, health club, and tennis courts. It also has a People Mover stop and a covered walk to the RenCen.

⊡ **Detroit Marriott Renaissance Center.**
✗ In the Renaissance Center;
  313-568-8000 $$$$
The pièce de resistance of the RenCen, this 73-story hotel has 1,342 rooms overlooking the Detroit River and downtown. Restaurants in the hotel include the 70th-floor **Summit.** More are in the RenCen. The hotel also has an exercise area.

✗ **Hockeytown Café.** *secondcity.com;*
  2301 Woodward Ave. (downtown);
  313-965-9500 $$
The bright, neon-lit cafe shares its location

with Second City Detroit comedy theater, and has Detroit Red Wings hockey memorabilia on display. Menu items include risotto crab cakes, grilled pork chops, and salmon in tomato-thyme barley. Outdoor dining on the upper levels.

✗ **Opus One.** 565 E. Larned St.;
   313-961-7766 $$$$
Generally considered one of the best restaurants in the city. Seasonally changing menu lists chef Tim Giznsky's imaginative, beautifully presented American regional dishes. Extensive wine list.

✗ **The Rattlesnake Club.** 300 River Pl. at
   Joseph Campau, in Rivertown district;
   313-567-4400 $$$$
With chef Jimmy Schmidt in charge, this windowed dining room in a renovated warehouse offers great meals served with flair in a sophisticated setting. The menu might include perch sautéed with citrus, capers, sweet peppers, and thyme. The wine list is superb.

✗ **Traffic Jam & Snug.** *traffic-jam.com;*
   511 W. Canfield just south of the
   Cultural Center and Wayne State Univ.;
   313-831-9470 $$
College students rub elbows with professors and professionals here. The menu stretches from vegetarian to turkey Reubens. Beer brewed in-house.

**Dowagiac** *map page 274, B-5*

✗ **Wicks Apple House.**
   52281 Indian Lake Rd., 8 miles northwest of Dowagiac; 616-782-7306 $
Enjoy a taste of Michigan on a 120-year-

old farm market and restaurant. The market, open for 50 years, sells fresh produce, jams, jellies, preserves, local honey, and maple syrup. The bakery makes all five varieties of pies from local fruit and a family recipe. Fresh apple bread and apple cake sell in fall. Watch on weekends as the cider mill presses "apple squeezin's." A gift shop sells holiday merchandise and items for the home. The Orchard View Room is in a garden setting. Everything is made fresh. Sandwiches use house-made breads, and the menu includes soups, quiche, and salads. Specialty is "the monster," a grilled Reuben the size of two regular sandwiches.

**Frankenmuth** *map page 274, D-4*

⊡ **Drury Inn.** 260 S. Main St.; 517-652-
   6881 $$
This modern, 78-room motel in the heart of downtown is accessible to everything. Indoor pool and complimentary breakfast.

*FRANKENMUTH BAVARIAN INN LODGE*

⊡ **Frankenmuth Bavarian Inn Lodge.**
✗ One Covered Bridge Lane;
   517-652-7200 $$$
This 354-room hotel is the city's largest and

one of the most popular for families to stay. A family fun center offers five indoor pools, three whirlpools, 18-hole indoor mini-golf course, jogging trails, and exercise area, with tennis courts and two restaurants.

☷ **Zehnder's Bavarian Haus.**
   1365 S. Main St.; 517-652-6144 $$
Located away from the crowds just south of downtown are these 137 rooms to choose from in a quiet setting, along with indoor and outdoor pools, exercise room, and breakfast nook *(see picture next page)*.

✕ **Bavarian Inn Restaurant.** 713 S. Main;
   800-228-2742 $$
First, stand outside to watch a 35-bell German glockenspiel tell the story of the Pied Piper of Hamelin. Then, head in to eat. Save the all-you-can-eat chicken for across the street and try German dishes instead, like the kasseler rippchen (smoked pork loin) or the sauerbraten (tender, spicy marinated beef).

✕ **Zehnder's Restaurant.** *zehnders.com;*
   730 S. Main; 800-863-7999 $$
It's America's largest family restaurant, and the menu is also huge, but most folks chow down on its famous family-style, all-you-can-eat chicken dinners with all the fixin's —fresh German stollen, stuffing, potatoes, giblet gravy, and ice cream. Order a sample of fried chicken livers too: you'll be hooked.

**Frankfort**   *map page 274, B-3*

☷ **Harbor Lights Motel and Condos.**
   *mlive.com/stayhere/focusharborlights.html;*
   15 Second St.; 800-346-9614 $$$

Located on 400 feet of Lake Michigan beach are 120 units, including 48 one-, two-, and three-bedroom condominiums, some with two-person whirlpools. All have full kitchens and decks overlooking the lake. Rooms are air-conditioned and have satellite television and free HBO. Rent by the week in July and August.

☷ **Knollwood Inn.**
   *laketolake/ knollwood/index.htm;*
   219 Leelanau Ave.; 231-352-4008 $$
Al and Irene Rice host guests in this turreted Victorian beauty. Four antique-filled guest rooms have private baths and queen beds. Breakfast served by candlelight in the formal dining room. There's also a two-bedroom carriage house rented by the week. Sleeping Bear Dunes is close by; Traverse City is about 45 minutes away.

**Gaylord**   *map page 274, C-3*

☷ **Treetops Resort.** *treetops.com;* on
   Wilkinson Rd., east of downtown. Follow the signs along M-32; 517-732-6711 or 888-treetops $$
One of northern Michigan's best four-season resorts. It's so named because it sits atop a hill outside Gaylord looking over the Pigeon River valley, home of Michigan's wild elk herd. There are 254 rooms, suites, condos, and homes, along with two restaurants, two pools, sauna, and fitness center. Summer brings over 81 holes of designer golf on courses by Robert Trent Jones Sr., Tom Fazio, and Rick Smith. In winter, enjoy downhill and cross-country skiing.

✕ **Sugar Bowl.** 216 W. Main St., Marsh Ridge; 517-732-5524 **$$**
Tucked amid a cluster of businesses downtown, this eatery is easy to miss, but don't. Opened in 1919 by the family who runs it today, it's among the oldest such restaurants in Michigan. If visiting during morel season (usually in May), be sure to ask if those prized mushrooms arc on the menu. Great breakfasts. Steak and fish specials at lunch and dinner; children's menu available.

### Grand Haven
*map page 274, B-4*

🛏 **Best Western Beacon Inn.** 1525 S. Beacon Blvd. (US-31), 1.5 miles from the beach; 616-842-4720 or 800-528-1234 **$$$**
New property with 107 rooms, indoor pool with whirlpool; whirlpool in some rooms.

🛏 **Grand Harbor Resort & Yacht Club.** ✕ 940 W. Savidge, Spring Lake, two miles from beach; 616-846-1000 **$$$**
Long a fixture of the Grand Haven scene, the resort features 121 rooms, indoor and outdoor pools, exercise area, whirlpool, sauna, and a restaurant.

🛏 **Lakeshore B&B.** *bbonline.com/mi/lakeshore;* 11001 Lakeshore Dr., West Olive, on the beach; 616-844-2697 or 800-342-6736 **$$$$**
Three rooms are open to guests at this 1935 4,500-square-foot mansion, with 275 feet of Lake Michigan beach out its front patio. Rooms are named after former Presidents for good reason: Locks of hair from Washington, Lincoln, and Kennedy; the Bible on which Harry Truman took the Oath of Office; and other Presidential memorabilia are on display. A beach bungalow is available as is a guest house (rented by the week). Dan and Jackie Hansen are innkeepers.

✕ **Bil-Mar Supper Club.** *grandhaven.com/ bil-mar;* 1223 Harbor Ave.; 616-842-5920 **$$**
Watch from the deck as sailboats and 600-foot freighters alike arrive at Grand Haven's harbor to dine at this restaurant, which has stood here since the 1950s. Specialties include fish in a bag, salmon baked in parchment, scallops, and vegetarian items. The deck, with umbrella-shaded tables, offers simpler fare such as good burgers, including a veggie burger.

✕ **Porto Bello.** 41 Washington St.; 616-1221 **$$**
A popular Italian eatery in downtown's Harbourfront Place shopping area.

### Grand Rapids
*map page 274, C-4*

🛏 **Amway Grand Plaza Hotel.** ✕ *amwaygrand.com;* 187 Monroe NW in downtown; 616-774-2000 or 800-253-3590 **$$$$**
Next to the Grand River, a wonderful marriage of the former Pantlind Hotel and a 30-story glass-exterior tower, adding up to 682 rooms. The high-ceilinged former Pantlind offers the elegance of a grand old hotel; in the west wing, modern rooms look out over city attractions across the river. Heated pool, saunas, whirlpool, racquetball and squash courts, tennis courts, three restaurants. **The 1913 Room** is a classy hotel

restaurant in period decor with an elegant menu and prices to match. Try the duck confit. The only must-have dessert is the Forbidden Apple, a mocha ice cream confection wrapped in a sugar coating colored to look just like an apple. Worth the price..

▦ **Fountain Hill B&B.**
  *fountainhillbandb. com;*
  222 Fountain NE; 800-261-6621 $$
A beautiful Italianate home built in 1874 in the historic Heritage Hill home district with four guest rooms, cable TV with video library access, down comforters, feather beds, and a full breakfast with breads, yogurts, and entrée. Sally Coburn is the host.

▦ **Peaches B&B.** *peaches-inn.com;*
  29 Gay Ave. SE; 866-732-2437 $$
This brick Georgian home was built in the Heritage Hill district in 1916. The living room is spacious and breakfasts are special, with fruit, breads, and gourmet entrees. Five guest rooms with four baths on the second floor; each room has down comforters, TV, and telephone. Exercise and TV room downstairs. Firenzi the dalmation is sweet and well-trained.

*PEACHES B&B*

✕ **Big Buck Brewery and Steakhouse.**
  2500 28th St. SE; 616-954-9635 $$$
Steaks and plenty of 'em, along with good house-brewed beers, top the menu of this large restaurant with an outdoor theme.

✕ **BD's Mongolian Barbecue.**
  2619 28th St. SE; 616-957-7500 $$
A fun restaurant. Choose from the selection of various meats and vegetables and hand them to one of the cooks, who'll sear it in a giant wok. Various recommended combinations are posted for the unsure.

✕ **The B.O.B. Restaurants.** *thebob.com;*
  20 Monroe Ave. NW (downtown); 616-356-2000 $$
Standing for "Big Old Building," the B.O.B. is a four-level entertainment and dining extravaganza. Four restaurants, a nightclub/comedy showcase, and a brewpub offer everything from steaks to comedy.

✕ **Pal's Diner.** 6503 28th St. SE.; 616-942-7257 $
An old-time refurbished diner once more hosts the hungry for solid American comfort food, from burgers to meat loaf.

## Grayling   *map page 274, C-3*

▦ **Gates Au Sable Lodge.** *gateslodge.com;*
  Stephan Bridge Rd.; 517-348-8462 $$
Lovers of rivers, especially trout streams, and those who like to fall asleep indoors to the sounds of the outdoors, head here: 16 rooms on what many consider the best trout stream east of the Mississippi give you fly fishing right outside your door. Owner Cal "Rusty" Gates manages a well-stocked

fly shop next to the small restaurant run by his wife, Julie. If you're not an angler, sit in the swinging chair and let the sounds of the river lull you to sleep.

⊡ **Hanson House B&B.**
*laketolake.com/ hanson/index.htm;*
604 Peninsula; 517-348-6630 $$
Mrs. Margarethe Hanson (the namesake of Lake Margarethe), wife of lumber baron Rasmus Hanson, wouldn't move from her home in Manistee to the wilds of Grayling unless her husband built her a "proper home." She moved to the complete Hanson house in 1883. At 6,500 square feet, it's a picture of Victorian elegance. There are seven bedrooms, and guests can choose from four, all furnished in period furniture including antiques original to the home.

Explore the library, with its 12-foot ceilings, original stained glass, and thick hand-made oak doors. In the hall, the original hand-painted murals depict scenes of Denmark, Hanson's birth country. Innkeepers David and Jill Wyman will take you into the rathskeller, a true "gentlemen's room" with dark wood and lumber camp murals, where, it's said, many a lumber deal was struck over brandy and cigars. Take breakfast—usually fruit, juice, muffins, perhaps crepes or French toast—in the large dining room. The Wymans also own the Icehouse quilt shop in town.

✕ **Patty's Town House.**
Business I-75 near the Holiday Inn;
517-348-4331 $$–$$$
This A-frame-style restaurant is one of the town's favorite spots. Steaks and seafood predominate the dinner menu, and other items for breakfast and lunch.

✕ **Stevens Family Circle.**
231 N Michigan Ave.; 517 348 2111 $
The soda fountain in this former drugstore is presided over by Russ Stevens, patriarch of the family running the show. Pull up a stool or slide into a booth and prepare to be wowed by old-fashioned sodas, creamy malteds, and even phosphates that could be ranked as gourmet by any ice cream aficionado. The sandwiches coming off the grill aren't bad, either.

## Harbor Springs
*map page 274, C-3*

⊡ **Kimberly Country Estate.**
2287 Bester Rd.; 231-526-7646 $$$$
This Colonial plantation style house with wide sweeping lawns is adjacent to Wequetonsing Golf Course. Back verandas with view of the swimming pool; six guest rooms. Deluxe buffet breakfast.

✕ **Juilleret's.** *May through December*
130 State St.; 231-526-2821 $–$$
A family restaurant since 1906, this seat-yourself eatery has a casual atmosphere, linoleum floor, tin ceiling, and paper napkins and placemats. Planked whitefish with duchess potatoes is the house specialty. The ice cream parlor boasts the first soda fountain in northern Michigan; it's famous for its all home-made Thunder Cloud and Velvet Sundaes.

✕ **Stafford's Pier Restaurant.** 102 Bay St.;
231-526-6201 $–$$$$
At this waterfront restaurant, diners dress as

formally or as casually as they choose. Waiters in tuxedos serve in the elite Pointer Room, while the Charts Room downstairs is casual; a nautical theme runs throughout the restaurant. Catch views of the yacht harbor and Little Traverse Bay from either room. A la carte menu featuring fresh fish.

## Harrisville  *map page 274, D-3*

⌑ **Alcona Beach Motel.**
   700 N. Lake Huron Shore Dr.;
   517-724-5471 $$
Owner Barbara Berl's great great grandfather—a farmer and the area's first justice of the peace—homesteaded the 56 acres surrounding this cozy six-unit motel in 1873. Berl's grandmother and brother built it in the mid-1950s, making sure it was a half-mile from the highway noise of US-23. Each room sleeps four and has a refrigerator, stove, and cable TV, but no telephone. Pets are allowed. Stroll the footpaths and logging roads through the lush pine, cedar, and maple forest on the property, or along the quarter-mile of Lake Huron beachfront. Room rental is a three-night minimum.

⌑ **Churchill Pointe Inn.**
✕ 5700 Bennett Rd., Hubbard Lake;
   517-727-2020 $$
Some inns are former homes, but this one, built in 1926, has always been an inn. The summery, neatly trimmed, blue-and-white-wood-frame building is nestled in the trees on the east side of a large lake and faces the its south end. Sharon and Donald Geib have looked after it since 1994.

There are eight rooms and one apart-ment. The apartment has a full kitchen and wood stove. Other rooms are decorated in country style and have private baths and cable TV. Natural cedar paneling lends a woodsy feel to the interior common rooms. Guests seeking some of the lake's walleye and panfish can dock boats on the grounds. Good swimming but no beach. Make reservations for the dining room on weekends. Nightly rate includes full breakfast for two.

Enjoy views of Hubbard Lake through windows on three sides of the **Churchill Pointe Inn Dining Room.** This 150-seat eatery is a great spot to experience northern Michigan. Pictures on the walls show the inn in the 1920s. Lake Huron whitefish, walleye, perch, seafood, steaks, and prime rib are always on the menu. If the weather cooperates, ask to sit on the outside deck.

⌑ **Widow's Watch B&B.** 401 Lake St.;
   517-724-5465 $$
In 1990, Bill and Becky Olson took over Widow's Watch, named after the room that used to be on top of this Victorian home built by lumber baron George Caldwell in 1866. The watch proved too heavy and was moved to the ground close to 100 years ago, where it remains. Four guest rooms are furnished with a variety of antiques. Sit on the wraparound porch and watch the salmon charter boats moor up in the harbor; enjoy breakfasts of pancakes or quiche; go fishing (the Olsons can book local charters); head for the beach before a movie at the Alco Theater (named for Alcona County); or go antiquing. The harbor antique show is held in early July; a wine and food festival featuring local restaurants takes

place in mid-July. Concerts are held at the harbor on Wednesday nights in summer.

X **Fieldstone's.** 676 N. Huron Rd. (US-23); 517-724-6338 $$
Named after the fieldstone fireplace, this venerable restaurant has served travelers since 1950 or so and specializes in German and European-style meals with occasional twists. Good bets are the wiener schnitzel, rouladen, Harrisville crabgrass, and the fettuccini (topped with fresh spinach, crabmeat, and parmesan cheese sauce). Children's menu available.

## Hillman    *map page 274, D-3*

⊡ **Garland Resort.** *garlandusa.com;*
X County Road 489, Lewiston, 12 miles north from M-72; 800-968-0042
$$–$$$
Luxury in the north country. Garland is the only four-diamond resort in the state, and it earns its reputation with outstanding lodging, dining, and services year-round. Turn off County Road 489 into a fairyland of lights. Pull up in front of the largest log lodge east of the Mississippi and enter the heavy twin wooden doors, and a woodsy, European hunting lodge feel envelops you.

Garland features 182 lodge rooms, 84 log cabin–style units from one to three bedrooms, and 16 two-bedroom villas on a lake or in the woods. There are 72 holes of golf, a big-game hunting club, outdoor hot tub, and a small indoor pool on the main lodge's lower level; cross-country skiing and snowmobiling, too. It doesn't get much better. Special winter weekend packages include one of Garland's romantic Zhivago Nights: a sleigh ride through the woods, followed by a gourmet dinner and live music in a hunting lodge on the property.

At **Herman's,** Garland's excellent restaurant, the hunting lodge theme continues with big-game trophies hung on the log walls. Wild game—pheasant, salmon, and trout or venison—is a specialty, as are locally picked morel mushrooms in season. Enjoy the view of the golf course or, in winter, of Nordic skiers gliding by. Be sure to take home a jar of Shelly's preserves—yum!

*THUNDER BAY GOLF RESORT*

⊡ **Thunder Bay Golf Resort.**
X *thunderbaygolf.com;* 27800 M-32, 22 miles west of Alpena; 800-729-9375
$$–$$$
In summer, Jack Matthias's resort in the woods just east of Hillman hosts cartsful of golfers. In winter, cross-country skiers come to ski the 12 km of trails on the course and along the Thunder Bay River, which flows on the northern edge of the fairways. Sleep in luxury condo lodging in villas near the restaurant or in log cabin chalets dotting the course, which can be split into smaller

rooms or set up for large groups (up to 12).

Also drawing thousands of visitors in snowy months are sleigh ride tours, which include a delicious dinner of classic American food. Sign up for this unique trip and you'll be carried over snow and across the river to a 150-acre preserve of tangled primeval forest, where a herd of elk roam. The sleigh rambles over several trails cut into the woods to view these magnificent creatures weighing up to 1,000 pounds. Matthias used to take guests to view part of Michigan's wild elk herd—the largest east of the Mississippi River—but concerns over feeding them ended that, so he built his own sanctuary.

Warm up before the fireplace at the **Elkhorn Cabin**, where dinner—five courses with an entree of crown roast of pork—simmers over wood cookstoves under the eye of wife Jan Matthias. Then hop into the sleigh for more elk-viewing on the trip back to the resort.

*ELKHORN CABIN*

**Holland** *map page 274, B-4*

☵ **Blue Mill Inn.** 409 US-31;
616-392-7073 $
A good, inexpensive stopover; 81 rooms.

☵ **Bonnie's Parsonage.** 6 E. 24th St.
(at Central Ave.); 616-396-1316 $$$
Bonnie McVoy–Verwys has turned this white-sided 1908 home into a quiet neighborhood inn. Relax on the glassed-in front porch. Two rooms with private baths. Morning begins with a gourmet breakfast.

*BONNIE'S PARSONAGE*

✕ **Backstreet Restaurant & Brew Pub.**
Between 6th and 7th off River Ave.;
616-394-4200 $$
Holland's only microbrewery pub. Menu items from pizza and pastas to prime rib.

✕ **The Piper.** 2225 South Shore Dr.,
Macatawa, along Lake Macatawa;
616-335-5866 $$
A contemporary restaurant with a nautical theme, with pastas and wood-fired pizzas as specialties.

✕ **Queen's Inn Restaurant.**
*dutchvillage.com/dvqueens.htm;*
12350 James St.; 616-393-0310 or
800-285-7177 $$
Billed as Holland's only authentic Dutch restaurant: old-country Dutch food as well as American favorites.

## Houghton   *map page 274, A-2*

▦ **Best Western-Franklin Square Inn.**
✕ 820 Shelden Ave.; 906-487-1700 $–$$
Seven-story, 104-room hotel with balcony
suites, spa, whirlpool, indoor pool, sauna.
The **Northern Lights** dining room offers
panoramic views of the city and hills.

*CHARLESTON HOUSE HISTORIC INN*

▦ **Charleston House Historic Inn.**
110 Shelden Ave.; 906-482-7790 or
800-482-7404 $$ $$$$
Two-story early 1900s Georgian house with
pillared double verandas and wicker chairs.
Four guest rooms, period furnishings, large
library with fireplace, extensive woodwork,
stained leaded-glass windows. Full breakfast
or breakfast-in-a-basket at your door.

## Houghton Lake
*map page 274, C-3*

*Looking for a cottage? Consult a map, available from local chambers of commerce. Some of the best places to stay here are on the lake's north side. Nearby Higgins Lake has some great lodgings, but they are harder to find and not widely advertised. Searching them out, however, can be well worth your time.*

✕ **Brass Lantern.** 729 Houghton Lake Dr.
(M-55), Prudenville; 517-366-8312 $$
A rustic, paneled "up north" atmosphere
envelops this restaurant across the road
from Michigan's largest inland lake. Steaks
and seafood for lunch and dinner.

✕ **Coyles Restaurant.** 9074 Old US-27,
On Houghton Lake's western shore;
517-422-3812 $
A pleasant, unassuming restaurant; good
for an inexpensive family breakfast, lunch,
or dinner. Lunch and dinner entrées include crab and frog legs as well as beef.

## Huron City   *map page 274, D-4*

▦ **Stafford House B&B.** 4489 Main St.
(M-25), Port Hope; 517-428-4554 $$
After a day on the road, relax in this de-
lightfully restored 1886 frame home with
four rooms (full or queen beds), a third of a
mile from Lake Huron. Woodwork is origi-
nal. Sit by the marble fireplace to enjoy a
complimentary evening dessert. Full break-
fast served. Borrow a bicycle to explore
nearby lighthouses, or take in a historic
walking tour. Owners Kathy and Greg
Gephart are happy to help you.

## Kalamazoo   *map page 274, C-5*

▦ **Radisson Plaza Hotel.**
✕ 100 W. Michigan Ave. (downtown);
616-343-3333 $$$
Well-appointed nine-story, 280-room hotel
attached to a shopping mall. Health club,
heated pool, whirlpool. **Webster's** restaurant is surprisingly good: large wine list and
entrées (such as seafood) hard to find in this
part of Michigan. *(See picture next page.)*

LODGING & RESTAURANTS

*RADISSON PLAZA HOTEL*

## Leelanau Peninsula
*map page 274, B-3*

*Between the sweeping orchard valleys of the Leelanau Peninsula lie literally scores of finger- and oval-shaped lakes, and nearly every one will have some sort of resort accommodations nestled along its shores. If you're searching for a cottage, check out the larger waters such as Glen Lake, Lake Leelanau, and Silver Lake, but don't ignore the smaller waters.*

▣ **Centennial Inn B&B.**
*laketolake.com/ centennial/index.htm;*
7251 E. Alpers Rd.; 231-271-6460 $$
Snuggle into the quilt on the four-poster bed in one of three rooms. In the morning, wake to the sound of a fire crackling in the country kitchen wood stove or the parlor fireplace in this restored 1865 centennial farm (a state award given to farms that have been in the same family 100 years). Owners Karl and JoAnne Smith serve a full breakfast of juice, fruit, and omelets or pancakes or French toast, locally made sausage, and muffins in the cozy dining room. Biking and Nordic ski trails just outside your door.

▣ **Manitou Manor B&B.**
*bbhost.com: 8008/manitoumanorbb/;*
147 Manitou Tr., 2.5 miles south of Leland; 231-256-7712 $$$
Bordered by century-old willows and accented by fruit trees and blue spruce, Manitou Manor is a former farmhouse, built in 1873 and added on to several times. The lodge has catered to vacationers since 1900 or so, when they arrived by steamer.

Explore the expansive lawn, rose garden, perennials, and maples or sunbathe on a deck on the house's west side. On spring evenings, watch for fawns romping in the orchard. The dining room, where guests enjoy a five-course breakfast, has country accents with maple hutches and windows on three sides. The living room features a granite fireplace, oak planking, and lots of Americana, from Native American baskets to carved birds and decoys. Rooms are done in country style; queen beds with quilts, some with lace canopies.

✕ **The Cove.** 111 River St., Leland; 231-256-9834 $$
In Michigan's north country, at least one whitefish meal is a must, and this restaurant specializes in it. Located beside the river and just upstream from the historic Leland Fishtown area, enjoy a window or patio table and the great views of Lake Michigan and the Manitou Islands in the distance. After an appetizer of seafood chowder, take your pick from several preparations, such as garlic parmesan, macadamia nut, or campfire whitefish—baked and served with key lime dressing and garnished with red and green peppers.

✕ **Hattie's.** *hatties.com;* 111 St. Joseph (M-22); 231-271-6222 $$$
Owner-chef Jim Milliman creates unique dishes in this former storefront seating 78 for dinner. Furnished in soft blues and grays, white tablecloths, wood accents, and opaque windows. The display of works by Michigan artists changes every two months. Popular menu items include sautéed lobster medallions with roasted red pepper butter sauce, and sautéed mushroom ravioli with locally picked morels. Wine list contains 180 labels. Early-bird dinner discounts.

## Mackinac Island
*map page 274, C-2*

*For a full list of other lodgings and restaurants along with other information on the island, visit www.mackinac.com.*

🛏 **Bay View Bed & Breakfast.** *mackinacbayview.com;* a short walk from downtown at Harborside; 906-847-3295 $$$
Stay in a famous Victorian, also the island's only B&B directly on the water. Built in 1891 for the Armour family, the house retains its Victorian charm. Guest rooms feature period furnishings, air conditioning, private bath, and phones. Three have TV and VCR (free movie library), private bath, and phones; three suites feature in-room whirlpools.

Enjoy the views over afternoon cookies and lemonade on the large second floor deck. Breakfast might include quiche, fresh-baked muffins, fruit, cereal and the inn's own coffee blend.

*GRAND HOTEL*

🛏 ✕ **Grand Hotel.** *grandhotel.com,* On a shelf of the island's main hill, a short ride from the ferry docks; 800-33-GRAND $$$$
First-time overnighters on the island can't do better than to stay at the Grand (a very inexpensive Grand Hotel. Festive decor shows the touch of New York interior designer Carleton Varney. Awake each morning by the clip clop of horse's hooves as carriages come and go. Enjoy cocktails and spectacular views in the cupola lounge. Swim in the kidney-shaped Esther Williams pool and relax in a rocking chaise on the 660-foot-long front porch. Rates include three meals. Do not, repeat, *do not* pass up the buffet lunch. Top off a five-course dinner with the Grand's famed pecan ice cream ball (coat and tie required for dinner). Afterwards, dance to a live orchestra.

▦ **Island House.** *theislandhouse.com*
✕ Lakeshore Dr., overlooking the harbor;
800-626-6304 $$$–$$$$.
Enjoy one of 97 rooms at the island's oldest Victorian hotel, built in 1852. Rooms range from modest to deluxe, with ceiling to floor windows looking onto the harbor. Three suites feature whirlpools; also an indoor pool and whirlpool. Relax on the porch overlooking the yacht harbor or dine indoors on dishes such as salmon with artichokes, or filet with stuffed scampi.

ISLAND HOUSE

▦ **Mission Point Resort.** *missionpoint.com*;
✕ One Lakeshore Dr., east of downtown;
906-847-3312 or 800-833-7711 $$$$
One of the few accommodations on the island to stay open in winter, the resort reflects has a northern Michigan lodge–style decor in its 242 rooms and 92 suites. Feather beds, cable TV, coffee makers and hair dryers. A few deluxe rooms also feature hot tubs. The heated outdoor pool is open in summer; also two hot tubs, a "kids' club" day care for 4- to 10-year-old guests, and a theater; bicycles and in-line skates available for rental. Four restaurants and a health club and spa. Children 18 and under stay free when sharing room with an adult.

CLOGHAUN

▦ **Cloghaun.** *cloghaun.com*
On Market Street, a block from the ferry docks; 888- 442-5929 $$$
Cloghaun is Gaelic for "stony ground," a perfect name for this clapboard bed and breakfast atop the island's rocky bluff. Built by an Irish immigrant fishing family in 1884, the inn is one of the island's oldest homes. Its 11 rooms are furnished in period antiques. The common library has a TV and VCR. Take afternoon tea in the sitting room or swing on the wide front porch. Breakfast in the dining room includes fresh coffee cake, muffins, fruit salad, oatmeal bagels, and other breads.

✕ **The French Outpost.**
On the west side of downtown at the foot of the Grand Hotel;
906-847-3772 $$
Dine outside or beside the stone fireplace in one of the island's most popular casual spots. Start with bread topped with pesto, parmesan, and goat cheese. Popular dinner entrées are a whitefish sautéed in capers, with baby corn, dried cherries, and citrus glaze. The Great Laker is an Asian-spiced salmon cake topped with house-made mustard and served on a sourdough roll with cucumber salad. Menu changes seasonally.

✕ **Pub Oyster Bar.** Across from the Arnold Line ferry dock; 906-847-3454 $$
Dark woods pervade the interior of this popular and intimate downtown eatery. The renovated interior retains much of the original decor; notably the pressed-tin ceiling and 120-year-old mirrored bar. Try the tournedos of beef tenderloin with potato gnocchi, or a chicken sandwich with Brie, honey mustard, apple butter, tomato, and lettuce on a whole-grain baguette. Gulf oysters are served on the half-shell with a citrus cocktail sauce. Seasonal menu.

✕ **The Woods.** About 1.2 miles from the Grand Hotel, near the Inn at Stonecliffe; 906-847-3331 $$–$$$
Owned by Grand Hotel, this restaurant is done in interior designer Carleton Varney's bright colors. Specializing in wild game and Bavarian dishes, the kitchen is also noted for six extremely creative appetizers, including martini of lobster with marinated rice noodles in a vodka glaze. Entrées include crispy lobster tail with seaweed salad, drawn butter, and spicy peanut sauce; venison loin with chestnut mashed potatoes in a wild berry demiglaze; and wiener schnitzel with red cabbage and celery root–potato salad. Get there via the shuttle carriage from Grand Hotel or from the Arnold Line ferry dock downtown.

✕ **Pink Pony.** Chippewa Hotel, One Main St., downtown; 906-847-3343 $
One of two establishments where islanders frequent, this restaurant specializes in light fare, from burgers to chicken.

**Mackinaw City**
*map page 274, C-2*

⌂ **The Beach House.** 1035 S. Huron St. (south on US-23); 616-436-5353 $$–$$$
This cabin resort, with a sand beach and views of the Straits of Mackinac and Mackinac Island, has 14 small 1950s cabins and 28 rooms with chenille bedspreads. Flowers bloom along the path to the outdoor grill. Heated indoor pool in the main lodge; coffee, juice, and hot muffins every morning. Beach toys on the clean swimming beach.

⌂ **Brigadoon Bed &Breakfast**
*Open May through October*
207 Langlade St.; 231-436-8882 $$$
The eight guestrooms at Brigadoon have whirlpool baths, fireplaces, wet bars, and balconies; gourmet breakfast is included. The inn is within walking distance of the Mackinac Island ferries and of the restaurants, shops, and beaches of Mackinac City. Hosts Doug and Lydia Yoder make this one of the most comfortable lodgings in town.

⌂ **The Deer Head Lodge.** *deerhead.com;* 109 Henry St.; 231-436-3337 $$–$$$$
Barry and Nancy Dean have decorated this B&B in one of Michigan's most-visited tourist towns with trophies of deer, bears, caribou, and fox. The warm wood, fireplaces, leather, and evergreens in this circa 1900 Mission-style home capture the spirit of northern Michigan. The four guest rooms are adjacent to shops and an island ferry. The full breakfast includes buffalo or venison on occasion.

⌸ **Ramada Convention Center.**
✗ 450 S. Nicolet; 231-436-5535 $$–$$$$
A full-service hotel with 162 rooms, 14
with whirlpools. Indoor pool, whirlpool,
and restaurant.

✗ **Audie's Restaurant.** 314 N. Nicolet
Ave.; 231-436-5744 $–$$
A very friendly, family-style restaurant that's
been serving tourists for about 25 years.
Casual dining and fast service. Daily specials are served in the Family Room, where
eggs and bacon are served all day. Leisurely
dining menu in the Chippewa Room.

⌸ **Dempsey Manor.** 506 Maple St.;
✗ 231-723-3767 $$$$
Manistee was once the home of more millionaires per capita than any other U.S. city.
James Dempsey's 30-room mansion, finished in 1894, is the largest survivor. This
12,000-square-foot monument to the past
was restored by Ed and Pat Kiefer, who run
it as an opulent Victorian B&B with six
rooms reserved for guests. Everywhere are
19th-century antiques: the Sleigh Room,
for example, features an antique sleigh bed;
one room is shrouded in romantic purple
velvet. Desserts such as raspberry chocolate
cake or cheesecake are served in the glassed-
in conservatory. Breakfast might include
cinnamon rolls, ham, or pecan-encrusted
French toast, with homemade custard for
dessert. Yes, dessert at breakfast! What used
to be the maid's room is now filled with
dolls and children's antiques. An elevator
serves the second floor, and the third floor
is a conference area.

*DEMPSEY MANOR*

✗ **River Street Station.** 350 River St.;
231-723-8411 $
Located in the heart of Manistee's historic
district and hard by the Manistee River (the
Riverwalk is right out the back) this popular casual eatery has a rustic/sports feel to it
and a menu to match. Split a Reuben, or
order a burger or Mexican entrée. Over 40
kinds of beer. A band plays most weekends.

**Manistee**   *map page 274, B-3*

⌸ **Stuart Avenue Inn B&B.**
*stuartaveinn.com;* 229 Stuart Ave.;
616-342-0230 $$
Actually *two* elegant pinnacled Victorian
homes in the Stuart Avenue historic dis-
trict, one being the former residence of the
Upjohn pharmaceutical family. Among the
19 rooms (all with private baths) are four
whirlpool suites, with an English garden
between them.

**Marquette**   *map page 274, B-2*

⌸ **Big Bay Pointe Lighthouse B&B.**
3 Lighthouse Rd., Big Bay;
906-345-9957 $$$–$$$$

This converted 1896 brick lighthouse on a Lake Superior bluff 25 miles northwest of Marquette has seven guest rooms, some with fireplaces and whirlpools. The 60-foot light tower boasts sunset views across Lake Superior and of the aurora borealis in the night skies. Hiking trails, full breakfast.

*BIG BAY POINTE LIGHTHOUSE*

🏨 **Landmark Inn.** 230 N. Front St.;
✕ 906-228-2580 $$–$$$$
Restored 1920s six-story hotel overlooking Marquette Harbor and Lake Superior, with 61 rooms, some furnished with fireplaces and whirlpools. Spa, three dining rooms. The traditional **Heritage Dining Room** off the original lobby has tall, graceful windows and chandeliers.

✕ **Harbor Brewery.** 119 S. Front St.;
906-228-3533 $–$$
Renovated 1883 saloon. Local artwork adorns the brick walls inside, and windows overlook Marquette Harbor. Menu features fresh, locally grown or gathered food (especially Lake Superior whitefish) for health-conscious diners.

✕ **Northwoods Supper Club.**
US-41 West and SR-28;

906-228-4343 $–$$
Renovated 1934 family-owned roadhouse. Gardens, full-service menu, and homemade breads and pies. Sunday brunch and Tuesday night smorgasbord. Log-frame rustic lounge with weekend entertainment.

**Marshall** *map page 274, C-5*

*NATIONAL HOUSE INN*

🏨 **National House Inn.**
✕ *nationalhouseinn.com;* 102 S. Parkview;
616-781-0600 $$
Stay in Michigan's oldest operating inn, a former stagecoach stop dating from 1835. Innkeeper Barbara Bradley cares for the 16 units overlooking Fountain Circle. The rooms, named for historic Marshall figures, are decorated with Victorian antiques; some rooms have half-baths and shared showers. A continental breakfast is included, and dinner is catered by appointment.

🏨 **Arbor Inn-Historic Marshall.**
15435 W. Michigan Ave.;
616-781-7772 $$
One-story economy motel with 48 rooms.

✕ **Schuler's Restaurant & Pub.**
*schulersrestaurant.com;* 115 S. Eagle St.;
616-781-0600 $$
Built to cater to Detroit-Chicago rail travelers in the early 1900s, Schuler's remains a traditional stop for auto travelers too. A state historic landmark, Schuler's prides itself on its warm atmosphere; poetic epigrams about food are inscribed on overhead beams. Favorites include prime rib and Lake Superior whitefish.

### Munising *map page 274, B-2*

⊞ **Homestead B&B.** 713 Prospect St.;
906-387-2542 $$
After 20 years in Alaska, nurse Barbara Carberry returned to her early 19th-century homestead in the hills above Lake Superior's Munising Bay, remodeled it, furnished it with family antiques and original Alaskan art, and made it a B&B. Six guest rooms, large breakfast, landscaped yard.

HOMESTEAD B&B

⊞ **Pinewood Lodge.** M-28 at AuTrain,
12 miles west of Munising;
906-892-8300 $$–$$$
Log lodge with six guest rooms, atrium, Finnish sauna, and porches. Gardens, boardwalks, and gazebo under tall pines on

a Lake Superior beach. You can walk for miles. Full homemade breakfast.

PINEWOOD LODGE

✕ **Dogpatch.** 820 Superior St.;
906-387-9948 $–$$
Northern version of Li'l Abner's Dogpatch. Illustrated menu featuring Dogpatch characters. Generous portions with salad bars.

### Muskegon *map page 274, B-4*

HACKLEY-HOLT HOUSE

⊞ **Hackley-Holt House.**
*dbonline.com/mi/ hhhbb/*
523 W. Clay; 888-271-5609 $$
Built in 1857 for the father of lumber baron Charles Hackley, this stately Victorian in the Heritage Village area has four first-floor rooms with king and queen beds, private

baths. Lots of antiques; big parlor and common room. Full breakfast.

**Port City Victorian Inn B&B.**
1259 Lakeshore; 231-759-0205 $$–$$$
This renovated 1877 home has five beautifully decorated upstairs rooms; note the original glass in the living room. Innkeepers Barbara and Frederick Schossau serve full breakfast. Some rooms have shared baths.

**Blue Country B&B.** 1415 Holton Rd., North Muskegon; 888-569-2050 $$
Children are not usually welcomed at heirloom-laden B&Bs, but this one, run by John and Barbara Stevens, welcomes kids of all ages. Infants stay in cribs equipped with stuffed animals. Toddlers wind down in the toy room. Older tykes play games, do puzzles, watch videos. Special menus for kids.

*DOUBLE JJ RESORT*

**Double JJ Resort.** *doublejj.com;*
5900 S. Water Rd., Rothbury, north of Muskegon on US-31; 800-DOUBLE JJ $$
A lot more than trail rides is offered at this dude ranch, one of several in Michigan and undoubtedly offering the most. The ranch is divided into an adult-oriented side, with rustic accommodations and no phones, TV, or air-conditioning. The family-oriented ranch, however, has water slides and wagons, tepees where young ropers can sleep, and beautiful log cabins big enough for an entire family. Learn to handle cows on the range during a two-hour cattle drive; play on The Thoroughbred, an Arthur Hills–designed 18-hole course rated one of the nation's best; or just relax and fish on the lake. Weekly, weekend, or three-days stays; packages include meals.

**Doo Drop Inn.** 2410 Henry St.; 231-755-3791 $
Family owned for more than a half-century, the restaurant offers good family meals, including lake perch.

**Rafferty's Dockside Restaurant.** *shorelineinn.com;* 231-722-4461 $$
Windows overlook the marina next door; the walls are bright; the furnishings are all light colors—a great place to enjoy casual fine dining. Entrées include pretzel-crumbed walleye and prime rib. In summer, watch the sun go down while you dine on the outdoor deck.

## Oscoda  *map page 274, D-3*

**Americinn of Oscoda.** 720 E. Harbor St.; 517-739-1986 $$
Close to the Au Sable River, this inn features 47 rooms, some with water views and some with whirlpools. Some even have fireplaces. There's also a heated pool and sauna. Continental breakfast comes with your stay, and boat tie-up is available.

**Huron House B&B.**
3124 N. US-23; 517-739-9255 $$$
Innkeepers Denny and Martie Lorenz specialize in making the 11 rooms of this

lodge retreats for couples. Private decks and hot tubs, two-person in-room whirlpool, fireplace, and breakfast served in your room help make this a special getaway.

✕ **Charbonneau's Family Restaurant.** 700 Lake St.; 517-739-5230 **$$**
A family-style restaurant for breakfast, lunch, and dinner overlooking the pleasure boat traffic on the Au Sable River. Try the roast chicken and weekend seafood buffet.

✕ **Garden View Coffee Mill.** 120 E. River Rd. (east of US-23); **$**
A block from the beach and surrounded by flowering gardens. Sisters Sandy Kowalski and Debbie Hamlin bake or cook everything (including the sandwich bread) they serve in this cottage-style shop. Soups too. The menu changes often, but count on offerings such as chicken and/or pasta salads. Stock up on Sandy's fresh-baked cinnamon rolls and strawberry-rhubarb pie.

## Petoskey/Bayview
*map page 274, B-3*

*INN AT BAY HARBOR*

⌂ ✕ **The Inn at Bay Harbor.** 3600 Village Harbor Dr.; 231-439-4000 **$$$–$$$$**

Corporate, neo-classical, over-the-top elegance is the theme. Golf, spa, and upscale dining are the rule at this bastion of conspicuous consumption. **Sagamore's** restaurant continues the soft raspberry-red and periwinkle-blue color schemes of the inn. White pillars frame the dining area adjacent to the terrace. In summer, choose from the "alfresco menu" and dine indoors or outdoors on the terrace.

⌂ **Stafford's Bay View Inn.** *staffords.com;*
✕ 2011 Woodland Ave. (US-31); 231-347-2771 **$$$**
A historic 1886 Victorian inn in the heart of the historic Bay View home district. Treat yourself to a stay in one of eight classic Edwardian-style rooms upstairs. Get settled in upstairs, then head for the bright **Roselawn** dining room, decorated in green, pink, and red, with clamshell-back chairs. Breakfast, lunch, dinner, and a large Sunday brunch are served. Dinner entrées include cherry-pepper steak—twin medallions of beef tenderloin dredged in cracked peppercorns and quickly seared and served with a rich port wine demi-glace laced with dried tart cherries.

*STAFFORD'S BAY VIEW INN*

◫ **Terrace Inn.** *theterraceinn.com;*
1549 Glendale, Bay View;
231-347-2410 $$$
This charming 1911 Victorian-style inn is a national historic landmark structure because it's located within the historic Bay View district. Lovingly looked after by Tom and Denise Earhart, the 43 rooms in the white clapboard building contain original furnishings; all have private baths, two have whirlpools. Natural wood, especially Michigan hemlock, abound in the interior, and the floors are dark hardwood. Guests have access to Bay View Association facilities, including its private beach and tennis court. Use of the inn's bicycles and snowshoes is complimentary, and golfers can book tee times at **Petoskey-Bay View Country Club.** Cross-country skiing, hiking, biking, and sleigh rides nearby, but no phones or TVs in rooms, and guests must smoke outdoors. And many say it's haunted and claim to have seen a woman in Victorian dress. The curious should try room 312.

*TERRACE INN*

◫ **Stafford's Perry Hotel.** *staffords.com;*
Bay and Lewis Sts.; 231-347-4000 $$$
When the Perry Hotel was about to crumble out of neglect, Stafford Smith of the Bay View Inn stepped in to save this historic former vacation retreat adjoining the Gaslight District. Built in 1899, the Perry is the only hotel in Petoskey surviving from that era. Eighty rooms and the common areas are decorated in Victorian style.

✕ **Andante.** 321 Bay St.; 231-348-3321 $$$
After strolling down the path through Andante's small garden, walking into this eatery is like stepping into the home of a good friend. Local art lines the walls on the two levels. The north window wall affords a panoramic view of Little Traverse Bay and the waterfront. Eclectic seasonal menu.

### Plymouth/Northville *map page 274, D-5*

◫ **Atchison House B&B.**
*laketolake.com/atchison/index.html;*
501 Dunlap St., Northville;
248-449-6699 $$$
Located in Northville's historic district, this 1882 Italianate home is run by Dave and Sherry Farhat. Five rooms are furnished in period antiques, with private baths.

◫ **Embassy Suites.** 19525 Victor Pkwy., ✕ Livonia (just south of Northville);
800-362-2779 $$$
Choose from 240 rooms in this hotel conveniently located just off I-275. Restaurant, an indoor pool, and other amenities.

◫ **Plymouth Hilton Garden Inn.**
✕ 14600 Sheldon Rd., Plymouth;
734-420-0001 $$$
Located outside Plymouth, this inn has 157 rooms, indoor pool and whirlpool, exercise area, and restaurant.

✕ **Café Bon Homme.**
844 Penniman Ave., Plymouth;
734-453-6260 $$$$
A very French restaurant, rated one of the state's best. The frequently changing menu lists items like southern French lamb pie.

✕ **MacKinnon's.** 126 E. Main St.,
Northville; 248-348-1991 $$$$
At this restaurant (rated among the nation's best) wild game dishes are the specialty.

✕ **Guernsey Farms Dairy.**
21300 Novi Rd., Northville;
248-349-1466 $
Ice cream–eaters are always satisfied when they leave this spot. In addition to 55 flavors of ice cream, sandwiches are served here too.

✕ **Uncle Frank's.** 550 Forest, Plymouth;
734-455-4141 $
For hot dog aficionados who've cut their teeth on a Detroit coney dog, this is the place to come for your advanced degree. Fifteen types of dogs go on buns here, from Italian to turkey to tofu .

## Port Austin   *map page 274, D-3*

*CAPTAIN'S INN B&B*

🏠 **Captain's Inn B&B.** 8586 Lake St.;
517-738-8321 $$–$$$
This rambling white-frame, two-story 1859 home is a great spot to base your Thumb tour. Rock in a rocker or swing on the front porch outside. Or relax inside on a mix of antique and traditional furniture. Enjoy a full breakfast on a rear patio or indoors. The five period-decorated rooms are named after owners Dave and Debbie Ramey's four children and granddaughter. Ask the Rameys to arrange charter boat fishing for salmon or perch as well as golf packages. They're happy to help. Take off your shoes and relax in the library or living room, both of which have fireplaces, which they'll light anytime anyone feels romantic.

🏠 **The Garfield Inn.** *garfieldinn.com;*
✕ 8544 Lake St. (M-25);
517-738-5254 $$
The innkeepers—the Pasant family—rent six rooms (three with private baths) here, and serve dinner too. Named after President James Garfield, who once spoke from its balcony, this French Empire Revival –style building is on both the Michigan and the National Registers of Historic Places. Most popular menu item is the reasonably priced prime rib; a children's menu is available as well. Breakfast includes complimentary champagne. *Open for dinner Monday through Saturday from May through October and on weekends the rest of the year.*

✕ **The Farm.** *Open April through October*
699 Port Crescent Rd.;
517-874-5700 $$
Many hungry travelers who've once stumbled across Jeff and Pam Gabriel's place end up coming back again and again. Inside this

100-year-old white-frame farmhouse, the Gabriels prepare dishes spiced with herbs and accompanied by produce grown in their own garden. Grandma Lizzie's chicken with lemon-thyme dumplings, and the boneless breast poached in wine are inspired by the owner's grandmother's recipe.

✕ **The Bank–1884.** Lake St. (M-25)
two blocks south of the harbor;
517-738-5353 $$–$$$
What do you do with an old and unused bank that survived the fires that wiped out forestry here in 1881? Make it a restaurant. Come here and dive into prime rib or fresh walleye. There's a children's menu.

## Port Huron  *map page 274, D-4*

🛏 **Blue Water Inn.** Just up the hill from the River Crab; 810-329-2236 $$
Each of the 21 differently decorated rooms at this comfortable inn is angled to face the river. Small swimming pool on the terrace.

🛏 **Lakeview Hills Country Club & Resort.**
✕ 6560 East Peck Rd.; Lexington;
810-359-7333 $$–$$$
A golfer's idea of a great vacation? Stay at a comfortable hotel a mile from Lake Huron with 36 holes to play, and other amenities to boot. Pick from 29 hotel rooms and four suites; go for an eagle and rent a home on the course for you and up to 11 of your closest friends; the motel-style rooms feature queen beds and cable TV. Staff will arrange charter-boat service for salmon fishing on Lake Huron. Beaches are nearby, too. Inside, the **Lakeview Hills Restaurant** looking onto the course and offers a menu listing seafood, steaks, and pasta.

## Port Sanilac  *map page 274, D-4*

🛏 **The Raymond House Inn.**
*laketolake.com/ raymond/index.htm;*
111 S. Ridge St.; 810-622-8800 or
800-622-7229 $$
This 1872 Victorian gingerbread home is 500 feet from the Lake Huron shore. Gary and Cristy Bobofchak run the inn and and adjacent gift shop and art gallery featuring Gary's photographs. Seven rooms (five with private baths) are decorated with antiques. Most have queen beds, one with canopy and some with antique frames. Stroll downtown to browse the antique shops, head to the beach, or visit the barn theater across the street for a local talent performance. Salmon- and steelhead-fishing charters are moored nearby in the harbor, and the historic lighthouse is but 300 feet away.

*RAYMOND HOUSE*

## Royal Oak  *map page 274, D-5*

🛏 **Sagamore Motor Lodge.**
30776 Woodward Ave.;
248-549-1600 $
Enjoy the exciting Woodward cruise from one of 79 economy-style rooms.

✗ **Memphis Smoke.** 100 S. Main St.;
248-543-4300 $$$
Ribs are top of the menu here. Beef brisket,
pulled pork, smoked turkey, pork ribs, and
other meats are slow-roasted over wood.
When the sun goes down, the live music—
often the blues—begins.

✗ **Royal Oak Brewery.** 215 E. 4th St.;
248-544-1141 $$
Soups, salads, sandwiches, gourmet pizzas,
and pastas are accompanied by house brews
in this casual eatery.

## St. Clair *map page 274, D-4*

▥ **St. Clair Inn.** 500 North Riverside Dr.
(M-29) in downtown St. Clair;
810-329-2222 $$–$$$
Dine on the boardwalk or inside by windows overlooking the St. Clair River.
Seafood, fresh lake fish (especially whitefish
and perch) are specialties at this Tudor-style
inn. Many of this English-style inn's 78 romantic rooms look out over the St. Clair,
with its parade of boats, freighters, and
ocean-going "salties." Whirlpool, indoor
pool. Close to the riverfront boardwalk.

▥ **Thomas Edison Inn.**
✗ 500 Thomas Edison Pkwy.;
810-984-8000 $$
Among the 149 rooms, best views are on
the river side, of course. Indoor pool, whirl-
pool, and exercise area. At the restaurant,
prime rib and paella are standouts; lunch
and breakfast, too. If you dine here in sum-
mer, you can watch the traffic on the St.
Clair River plow through the standing
waves and fast current created where Lake
Huron narrows into the river.

✗ **River Crab.** 1137 N. River Rd. (M-29),
St. Clair township; 810-329-2261 or
800-468-3727 $$
The small community of St. Clair town-
ship—just south of Port Huron and north
of St. Clair—was chosen by the late Chuck
Muer for one of his landmark restaurants.
Sadly, Muer died in a storm off the Bahamas, but his restaurants live, as do the
charities he launched from them: the
Salmon Stakes funds counseling centers for
victims of child abuse. Buy a raffle ticket,
and you can take off its cost from your dinner check here. The River Crab specializes
in seafood: one of the best dishes is the
Pasta Pagliara: shrimp, scallops, and chunks
of salmon surrounded by mussels in a light
garlic sauce over homemade linguine. Great
Sunday brunch. Lots of waterfront memorabilia, including a racing shell hanging
from the ceiling and paintings of freighters
on the paneled walls.

✗ **Diana Sweet Shoppe.** 307 Huron;
810-985-6933 $
Bill and Leo Deliganis know how to run an
old-fashioned sweet shop. Great sandwiches, too. It's been serving ice cream, malteds,
and other treats since 1926, when Bill and
Leo's father and uncle opened the place.
Sauces are still made in the store, in a copper pot. Sit in a booth and dig into a lemon
soda or the sundae of all sundaes here:
vanilla ice cream, chocolate sauce, various
toppings, and a cherry, served in a souvenir
plastic Detroit Tigers baseball hat. Breakfast, lunch, dinner; some vegetarian dishes.

✗ **The Fogcutter.** 511 Fort St., atop the
Port Huron Office Center;
810-987-3300 $$

Great views of Lake Huron, the Bluewater Bridge, and the river. Steaks and seafood for lunch, dinner; children's meals available.

⊞ **Harbour Pointe Lakefront Lodging.** 797 N. State St.; 906-643-9882 or 800-642-3318 $$$
This 150-room lodge has balconies on Lake Huron, giving you a view of the nightly beach bonfires. Indoor and outdoor pools, spas, game room, and yard games. Suites have jacuzzis. Three stories, no elevator. Continental breakfast.

⊞ **K-Royale Motor Inn.**
*Open April through October*
1037 N. State St.; 906-643-7737 or 800-882-7122 $
Summer lodge on 600 feet of private sand beach on Lake Huron. Balconies overlook the lake, a large playground, and picnic area. Some 95 rooms and suites. Three stories, no elevators.

✕ **The Galley Restaurant & Bar.**
*Open May to mid-October*
214 N. State St.; 906-643-7960 $–$$
Views of Moran Bay and Mackinac Island. All-service menu specializing in fish fresh from the bay; hard-to-find whitefish livers.

✕ **Huron Landing**. 441 N. State St., 906-643-9613 $–$$
Cozy harborfront dining room steps from a mile-long boardwalk along Moran Bay. The winter view is of snowmobiles towing sleds loaded with hay and other supplies as they cross the ice road of the bay to Mackinac Island. Italian dishes and ethnic specials.

## St. Joseph   *map page 274, B-5*

⊞ **The Boulevard Inn.** 521 Lake St.; ✕ 616-983-6600 $$$$
The hostelry features 82 rooms next to the Lake Michigan channel, a few with lake views. There's a restaurant in the inn.

*SOUTH CLIFF INN B&B*

⊞ **South Cliff Inn B&B.**
1900 Lakeshore Dr.; 616-983-4881 $$–$$$
Renovated B&B on a Lake Michigan bluff. The brick exterior and formal perennial garden call to mind an English cottage. Inside you'll find custom-made furniture and many antiques. Seven guest rooms: some have fireplaces, whirlpool tubs, and/or balconies overlooking the lake; all have private baths. Decks overlook the lake. Innkeeper Bill Swisher is a retired chef, so expect a great breakfast. Handicapped-accessible.

✕ **Clementine's.** 1235 Broad St. (downtown); 616-983-0990 $$
Marina view and huge club sandwiches. Try the lake perch: it's lightly dusted, pan fried, then served with garlic bread and coleslaw. Children's menu is available.

✕ **Lighthouse Depot Restaurant & Brewpub.**
128 North Pier; 616-98-BREWS $$
Located in a renovated Coast Guard lighthouse service building, hence the name. Great outdoor dining; or eat indoors on a rustic upper floor. Sip a house ale and scan the menu for steaks, lake fish, and seafood.

✕ **Schu's Grill and Bar.** 501 Pleasant St.; 616-983-7248 $$
Cozy location downtown; traditional American fare from burgers to steaks to pasta. Rustic atmosphere, with outdoor dining.

## Saugatuck/Douglas
*map page 274, B-5*

*This must be Michigan's B&B center: 38 are listed on the local visitors bureau website. Most downtown Saugatuck businesses don't need an address, as the area is so compact: just drive down Water Street and you'll see them.*

⌂ **Fairchild House.** 606 Butler St.; 616-857-5985 $$
A traditional New England–style B&B with European featherbeds and fine antiques. Champagne breakfasts are served, and a garden gazebo is a favorite for weddings. Air-conditioning, no smoking.

⌂ **Goshorn Lake Family Resort.**
*saugatuck.com/sbonline.htm;*
3581 65th St.; 616-857-4808 or 800-541-4210 $$$
Old-style cottage resorts are fast disappearing into condo developments, so this one is nice to see: 19 housekeeping cottages (rent by the week) on Goshorn Lake.

*GOSHORN LAKE RESORT*

⌂ **Park House B&B Inn.**
*bbonline.com/mi/parkhouse;*
888 Holland St.; 616-857-4535 or 800-321-4535 $$$
Built in 1857 by lumberman H. D. Moore, this is Saugatuck's oldest home and is listed on the National Register. Susan B. Anthony was a guest. Eight rooms with queen beds, one family suite, and two suites with fireplaces and whirlpool tubs. All have private baths and air-conditioning; large continental breakfast. The Park House also has three cottages, including the oft-photographed Peterson's Mill on the north edge of town.

*PARK HOUSE B&B INN*

✕ **Coral Gables.** Overlooking the river;
616-857-2162 $$
The nautical theme and dockside dining in warm weather tell the tale. Food ranges from burgers to seafood on the eclectic lunch and dinner menus.

✕ **Crane's Pie Pantry.**
M-89 bet. Saugatuck and Fennville;
616-561-2297 $
Perhaps best known for apple cider and for pies full of fresh orchard fruit, Crane's also serves good food for lunch and dinner.

✕ **Ida Red's.** Water St., downtown Saugatuck; 616-857-5803 $
Named for a famous folk song (on which Chuck Berry's "Maybellene" was based, Ida Red's serves good Italian and Greek dishes. Burgers, too.

### Sault Ste. Marie
*map page 274, C-2*

⊞ **Ojibway Hotel.** 240 W. Portage Ave.;
✕ 906-632-4100 or 800-654-2929 $–$$
With 71 rooms and suites, this restored 1920s hotel offers an indoor pool and spa. At **Freighters Restaurant**, tall windows give diners panoramic views of Soo Locks and of Great Lake ships traveling up and down St. Marys River. Casual upscale menu.

✕ **The Antlers.** 804 E. Portage Ave.;
906-632-3571 $–$$$
A rustic old bar decorated with bric-a-brac (canoes, logging tools, deer antlers) hanging from ceiling rafters and walls. Family-sized hamburgers, steak, and lobster.

### Seney *map page 274, B-2*

✕ **Golden Grill.** South side of M-28 in the village and adjacent to IGA store;
906-499-3323 $–$$
The hearty country menu includes homemade pies, bread, pastries, and donuts. Breakfast buffet and 4 P.M. daily smorgasbord. Closed Sundays.

### Stevensville *map page 274, B-5*

✕ **Grand Mere Inn.**
5800 Red Arrow Hwy.;
616-429-3591 $$
An elegant restaurant on a bluff looking over Lake Michigan. Seafood and fresh water fish including perch and bluegill, ribs, parboiled and served with house-made sauce, plus steaks are specialties and a children's menu is available.

✕ **Schuler's.** 5000 Red Arrow Hwy.; 616-429-3273 $$$
This restaurant has an "up north" feel, with log and barnwood-style wall treatment. Steaks like New York Strip charred and served with a roasted three onion salad and lobster coral butter and baked sweet potato, and Atlantic salmon glazed with house sweet and sour accompanied by Basmati rice and crispy fried leeks are two entrees.

✕ **Tosi's Restaurant.** *tosis.com;* 4337 Ridge Rd.; 800-218-7745 $$
Begun by Emil Tosi in 1948 using many of his mother's Old World recipes, Tosi's serves excellent northern Italian cuisine and has a wine cellar voted by *Wine Spectator* as one

of the top in the world. The huge menu include pizza baked in a wood-burning oven and cannelloni, plus nine other pasta dishes. Steaks available too.

## Tawas City & East Tawas   *map page 274, D-3*

☵ **Tawas Bay Holiday Inn Resort.** 300 East Bay (US-23); 517-362-8601 $$
Heading for the beach and want a place to stay? Take care of both here. Select one of the 103 rooms, many with shoreside views of the 900-foot sand beach on Tawas Bay, where there is great swimming. There's also an indoor pool. Walk to downtown's shops or the small local movie theater.

☵ **Bambi Motel.** 1100 East Bay (US-23); 517-362-4582 $
A well-kept mom and pop motel with lake access. Rooms aren't fancy but are clean and the price is right.

☵ **East Tawas Junction B&B.** *laketolake.com/easttawas/index.htm;* 514 W. Bay (US-23); 517-362-8006 $$$
Ask innkeeper Leigh Mott the history of this turn-of-the-century home built by a president of the Detroit and Mackinac Railroad, whose tracks still run by the home, albeit under a different name now. She and husband Donald purchased the five-room mansion nestled on a treed, manicured estate-size lot in 1996. All rooms have private baths. Relax on the sundeck, next to the fireplace, or in the library. The wraparound porch has been glassed in, and the original wavy glass is intact. It was done apparently after the house was moved back

from the rails decades ago after a passing train derailed and knocked off the original porch. Trains still rumble by, but well out of range now. Leigh's breakfasts are sumptuous, including raspberry crepes or cheese soufflé, with homemade bread and rolls. The inn is a short walk from downtown and across US-23 from the beach.

✕ **Genii's Fine Foods.** 1100 E. Bay (US-23); 517-362-5913 $
Genii's has been an East Tawas fixture for more than 40 years, serving breakfast, lunch, and dinner.

✕ **Marion's Dairy Bar.** 111 E. Bay (US-23;. 517-362-2991 $
After dinner, head here for dessert, because Marion's specializes in ice cream—over 32 flavors of it. Cones, malts, sundaes.

## Traverse City   *map page 274, B-3*

☵ **Waterfront Inn.** 2061 US-31; ✕ 231-938-1100 $$$
One of the best places to stay of the scores of places ringing the crescent necklace of a beach of Grand Traverse Bay's West Arm. Four-story building (127 rooms) surrounded by trees. Play on nearly 800 feet of beach or in the pool, saunas, and whirlpool.

Atop the inn, **Reflections** offers views of Grand Traverse Bay that suit the fine, sophisticated fare. Best dishes include seafood, whitefish, and brandy-pecan walleye.

☵ **Grand Traverse Resort.** 100 Grand Traverse Village Blvd. (just north of Traverse City off US-31); 231-938-2100 $$$

The gleaming blue-gray glass of northern Michigan's tallest structure can be seen for miles around. The 665 rooms are divided between a 17-story tower and housekeeping units scattered at its base. Also marching on the property is the resort's main summer draw, 54 holes of golf (including the Jack Nicklaus–designed Bear course), along with indoor tennis, racquetball courts, exercise area, and a beach on Grand Traverse Bay.

*GRAND TRAVERSE RESORT*

☵ **Chateau Chantal B&B.**
*chateauchan tal.com;* 15900 Rue de Vin; 800-969-4009 $$$$

*CHATEAU CHANTAL B&B*

Turn onto the private road off M-37 on the Old Mission Peninsula and you'll swear you were in California or France when you pass by row upon row of grape trellises. Tour the wine cellar and sample a few vintages before retiring to one of the two suites or a queen-sized bedroom in this French chateau-inspired home. Guests sip wine by a majestic fireplace in the Great Room. Full breakfast is served each morning.

✕ **Boone's Long Lake Inn.**
7208 Secor Rd.; 231-946-399 $$
Traverse City's steak and seafood favorite has been feeding hungry locals and tourists for more than 20 years. The menu includes an 18-ounce New York strip that will convert the most ardent vegetarian. Finish with a piece of chocolate mousse pie.

✕ **Bowers Harbor Inn.**
13512 Peninsula Dr.; 231-223-4222 $$$
Diners are transported to New England at this white-gabled inn, tucked into a cove on Grand Traverse Bay's Old Mission Peninsula. Seafood, steaks, chicken, and a few pasta dishes prevail, as do wonderful views of sunsets and sailboats in the harbor.

## Union Pier *map page 274, B-5*

☵ **Inn at Union Pier.** 9708 Berrien St.; 616-469-4700 $$$
Choose from 16 spacious guest rooms in this lakeside retreat, built in the 1920s as a summer resort. Bill and Madeleine Reinke purchased it in 1983, restored it, and in 1985 opened it as the area's first B&B. Each room has a mix of Danish and Swedish antiques and reproductions (such as antique *kakelugns,* Swedish wood-burning fireplaces in 13 of the rooms); all have private baths

and air-conditioning. Many rooms have a porch or balcony. Breakfast usually features blueberries: this is the state's fruit belt, and boasts the top U.S. blueberry crop. Chocolate chip–oatmeal cookies are set out each day along with seasonal soft drinks (lemonade in summer, hot cocoa in winter). Relax in the hot tub or sauna, or borrow a bike from the inn to explore the countryside.

✗ **Miller's Country House.**
16409 Red Arrow Hwy., New Buffalo; 616-469-5950; grill items $, dinner $$
A Harbor Country fixture since the 1930s, when this roadhouse-style restaurant served travelers on the former main route from Michigan to Chicago. The walls are stucco outside and in; three dining areas boast the original walls. Best seats in the house are along the rear wall, a length of windows looking over a lovely garden. The Woodland Room features a mural of Harbor Country; the Hardwood Room contains a 130-year-old bar where casual lunch fare (burgers, salads, sandwiches) is served. Many dinner entrées include seafood: recent menu items have included a crab-crusted sea bass, and a planked whitefish in brown sugar–vodka sauce. Rack of lamb

with mango chutney sauce is also great. Dress is resort casual.

## Ypsilanti *map page 274, D-3*

✗ **Cady's Grill.** 36 E. Cross St.;
734-483-2800 $-$$
Fun atmosphere, with food that is based more on dinners than on sandwiches.

✗ **Cross Street Station.** 511 W. Cross St.;
734-485-5050 $$
The music gets a bit far out, but if you're looking to dance, this could be the place.

✗ **Sidetrack Bar & Grill.** 56 E. Cross St.;
734-483-1035 $-$$
Award-winning burgers plus an eclectic decor make this a great place to stay a few hours beyond dinner.

✗ **Sticks.** 39 E. Cross St.; 734-483-1870 $
Pretty good, as basic bar food goes, and a great place to shoot stick and toss darts.

✗ **The Tap Room.** 201 W. Michigan Ave.;
734-482-5320 $-$$
Music that's a bit more bluesy, though Sunday's karaoke might give you the blues.

---

### METRIC CONVERSIONS

degrees C = (degrees F − 32) x $5/9$
meters = feet x .3
kilometers = miles x .62
kilograms = pounds x .45

# I N D E X

# COMPASS AMERICAN GUIDES

*Compass American Guides are available in general and travel bookstores, or may be ordered directly by calling (800) 733-3000. Please provide title and ISBN when ordering.*

**Alaska**
(2nd edition)
$19.95 ($27.95 Can)
0-679-00230-8

**Arizona**
(5th edition)
$19.95 ($29.95 Can)
0-679-00432-7

**Boston**
(2nd edition)
$19.95 ($27.95 Can)
0-679-00284-7

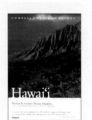

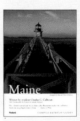

**Chicago**
(2nd edition)
$18.95 ($26.50 Can)
1-878-86780-6

**Coastal California**
(2nd edition)
$21.00 ($32.00 Can)
0-679-00439-4

**Colorado**
(5th edition)
$19.95 ($29.95 Can)
0-679-00435-1

**Florida**
(1st edition)
$19.95 ($27.95 Can)
0-679-03392-0

**Georgia**
(1st edition)
$19.95 ($29.95 Can)
0-679-00245-6

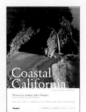

**Gulf South**
(1st edition)
$21.00 ($32.00 Can)
0-679-00533-1

**Hawaii**
(4th edition)
$19.95 ($27.95 Can)
0-679-00226-X

**Idaho**
(1st edition)
$18.95 ($26.50 Can)
1-878-86778-4

**Las Vegas**
(6th edition)
$19.95 ($29.95 Can)
0-679-00370-3

**Maine**
(3rd edition)
$19.95 ($29.95 Can)
0-679-00436-X

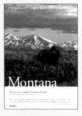

**Manhattan**
(3rd edition)
$19.95 ($29.95 Can)
0-679-00228-6

**Minnesota**
(2nd edition)
$19.95 ($29.95 Can)
0-679-00437-8

**Montana**
(4th edition)
$19.95 ($29.95 Can)
0-679-00281-2

**Nevada**
(1st edition)
$21.00 ($32.00 Can)
0-679-00535-8

**New Mexico**
(4th edition)
$21.00 ($32.00 Can)
0-679-00438-6

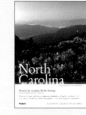

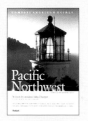
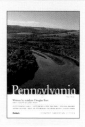

**New Orleans**
(4th edition)
$21.00 ($32.00 Can)
0-679-00647-8

**North Carolina**
(2nd edition)
$19.95 ($29.95 Can)
0-679-00508-0

**Oregon**
(3rd edition)
$19.95 ($27.95 Can)
0-679-00033-X

**Pacific Northwest**
(2nd edition)
$19.95 ($27.95 Can)
0-679-00283-9

**Pennsylvania**
(1st edition)
$19.95 ($29.95 Can)
0-679-00182-4

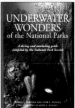

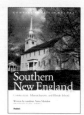

**San Francisco**
(5th edition)
$19.95 ($29.95 Can)
0-679 -00229-4

**Santa Fe**
(3rd edition)
$19.95 ($29.95 Can)
0-679-00286-3

**South Carolina**
(3rd edition)
$19.95 ($29.95 Can)
0-679-00509-9

**South Dakota**
(2nd edition)
$18.95 ($26.50 Can)
1-878-86747-4

**Southern New
England** (1st ed)
$19.95 ($29.95 Can)
0-679-00184-0

**Southwest**
(3rd edition)
$21.00 ($32.00 Can)
0-679-00646-X

**Texas**
(2nd edition)
$18.95 ($26.50 Can)
1-878-86798-9

**Underwater Wonders
of the National Parks**
$19.95 ($27.95 Can)
0-679-03386-6

**Utah**
(4th edition)
$18.95 ($26.50 Can)
0-679-00030-5

**Vermont**
(1st edition)
$19.95 ($27.95 Can)
0-679-00183-2

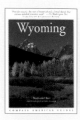

**Virginia**
(3rd edition)
$19.95 ($29.95 Can)
0-679-00282-0

**Washington**
(2nd edition)
$19.95 ($27.95 Can)
1-878-86799-7

**Wine Country**
(3rd edition)
$21.00 ($32.00 Can)
0-679-00434-3

**Wisconsin**
(2nd edition)
$18.95 ($26.50 Can)
1-878-86749-0

**Wyoming**
(3rd edition)
$19.95 ($27.95 Can)
0-679-00034-8

## ■ ABOUT THE AUTHORS

**Dixie Franklin** left her home state of Texas in 1963 and fell head-over-heels in love with Michigan and the Great Lakes. As a full-time, prize-winning freelancer, she roams the cities, byroads, and lakeshores, contributing to the *Chicago Tribune, Midwest Living, Lake Superior Magazine,* and AAA *Home & Away,* among others. Books include *Michigan, Faces of Lake Superior,* and *Haunts of the Upper Great Lakes.* Awards she has won include the Michigan Outdoor Writers Association (1988, '90) and the Society of American Travel Writers (1989). She has two daughters and three grandchildren.

**Bill Semion** is a freelance writer who has lived in and explored Michigan all of his life. He is a board member of the Michigan Outdoor Writers Association(currently board chairman), the North American Snowsport Journalists Association and the Midwest Travel Writers Association writes extensively about the state. He lives in Canton Township.

After contributing to this book, freelance writer **Dan Stivers** moved back to Ann Arbor with his wife and daughter. His articles have appeared in a number of magazines, and he has co-authored books for Fodor's Travel Publications and *CliffsNotes.*

## ■ ABOUT THE PHOTOGRAPHER

**Dennis Cox** is a Detroit-based photographer whose work has appeared in more than 200 different publications, including *GEO, Midwest Living Smithsonian, Time, Newsweek, Forbes,* and *Business Week.* In 1984, his portfolio on China in the *Minolta Mirror* won an Award of Excellence from *Communication Arts.* An executive board member of the Michigan Chapter of the American Society of Magazine Photographers and of the Art Directors Club of Detroit, he is listed in *American Photographers*—the "who's who" of American photographers.